ASCENT
CENTER FOR TECHNICAL KNOWLEDGE

Creo Parametric 6.0
Behavioral Modeling

Learning Guide
1ˢᵗ Edition

ASCENT - Center for Technical Knowledge®
Creo Parametric 6.0
Behavioral Modeling
1st Edition

Prepared and produced by:

ASCENT Center for Technical Knowledge
630 Peter Jefferson Parkway, Suite 175
Charlottesville, VA 22911

866-527-2368
www.ASCENTed.com

Lead Contributor: Scott Hendren

ASCENT - Center for Technical Knowledge (a division of Rand Worldwide Inc.) is a leading developer of professional learning materials and knowledge products for engineering software applications. ASCENT specializes in designing targeted content that facilitates application-based learning with hands-on software experience. For over 25 years, ASCENT has helped users become more productive through tailored custom learning solutions.

We welcome any comments you may have regarding this guide, or any of our products. To contact us please email: feedback@ASCENTed.com.

AS-CRP6-BMX1-SG   //   RS-CRP6-BMX1-SG

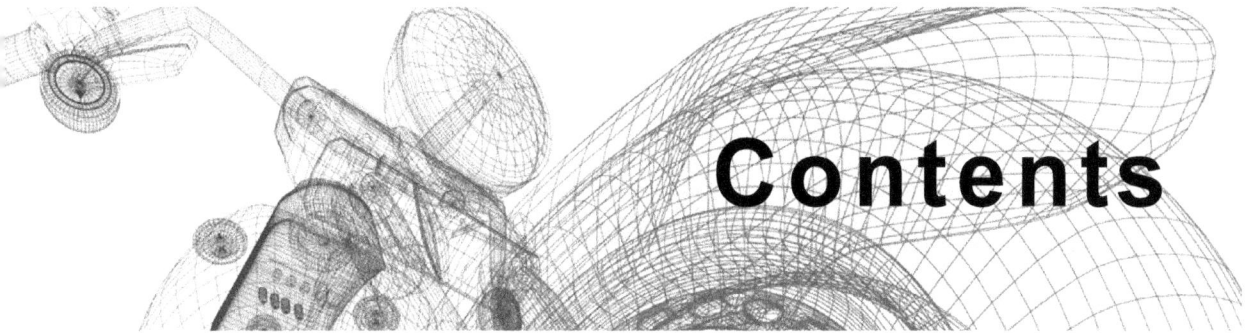

Contents

Preface

The *Creo Parametric 6.0: Behavioral Modeling* learning guide introduces the analysis tools available in the Behavioral Modeling Extension (BMX) for establishing and analyzing design goals. You will learn how to create analysis features and sensitivity and feasibility studies. Behavioral Modeling provides the ability to automatically change dimensions and parameters to meet specific design goals.

Topics Covered:

- Capabilities of BMX

- Analysis Features

- Sensitivity Analysis

- Feasibility and Optimization Analysis

- Multi-Objective Design Studies

- Graph Matching

- Excel Analysis

- Motion Analysis

Prerequisites

- Access to the Creo Parametric 6.0 software. The practices and files included with this guide might not be compatible with prior versions. Practice files included with this guide are compatible with the commercial version of the software, but not the student edition.

- It is highly recommended that you have completed the *Creo Parametric 6.0: Introduction to Solid Modeling*. Experience with MS Excel and Creo Mechanism Design is useful, but not required.

Note on Software Setup

This learning guide assumes a standard installation of the software using the default preferences during installation. Lectures and practices use the standard software templates and default options for the Content Libraries.

This guide was developed using Creo Parametric 6.0, Build 6.0.4.0.

Lead Contributor: Scott Hendren

Scott has been a trainer and curriculum developer in the PLM industry for over 20 years, with experience on multiple CAD systems, including Creo Parametric, Creo Parametric, and CATIA. Trained in Instructional Design, Scott uses his skills to develop instructor-led and web-based training products.

Scott has held training and development positions with several high profile PLM companies, and has been with the Ascent team since 2013.

Scott holds a Bachelor of Mechanical Engineering Degree as well as a Bachelor of Science in Mathematics from Dalhousie University, Nova Scotia, Canada.

Scott Hendren has been the Lead Contributor for *Creo Parametric: Behavioral Modeling* since 2017.

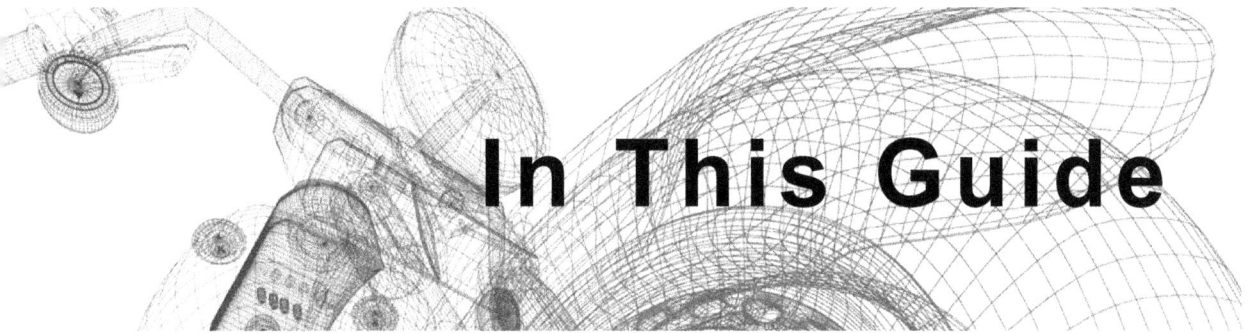

In This Guide

The following highlights the key features of this guide.

Feature	Description
Practice Files	The Practice Files page includes a link to the practice files and instructions on how to download and install them. The practice files are required to complete the practices in this guide.
Chapters	A chapter consists of the following - Learning Objectives, Instructional Content, Practices, Chapter Review Questions, and Command Summary. • **Learning Objectives** define the skills you can acquire by learning the content provided in the chapter. • **Instructional Content**, which begins right after Learning Objectives, refers to the descriptive and procedural information related to various topics. Each main topic introduces a product feature, discusses various aspects of that feature, and provides step-by-step procedures on how to use that feature. Where relevant, examples, figures, helpful hints, and notes are provided. • **Practice** for a topic follows the instructional content. Practices enable you to use the software to perform a hands-on review of a topic. It is required that you download the practice files (using the link found on the Practice Files page) prior to starting the first practice.
Appendices	Appendices provide additional information to the main course content. It could be in the form of instructional content, practices, tables, projects, or skills assessment.

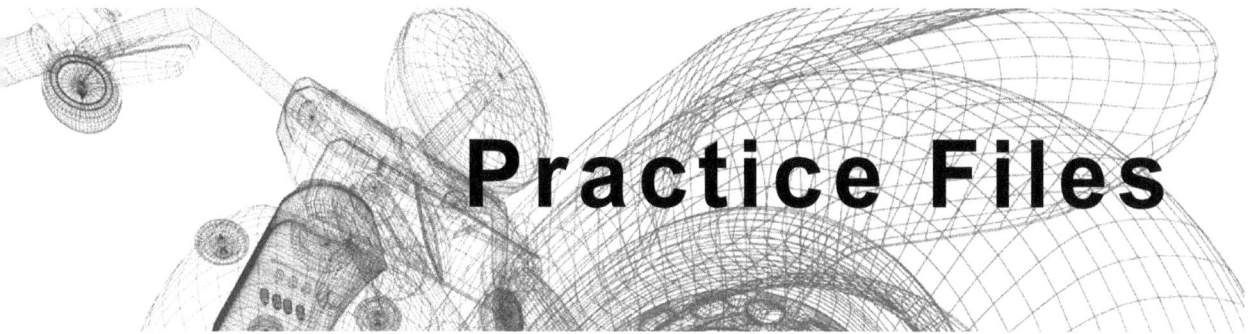

Practice Files

To download the practice files for this guide, use the following steps:

1. Type the URL *exactly as shown below* into the address bar of your Internet browser, to access the Course File Download page.

   Note: If you are using the ebook, you do not have to type the URL. Instead, you can access the page simply by clicking the URL below.

   ## https://www.ascented.com/getfile/id/bryobium

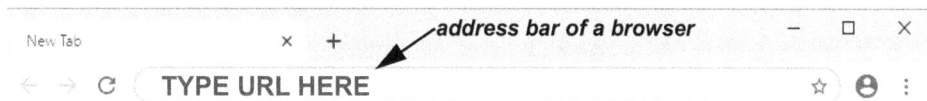

   address bar of a browser

2. On the Course File Download page, click the **DOWNLOAD NOW** button, as shown below, to download the .ZIP file that contains the practice files.

   DOWNLOAD NOW ▶

3. Once the download is complete, unzip the file and extract its contents.

   The recommended practice files folder location is:
   C:\Creo Parametric Behavioral Modeling Practice Files

   Note: It is recommended that you do not change the location of the practice files folder. Doing so may cause errors when completing the practices.

   Stay Informed!
   To receive information about upcoming events, promotional offers, and complimentary webcasts, visit:
   www.ASCENTed.com/updates

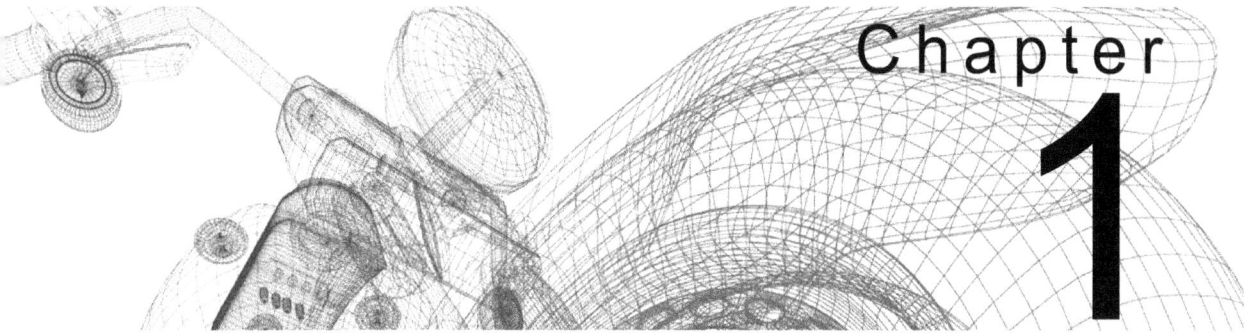

Introduction to Behavioral Modeling

The Behavioral Modeling Extension (BMX) is an analysis tool for Creo Parametric models. BMX enables you to subject the model to a series of real world situations and problems. With BMX, you can test the behavior of your model before a physical model is created to generate and test the prototypes, saving time and money. This course provides examples and explanation of how behavioral modeling can be used to build a robust design.

Learning Objectives in This Chapter

- Review the capabilities of BMX.
- Understand where to use BMX.
- Learn the building blocks of BMX.

1.1 Capabilities of the Behavioral Modeling Extension

Unlike other analysis tools, the Behavioral Modeling Extension (BMX) works in a flexible environment. It enables you to capture the design intent that lies outside of that captured using standard dimension schemes. The results can then be used to drive the dimensions and features of your model.

BMX can be used to solve some of the following situations:

- Trial and error iteration of one or more design variables.

- Repetitive construction of a feature.

- Repetitive measurement of a feature.

- Feasibility or optimized solutions to a problem.

- Analyzing your model when standard functionality does not exist.

A BMX analysis is accomplished using Analysis features. The Analysis feature is not confined to a specific analysis type, but can be applied to extract virtually any type of data required from the Creo Parametric model. This enables you to apply BMX to many different analysis scenarios.

BMX enables you to do the following:

- Create feature parameters that result from measurement, model, surface, or curve analyses. For example, you can create a parameter that measures the length of a bolt. This parameter could then be placed in a family table.

- Create datum features based on analysis results from your model. For example, you can create datum points or a coordinate system on the model's center of mass.

- Create an Excel Analysis that integrates an Excel spreadsheet directly into a Creo Parametric model. Creo Parametric dimensions, parameters, and other analysis parameters are matched with corresponding cells in the spreadsheet.

- Create a User-Defined Analysis (UDA) feature specific to your design requirements.

- Create a Sensitivity Analysis to show how a design parameter reacts when a design variable is changed within a specific range.

- Create a Feasibility Study that adjusts design variables to meet specific design constraints. It determines if a feasible solution exists given the range of values for the design variables.

- Create an Optimization Study to adjust the design variables to meet specific design constraints. It optimizes the model with respect to a specific goal while maintaining design constraints.

- Create a Multi-Objective Design Study to report all of the values of the design parameters across a variation of design variables. The Multi-Objective Design Study provides access to all permutations and variations of a model within the bounds of the design variables.

- Compare two graphs to determine the difference in the distribution of one parameter along another parameter.

- Create a Motion Analysis that graphs design parameters with respect to time. This can only be created in the Assembly mode.

- Create a Simulation analysis that uses the results from a Creo Simulate analysis.

BMX Example

Creo Parametric has no standard solution for determining the holding capacity of a container (e.g., a bottle). You can solve this problem by using BMX analysis tools to create two volume calculations: one to measure the solid volume of the bottle and another to measure the volume of the bottle after it is shelled, as shown in Figure 1–1. You can then create a Relation analysis feature to measure the difference between solid and shelled volumes to determine the holding capacity of the bottle. The Relation analysis feature updates if changes are made to the model.

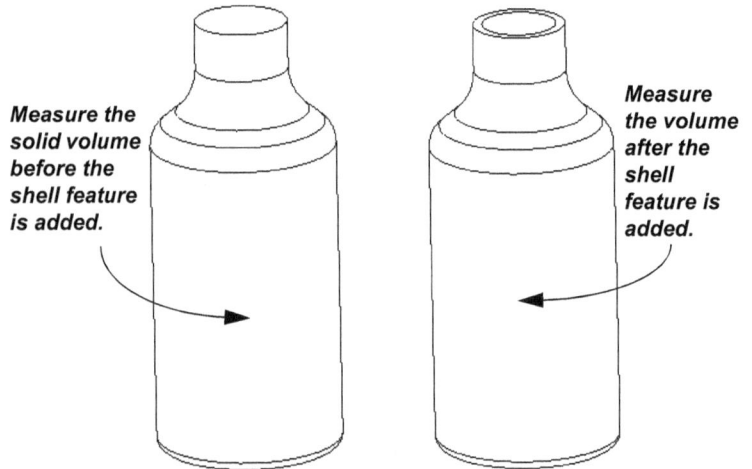

Measure the solid volume before the shell feature is added.

Measure the volume after the shell feature is added.

INTERNAL_VOL = SOLID_VOL - SHELLED_VOL

Figure 1–1

1.2 Building Blocks of BMX

In the past, standard CAD tools were limited to capturing design intent in the form of an electronic model. Some of the important design information could be transferred to the model using relations or dimension schemes, while other design requirements could not be incorporated. For example, CAD was used for design documentation. In many situations, the Engineering design of the model has been independent from the CAD system. BMX provides tools in Creo Parametric that enable you to further integrate your design goals with CAD modeling (e.g., minimize model weight).

The following describes some of the building blocks used in BMX:

- Analysis Features
- Field Points
- Construction Groups
- User-defined Analyses
- Design Studies

Analysis Features

An Analysis feature takes the Analysis setup and results and stores this information in a feature, as shown in Figure 1–2. The results can be stored as parameters. These parameters are updated each time the model is modified.

Analysis features are discussed in more detail in later chapters.

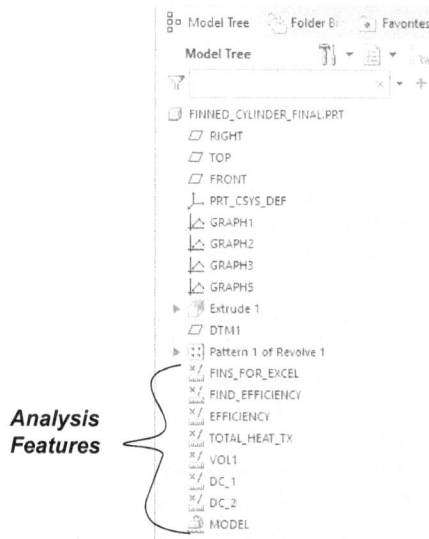

Figure 1–2

Field Points

Field points are special datum point features used in user-defined analyses (UDA). A field point is placed on a reference (i.e., curve, surface, quilt), but is not rigidly constrained. Therefore, it can capture data from anywhere on the geometry. Figure 1–3 shows a field point that was placed on a surface feature, which can be used to measure the shortest distance between the surface and the pipe.

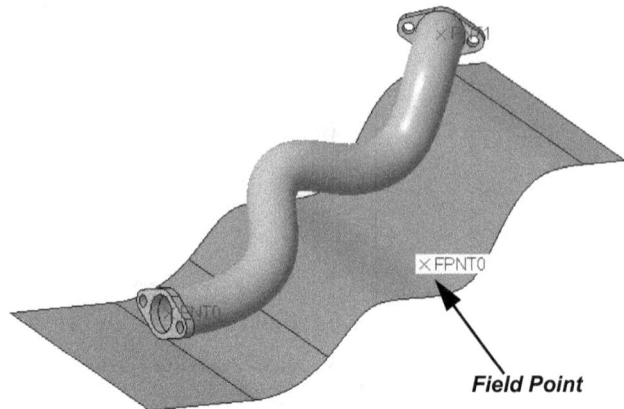

Field Point

Figure 1–3

Construction Groups

Construction Groups are discussed in more detail in later chapters.

A construction group (shown in Figure 1–4) is a group of features used to measure a design variable.

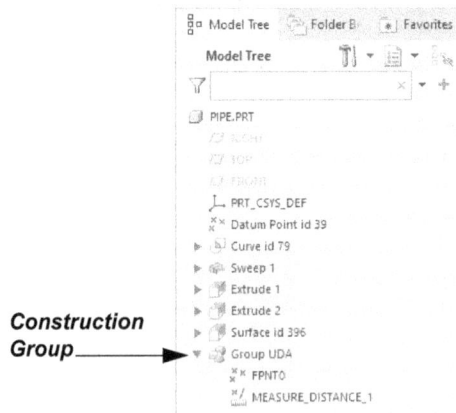

Construction Group

Figure 1–4

User-Defined Analyses

A User-defined analyses (UDA) provides modeling solutions that meet your user-defined constraints. To create a UDA, you have to define a construction group.

- UDAs are discussed in more detail in later chapters.

Design Studies

Design studies are discussed in more detail in later chapters.

Once Analysis features are added to the model to represent the design possibilities, you can run design studies that enable you to perform the following additional studies:

- "What if " analysis (Sensitivity Analysis)

- Goal-seeking analysis (Feasibility/Optimization)

- Simultaneous goal analysis (Multi-Objective Design Study)

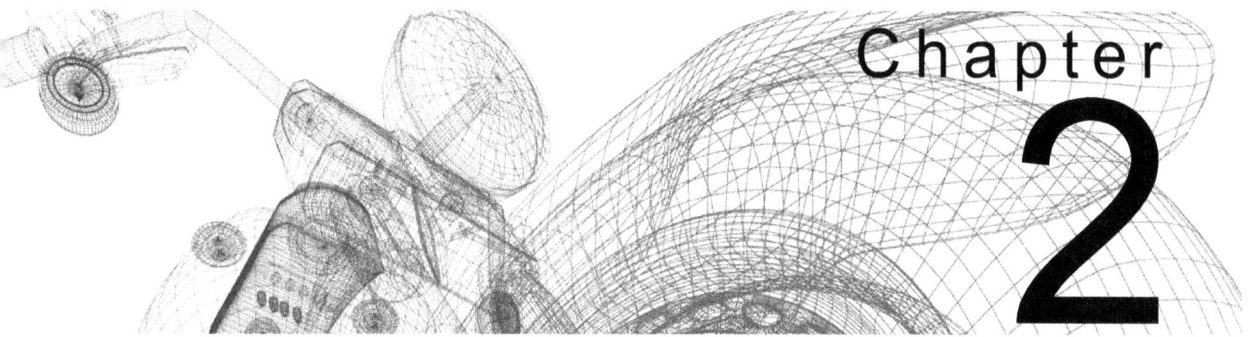

Analysis Features

Analysis features are used to generate parameters and datum features based on an analysis calculation on the model geometry.

Learning Objectives in This Chapter

- Learn how to create analysis features.
- Recognize the various analysis feature types and techniques.

2.1 Analysis Features

An analysis feature can be used to generate parameters and datum features based on an analysis calculation on the model geometry. An analysis feature, plus any dependent features and relations, update automatically when changes are made to the design.

An analysis feature has the following properties of a standard Creo Parametric feature:

- It is stored with the model.

- It is added as a feature to the Model Tree ( ).

- It can be suppressed, reordered, deleted, etc.

- It reacts to feature order.

Figure 2–1 shows the Model Tree with multiple analysis features.

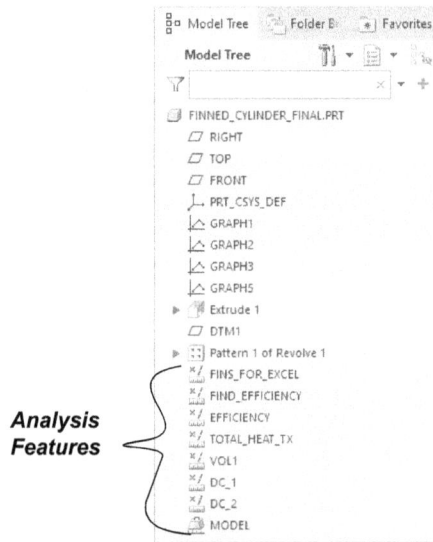

Figure 2–1

Once the analysis feature has been defined, the resulting parameters can be used in a relation. The relation can be written in the following way:

result_parameter_name: fid_analysis_feature_name

Where:

> **result_parameter_name** = The name of the results parameter created as a result of the analysis.

> **analysis_feature_name** = The name of the analysis feature.

In the example shown in Figure 2–2 and Figure 2–3, sweeping a section along a datum curve creates the solid geometry and the dimension d14 drives the height of the section of the geometry. The design intent of the part is to have the height of the protrusion equal to 50% of the distance around the trajectory. To accomplish this, a datum analysis feature is created to measure the distance around the trajectory. The analysis feature is then used in a relation to capture the design intent.

Before Analysis:

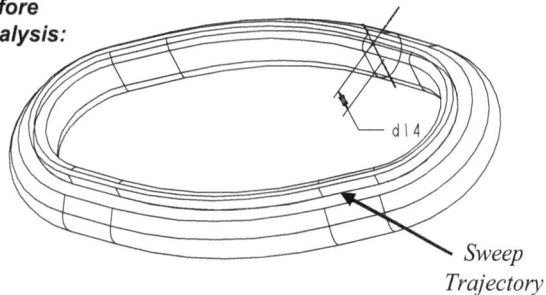

Sweep Trajectory

Figure 2–2

After Analysis:

Analysis Information:
analysis_feature_name = ANALYSIS_LENGTH_1
results_parameter_name = LENGTH

Analysis created using the Length dialog box.
A measurement of the sweep trajectory length is generated.

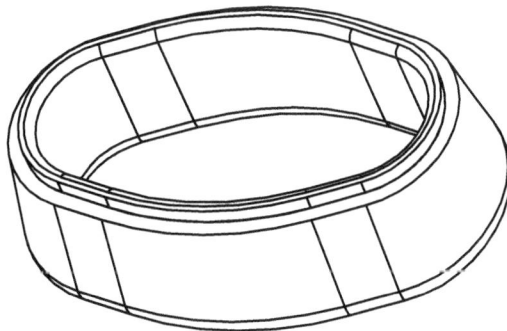

Relation:
d14 = 0.5 * LENGTH:fid_ANALYSIS_LENGTH_1

Figure 2–3

If parameters are defined in a part or assembly, they can be inserted directly into a relation. To insert a parameter into a relation, expand the *Local Parameters* area in the Relations dialog box and select the parameter name. Right-click and select **Insert to Relations**, as shown in Figure 2–4.

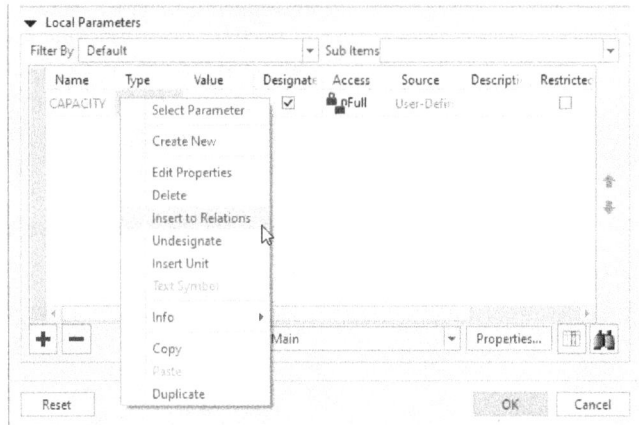

Figure 2–4

Creo Parametric enables you to create the following analysis types:

Analysis Type	Description
Measure	Measures distance, length, angle, area, volume or diameter of selected references. To create this type of analysis, select the *Analysis* tab, click (Measure), and select the appropriate option from the Measure dialog box, as shown below.
Model Report	Calculates model mass properties, finds short edges, or measures thickness of selected entities. To create this type of analysis, select the *Analysis* tab, and select the appropriate option, as shown below.

Inspect Geometry	Measures radius, curvature, dihedral angle, deviation, and slope of selected references. To create this type of analysis, select the *Analysis* tab, and select the appropriate option, as shown below. Geometry Report ▼ Pairs Clearance ▼ Curvature ▼ Draft Mesh Surface Build Direction Dihedral Angle Inspect Geometry ▼ Offset Analysis Radius Deviation Shadow Reflection Knots Slope Connection
Custom	This group contains **User-Defined**, **Excel**, **External**, **Mathcad**, and **Prime**, as shown below. The analysis available depends on the license available. Some of the more commonly used analysis in this group are **Excel** and **User-Defined**. User-Defined Analysis Mathcad Analysis Excel Analysis Prime Analysis Toolkit-Based External Analysis Custom
Relation	This type of the analysis feature is defined by means of a relation(s). Relations enable you to define analysis feature parameters. To create this type of analysis, select the *Tools* tab and click $d=$ (Relations).

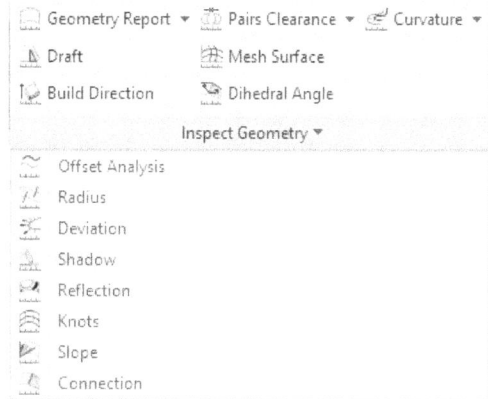

2.2 Analysis Feature Types

All the analysis features are created in the *Analysis* tab. The following types of analyses that can be created in an analysis feature:

- Measure

- Model Analysis

- UDA (User-Defined Analysis)

- Relation

- Excel Analysis

- Motion Analysis (Assembly mode only)

- Simulate

Measure

The Measure analysis feature enables you to conduct a measurement on the model, including:

- Length

- Distance

- Angle

- Diameter

- Area

- Volume

- Transform

How To: Create a Measure Analysis Feature

1. Select the *Analysis* tab. It activates as shown in Figure 2–5.

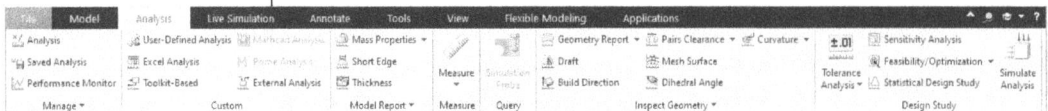

Figure 2–5

2. Select the type of analysis from the groups that you want to add to your model. A dialog box opens corresponding to the analysis type.

For example, if you click ✎ (Measure), the Measure dialog box as shown in Figure 2–6.

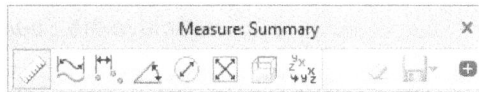

Figure 2–6

3. When the Measure dialog box opens, you can select the type of measurement that you want to create and then click

   ⊕ (Expand The Dialog) to expand the dialog box, as shown in Figure 2–7.

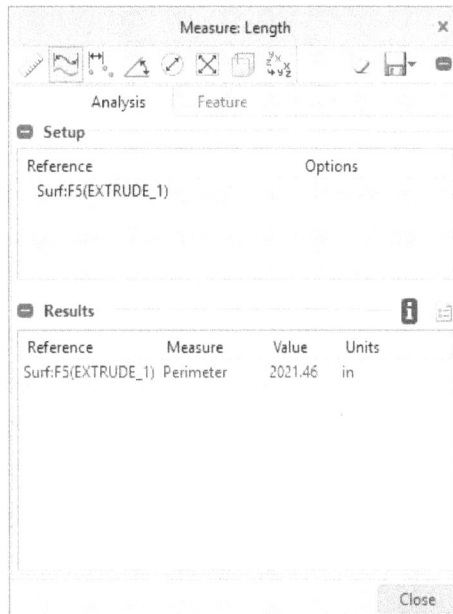

Figure 2–7

The item to measure can be preselected or selected when the *Analysis* tab is active and displays in the Measure dialog box. The results also display in the View window.

4. Click 📄 (Open Options) in the Measure dialog box to set various options. For example, you can toggle the **Show Feature Tab** option, as shown in Figure 2–8. This will show or remove the *Feature* tab in the dialog box.

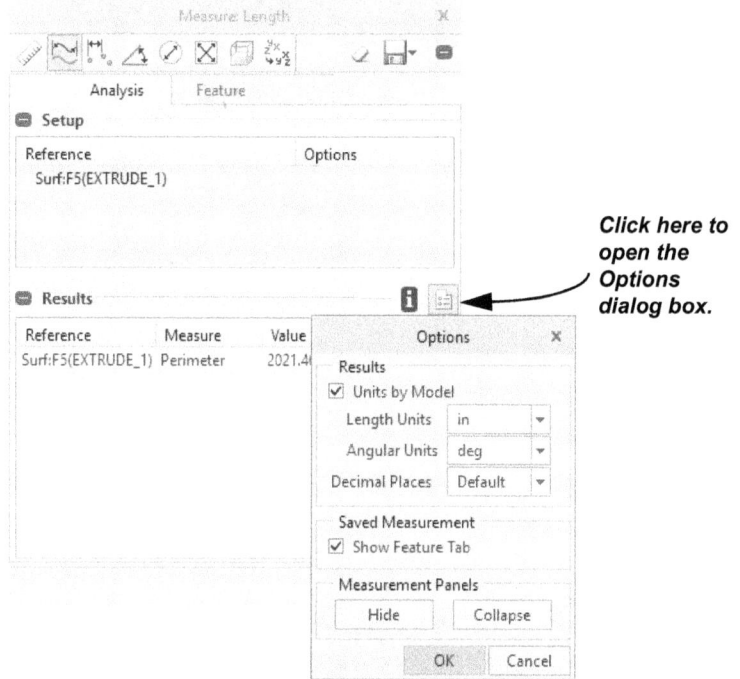

Click here to open the Options dialog box.

Figure 2–8

Select the *Feature* tab shown in Figure 2–9 to display the parameter.

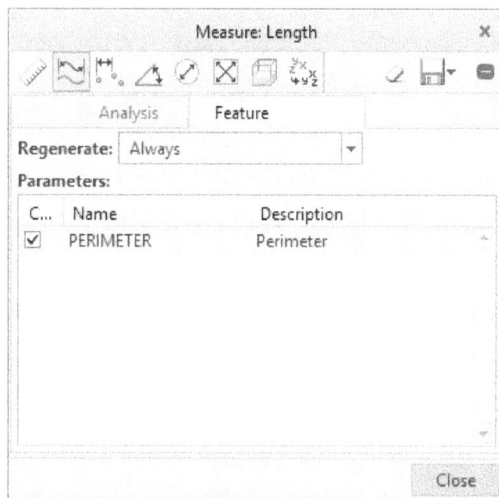

Figure 2–9

The Regenerate drop-down list enables you to assign when the analysis feature regenerates. The options include the following:

- **Always:** Regenerates the analysis feature during model regeneration.
- **Read Only:** Excludes the analysis feature from the model regeneration.
- **Design Study:** Only regenerates the analysis feature when it is used by a design study.

In the *Parameters* area, you can specify whether you want to create the displayed parameters. You can edit the names of these parameters as required.

*Note that when you click **Save Analysis** or **Make Feature**, any parameter names you changed will be saved correctly with the analysis, but will revert to the original names in the dialog box. This way, you can use the dialog box to save multiple analyses without closing it.*

5. By default, the **Make Feature** option is preselected in the Measure dialog box. The **Feature** option creates an analysis feature. Enter an appropriate name for the analysis feature. By default, the default name identifies the analysis type (e.g., **MEASURE_LENGTH_#** for length analysis feature). The updated dialog box is shown in Figure 2–10.

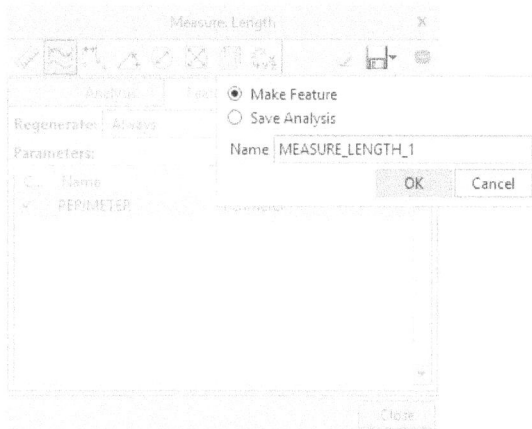

Figure 2–10

6. Click **OK** and then **Close** in the Measure dialog box to complete the feature.

Model Analysis

A model analysis feature calculates any of the following properties:

- Model Mass Properties

- X-section Mass Properties

- Clearance and Interference

Figure 2–11 shows the Mass Properties dialog box used to calculate and define the required information.

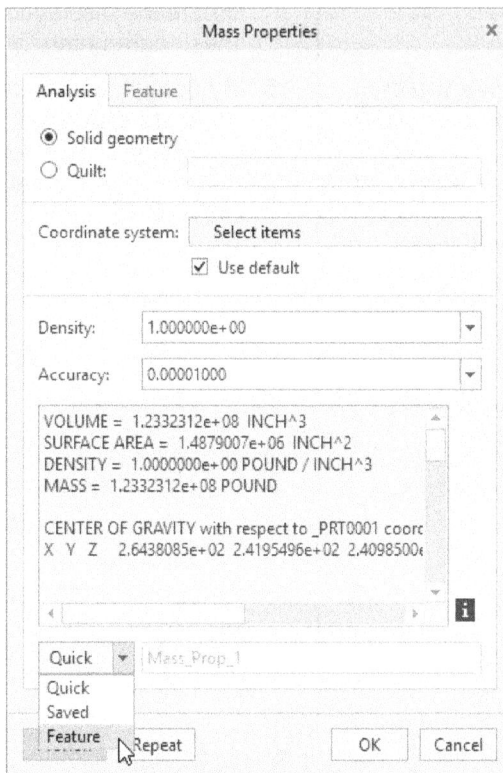

Figure 2–11

Model Analysis Example

The designer needs to ensure the center of gravity is correctly located on the model (shown in Figure 2–12) so that it does not tip over once used. You can create a Model Analysis analysis feature that measures the location of the center of gravity and creates a coordinate system at this location. The location updates as changes are made to the model, ensuring that design changes reflect in an updated center of gravity.

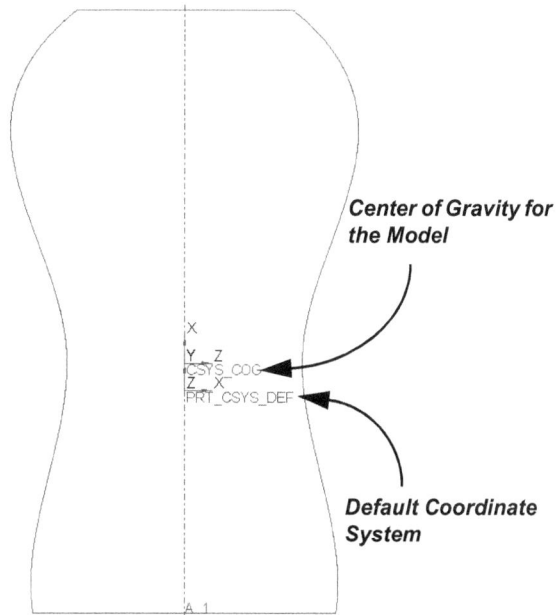

Center of Gravity for the Model

Default Coordinate System

Figure 2–12

UDA

The UDA analysis feature enables you to define, perform, and store non-standard geometric analyses.

A group must be defined consisting of all the datum features. The last feature in the group must be an Analysis feature. If the group contains a field point as the first feature, the measurement is used throughout the entire domain of the field point. The resulting parameters are the maximum and minimum values of the Analysis feature in the created group.

The analysis is performed during regeneration, so the location of the feature can impact results. These values can be used in other Analysis features later in the regeneration cycle.

UDA Example:

You must determine the distance between the two cylinders. A measurement between the two surfaces only reports the closest distance. You will require the distance at all locations.

How To: Perform a UDA Analysis

1. In the *Model* tab, in the Datum group, expand $\overset{x\,x}{x}$ (Point) and select $\overset{x}{\underset{\square}{}}$ (Field). Select anywhere on the surface of one of the cylinders to place the point, as shown in Figure 2–13. The location does not matter because when it is used in the Analysis feature, it is permitted to move over the entire surface.

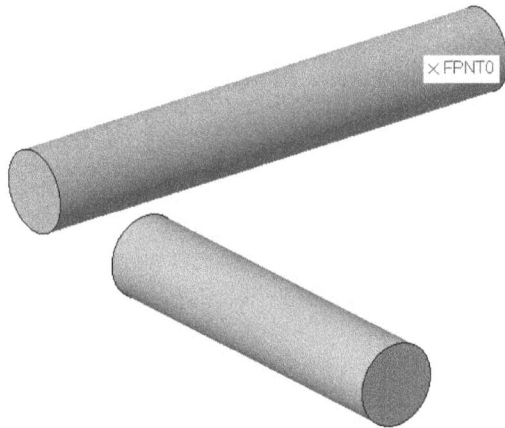

Figure 2–13

2. Create a distance measurement analysis feature with its associated parameter. This feature determines the distance between the field point and the other cylinder.
3. To run a user-defined analysis, a local group must be created that groups the analysis and field datum point feature. In the Model Tree, select the field point and analysis feature, and click $\overset{\text{⬚}}{}$ (Group) in the mini toolbar. Edit the group name in the Model Tree, to make it meaningful.

4. In the *Analysis* tab, in the Custom group, click

 (User-Defined Analysis). The dialog box displays as shown in Figure 2–14.

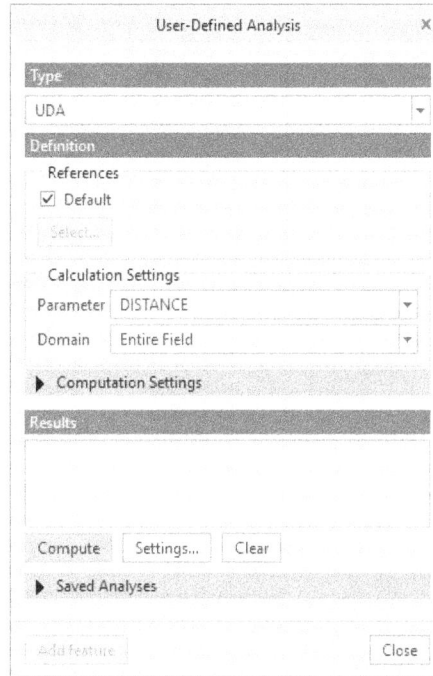

Figure 2–14

The elements in the dialog box required to create a User-Defined Analysis feature are described as follows:

Element	Description
Type	Select the UDA local group to analyze.
References	Enable the **Default** option to use default UDA references. In the example, the distance between the two protrusions was reported for the top surface. If the same information was required for the bottom surface, the references must be switched by clearing the Default checkbox and using **Select** to select the new references.
Calculation Settings Parameter	Lists all parameters belonging to the analysis in the UDA local group. Only one parameter can be analyzed at a time by the UDA.
Calculation Settings Domain	**Entire field -** Calculates the parameter for all the geometry associated with the field point. Reports a fringe plot. **Selected Point -** Prompts you to select a point on the geometry. Reports a single value in the results field.

The results of the analysis for the entire field are shown in Figure 2–15.

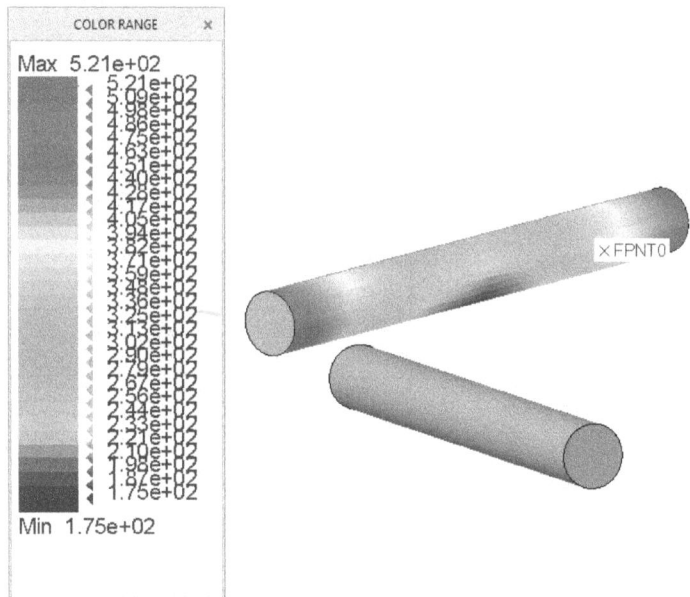

Figure 2–15

Relation

The Relation analysis feature enables you to write a relation that calculates model information that cannot be directly derived from another type of analysis. A relation is written using the standard Creo Parametric editor.

Relation Analysis Example

For example, the vase shown in Figure 2–16 has been created by shelling a solid protrusion. If the internal volume of the vase is required, a Relation Analysis feature can be created that subtracts the volume of the vase before and after the shell feature. The parameter **INTERNAL_VOL** can then be optimized or included in other design studies.

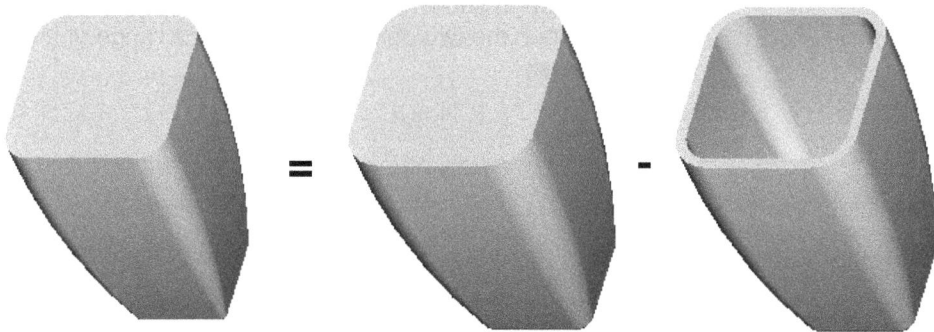

INTERNAL_VOL = SOLID_VOL - CUT_VOL

Figure 2–16

Motion Analysis

The Motion Analysis analysis feature enables you to evaluate parameters based upon the entire range of motion for an assembly. As the assembly is put in motion, results of the design parameters can be graphed with respect to time. This type of analysis feature is only available in the Assembly mode.

Motion Analysis is discussed further in a later chapter.

Motion Analysis Example

Figure 2–17 shows a model where a shaft rotates on its pin connection with a block. Two datum points have been created on each part. A Measure analysis feature was created to track the distance between the two points as the shaft rotates.

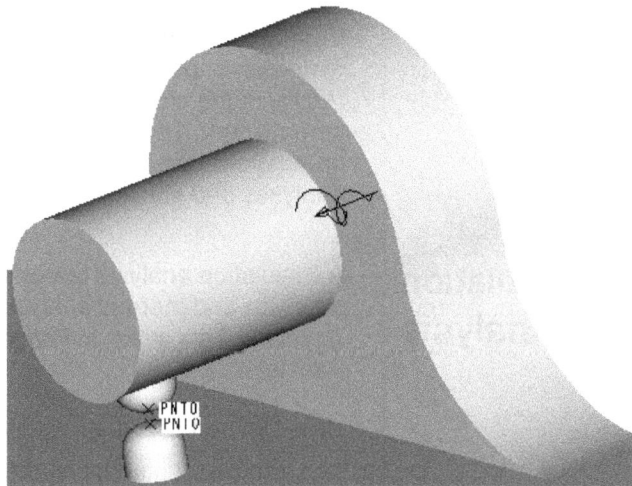

Figure 2–17

The graph shown in Figure 2–18 tracks the displacement between the two points throughout the range of the motion analysis.

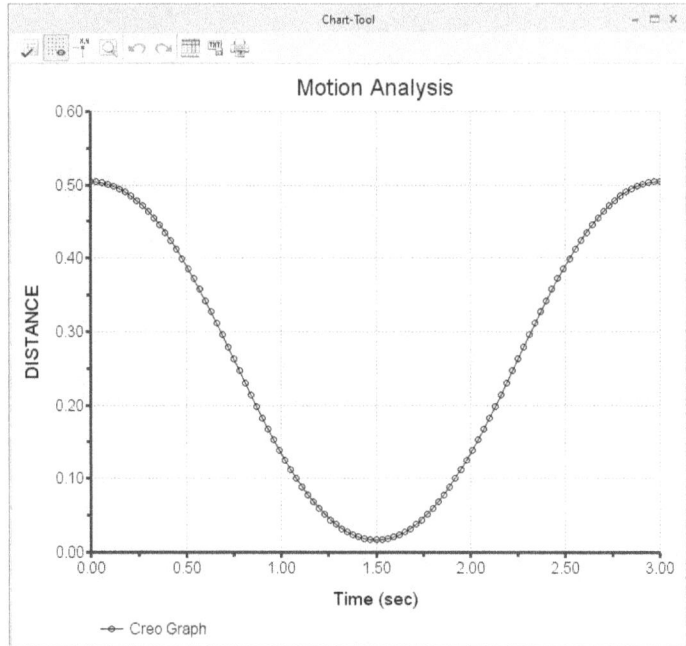

Figure 2–18

Excel Analysis

An Excel analysis feature enables you to use an Excel spreadsheet to define the analysis that is run on the Creo Parametric model. The spreadsheet links with Creo Parametric dimensions, parameters, and other analysis parameters. The results of the analysis can then be output and stored in the Excel spreadsheet. The data that is output can be stored as a feature parameter in the Excel Analysis feature and used in downstream analyses and studies.

Simulation Analysis

A Simulation analysis feature enables you to run both the structure and thermal analyses that have been defined in Creo Simulate. This analysis feature requires a license of Creo Simulate.

User-Defined, Relation, Excel, Motion and Simulate analyses can also be created using the $\overset{\times f}{\underset{\dots}{}}$ (Analysis) option in the *Manage* group in the *Analysis* tab.

How To: Create an Analysis Feature in the Manage Group, in the *Analysis* tab

1. To create an analysis feature, in the *Analysis* tab in the Manage group, click ⬚ (Analysis). The ANALYSIS dialog box opens as shown in Figure 2–19. Enter a new name for the Analysis feature and press <Enter>. The default name is **Analysis#**.

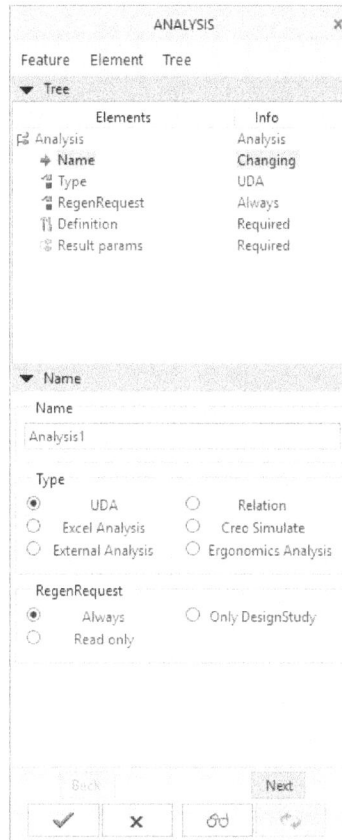

Figure 2–19

The *Tree* area in the Analysis dialog box lists the elements required for the selected Analysis feature. The elements required for the creation of an Analysis feature are described as follows:

Element	Description
Name	Defines the name of the Analysis feature. You must press <Enter> for the name to be assigned.

Type		Defines the type of Analysis feature. The image below shows the available options. The Motion Analysis option is only available in Assembly mode. 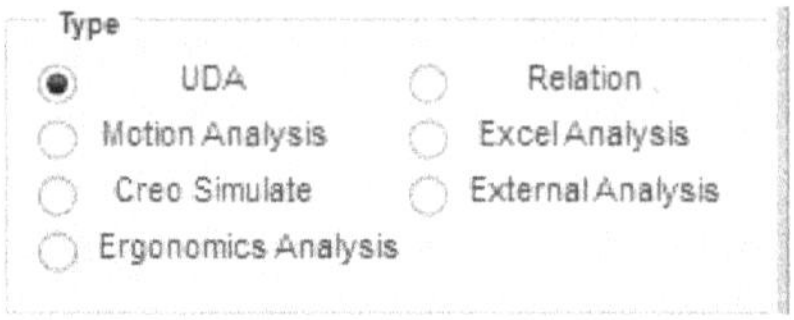
Regen Request		Defines how regeneration affects the Analysis feature. The *RegenRequest* options are shown below. 
	Always	The Analysis feature is regenerated each time the model is regenerated.
	Only DesignStudy	The Analysis feature is only regenerated when running a design study
	Read only	The Analysis feature is never regenerated.
Definition		Defines the calculations for the Analysis feature. This varies depending on the type of Analysis feature. This is accessed by selecting **Next** in the ANALYSIS dialog box.
Result Params		Defines the parameters that are added to the Analysis feature. This is only available for certain Analysis features. To add a parameter, select it in the *Result params* area, select **YES**, and enter a name, as shown below. 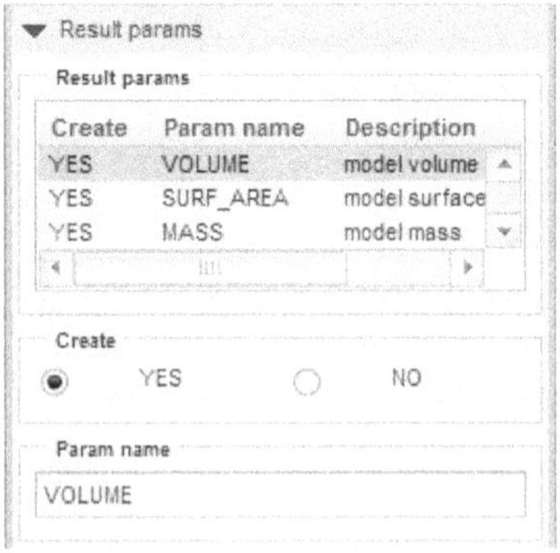

Result Datums	Defines the datum features that are added to the Analysis feature. This is only available for certain Analysis features. To create a datum feature, select it from the *Result datums* area, select **YES**, and enter a name, as shown below.

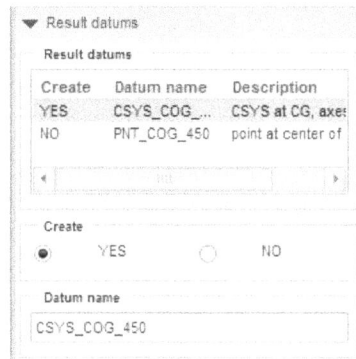

Persistent Display

For Curve, Surface and User-Defined Analysis (UDAs) features, their calculations generate graphs or a color fringe plot. In these situations, you have the ability to control the display of these features. The display properties can be accessed either through the Analysis feature or by clicking (Saved Analysis) in the Manage group of the *Analysis* tab. The Saved Analysis dialog box is shown in Figure 2–20.

Figure 2–20

You can select the Analysis feature, expand **All** and click **Hide All** or **Unhide All** to toggle the display.

2.3 Customizing Graphs

Many analyses allow you to create graphs of the results. The Chart-Tool window can be customized to change titles, fonts colors, and so on.

In the image shown in Figure 2–21, the chart on the left is the default graph and the image on the right is a customized graph.

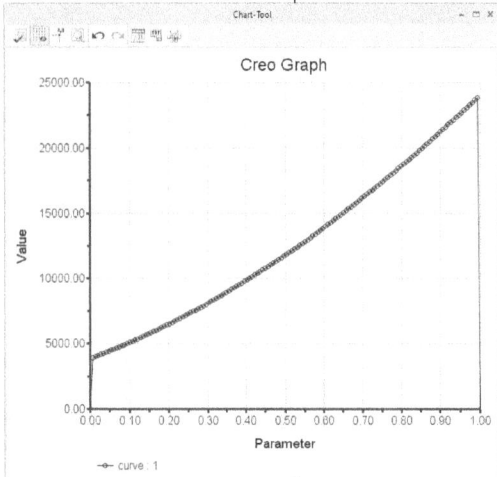

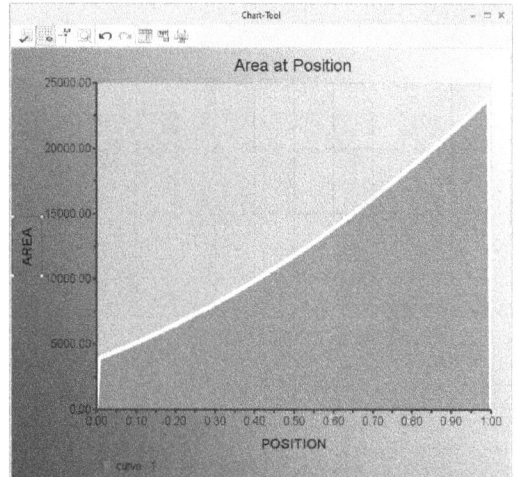

Figure 2–21

To customize a graph, click ✓ (Customize Graph) in the toolbar at the top of the Chart-Tool window. The window expands to show the customization options shown in Figure 2–22.

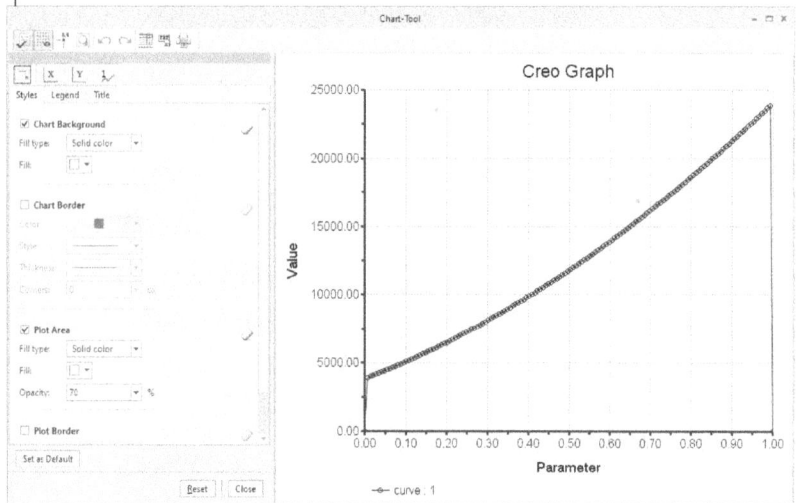

Figure 2–22

There are four areas you can customize:

- ⬚ (Format Chart) - Format the overall chart style and legend and title areas.

- ⬚ (Format X-Axis) - Format the x-axis style, gridlines, title and setup. The setup customizations include setting a user defined range, linear or logarithmic scale, and so on.

- ⬚ (Format Y-Axis) - Format the y-axis with the same options as the x-axis.

- ⬚ (Format Trace) - Format the curve and data point styles as well as the setup which include the ability to switch from a line chart to a column chart.

Select the appropriate option from the customization area, and the available options display. In Figure 2–23, the ⬚ (Format Chart) option is selected.

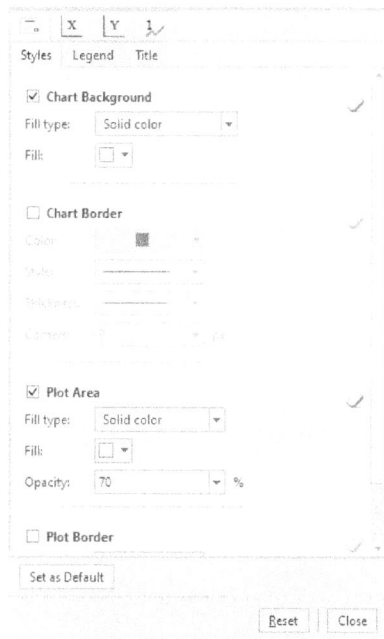

Figure 2–23

The background color can be changed by selecting a color from the color swatch. It can also be changed from a solid color to gradient. When the **Gradient** option is selected, two color swatches are available as well as an angle values, so you can select two colors and an angle, and the background will blend between them, as shown in Figure 2–24.

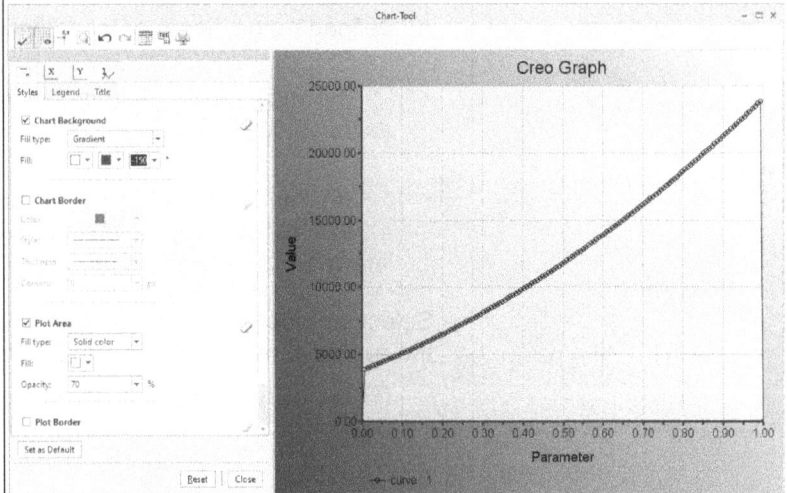

Figure 2–24

The *Legend* tab, shown in Figure 2–25, controls the display of the legend. The *Title* tab, also shown in Figure 2–25, controls the display of the chart title.

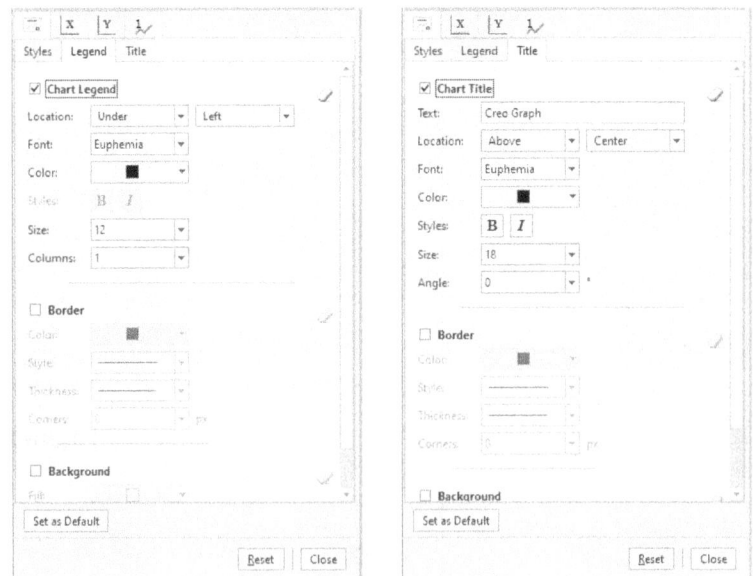

Figure 2–25

Similarly, you can make changes to the X and Y axis areas and the data curve.

Changes can be reset to default in multiple ways:

- Any individual changes can be reset to the original by clicking ✎ (Clear Formatting).

- All settings can be set to defaults by clicking **Reset**.

You can define the default style for new charts by making the edits you want and clicking **Set as Default**.

Graphs and underlying data are exported to an Excel spreadsheet by clicking ▦ (Export To Excel). Note that customizations to the graph such as background color will not be carried forward into the Excel graph, although changes to the X and Y axis Titles will, as shown in Figure 2–25.

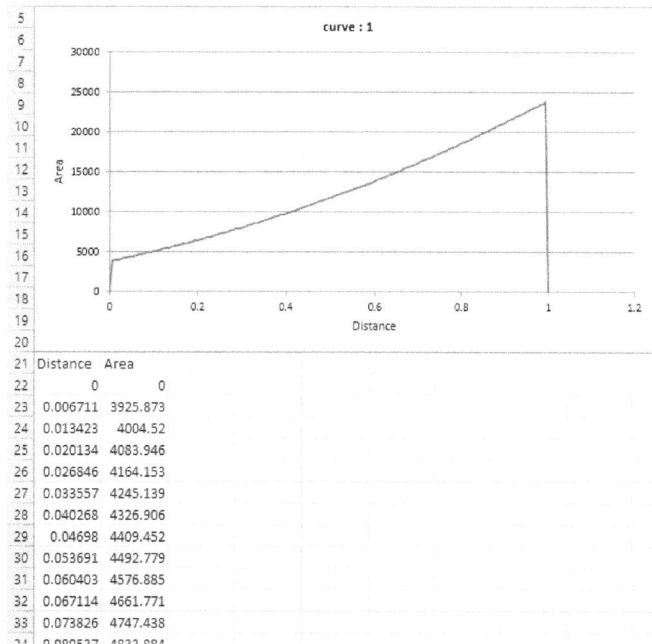

	Distance	Area
21	Distance	Area
22	0	0
23	0.006711	3925.873
24	0.013423	4004.52
25	0.020134	4083.946
26	0.026846	4164.153
27	0.033557	4245.139
28	0.040268	4326.906
29	0.04698	4409.452
30	0.053691	4492.779
31	0.060403	4576.885
32	0.067114	4661.771
33	0.073826	4747.438
34	0.080537	4833.884

Figure 2–26

Practice 2a	# Analysis Features I

Practice Objectives

- Create a Measure Analysis feature.
- Create a Relation Analysis feature.
- Add Analysis feature parameters to the Model Tree.

In this practice, you will create three Analysis features to determine the internal volume of a canister. A shell feature is used to remove the material in the canister. The first two Analysis features measure the liquid volume that the model holds below a specified fill line. One of these Analysis features calculates the entire volume of the model, without the shell, and the second measures the volume with the shell. A final Analysis feature is added to the model as a relation to subtract the values for the solid and shell parameters.

Task 1 - Open the canister.prt model.

1. Set the working directory to *Analysis_Features_I*.

2. Open **canister.prt**.

3. Set the model display as follows:

- ⋮⁄⊹ *(Datum Display Filters)*: Only 🔲 (Plane Display)
- *View* tab: 🔲 (Plane Tag Display)
- ⊱ *(Spin Center)*: Off
- ⬜ *(Display Style)*: 🔲 (Shading With Edges)

The model displays as shown in Figure 2–27.

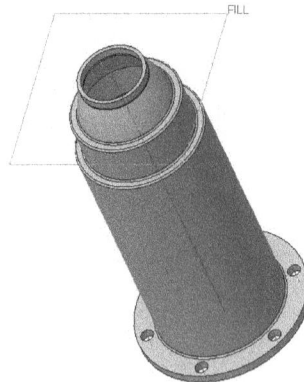

Figure 2–27

Task 2 - Use the Model Player to investigate the model.

1. Select the *Tools* tab.

2. In the Investigate Group, click ◢ (Model Player).

3. Click ◄ (Go To Beginning) to rewind to the beginning of the feature list.

Note that the first four features are hidden datums, so they will not display while using the Model Player.

4. Click ▶ (Step Forward) repeatedly to review each feature in the feature list. The shell feature was added to the canister to create an internal cavity. The **FILL** datum plane was added to the model to mark the location of the water line for the canister.

Task 3 - Create the first Analysis feature.

1. Select the *Analysis* tab.

2. In the Measure group, expand ◢ (Measure) and select ▢ (Volume). The Measure: Volume dialog box displays as shown in Figure 2–28.

Your dialog box may already display as expanded.

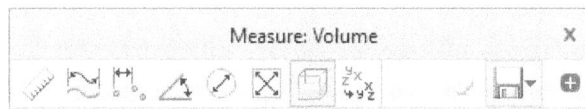

Figure 2–28

3. In the Measure: Volume dialog box, click ⊕ (Expand The Dialog), if not already expanded.

4. Click in the *Plane* field and select the **FILL** datum plane from the model.

5. Note that if you are unable to click in the *Plane* field, right-click on **CANISTER.PRT** in the *Reference* area and select **Remove**. Then, select **CANISTER.PRT** in the Model Tree and the *Plane* field activates.

6. If required, click ⚹ (Measure Other Side) to flip the direction of the arrow so that it points down into the part, as shown in Figure 2–29.

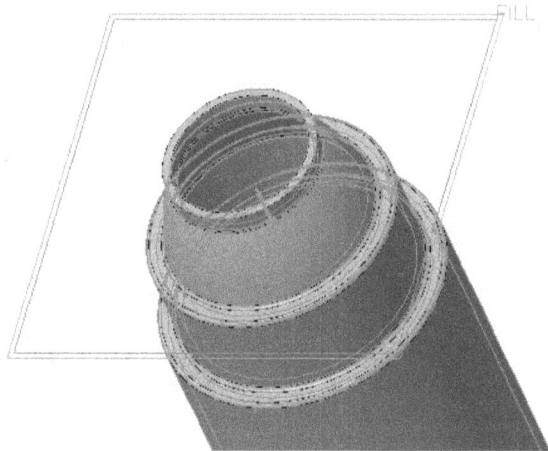

Figure 2–29

7. The part volume beneath the **FILL** datum plane is 926352 mm^3 (or approximately 1.0 L), as shown in Figure 2–30.

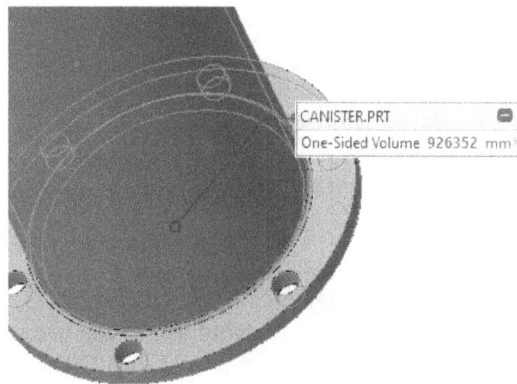

Figure 2–30

8. In the Measure: Volume dialog box, select the *Feature* tab.

9. Ensure that **Always** is selected as the default *Regenerate* option.

10. Select **ONE_SIDED_VOLUME** in the *Name* column, edit the parameter name to **CUT_VOL** and press <Enter>.

*After saving, the parameter name may change back to **ONE_SIDED_VOLUME** but this does not impact the analysis you just saved.*

Like all Creo Parametric features, Analysis features obey the regeneration order.

11. In the Measure: Volume dialog box, click 🖫▾ (Save).

12. Ensure that **Make Feature** is selected, set the name to **CUT**, and press <Enter>.

13. Click **Close** in the Measure: Volume dialog box.

Task 4 - Create a second Model Analysis feature.

1. In the Measure group, expand ⟋ (Measure) and select ▢ (Volume).

2. Click in the *Plane* field and select the **FILL** datum plane from the model.

3. If required, click ⟋ (Measure Other Side) to flip the direction of the arrow so that it points down into the part.

4. Select the *Feature* tab.

5. Ensure that **Always** is selected as the default *Regenerate* option.

6. Select **ONE_SIDED_VOLUME** in the *Name* column, edit the parameter name to **SOLID_VOL**, and press <Enter>.

7. In the Measure: Volume dialog box, click 🖫▾ (Save).

8. Ensure that **Make Feature** is selected, set the name to **SOLID**, and press <Enter>.

9. Click **Close** in the Measure: Volume dialog box.

Task 5 - Show the feature parameters in the Model Tree.

1. In the Model Tree, click 🗍 ▾ (Settings)>**Tree Columns** from the drop-down list.

2. In the Type drop-down list, select **Feat Params**.

3. Enter **CUT_VOL** in the Name field and select ≫ (Add Column).

4. Enter **SOLID_VOL** in the Name field and click ⟫ (Add Column) to add it to the *Displayed* column. The Model Tree Columns dialog box displays as shown in Figure 2–31.

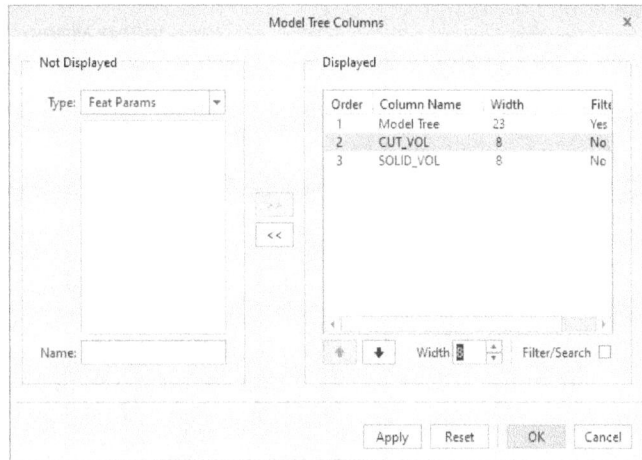

Figure 2–31

5. Click **OK**.

6. The new parameters display in the Model Tree, as shown in Figure 2–32. Note that both parameters have the same volume. This is because they were both created at the same point in the feature list.

Figure 2–32

Task 6 - Reorder the SOLID and CUT Analysis features.

Design Considerations

You want to determine the difference between the solid volume and the shelled volume, which is the carrying capacity of the container. So the SOLID measurement has to be made prior to shelling the container, and the CUT analysis feature after the shell feature.

1. In the Model Tree, drag the SOLID analysis feature and drop it so that it comes before the **Shell 1** feature, then drag the CUT analysis feature so that it comes after **Shell 1**. The Model Tree displays as shown in Figure 2–33.

Analysis features behave like other features; their feature order can affect the resulting parameter values.

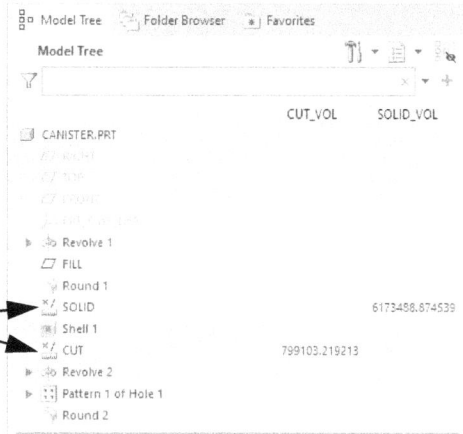

Reorder the SOLID Analysis feature before the Shell and CUT after the Shell

Figure 2–33

The **solid_vol** (6173488.87 mm^3) and **cut_vol** (799103.22 mm^3) will be used in a Relation Analysis feature to calculate the internal volume.

Task 7 - Create a Relation Analysis feature.

Design Considerations

In this task, you will add a relation to calculate the capacity. The relation will be of the form:

CAPACITY = SOLID_VOL:FID_SOLID - CUT_VOL:FID_CUT

The relation can be typed in as written or you can use the tools in the Relations dialog box to select the parameters.

In this relation, the two parameters **solid_vol** and **cut_vol** are subtracted. These parameters exist at the feature level and not at the part level. To indicate this, the feature name must be specified, as shown in Figure 2–34.

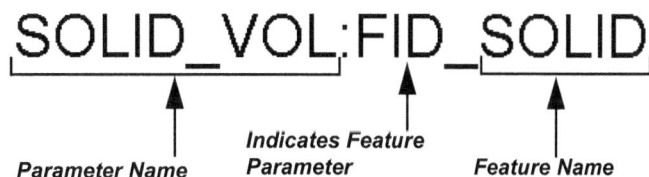

SOLID_VOL:FID_SOLID

Parameter Name   **Indicates Feature Parameter**   **Feature Name**

Figure 2–34

1. In the Manage group in the ribbon, click $\overset{\times}{\underset{\ldots}{/}}$ (Analysis).

2. In the Name field of the ANALYSIS dialog box, type **internal** and press <Enter>.

3. In the *Type* area, select **Relation**.

4. Ensure that **Always** is selected as the default *RegenRequest* option.

5. Click **Next**. The Relations dialog box displays, where you can enter the relation.

6. Type **CAPACITY =**.

7. In the Relations dialog box, click [ ] (Insert Parameter Name) and the Select Parameter dialog box opens, as shown in Figure 2–35.

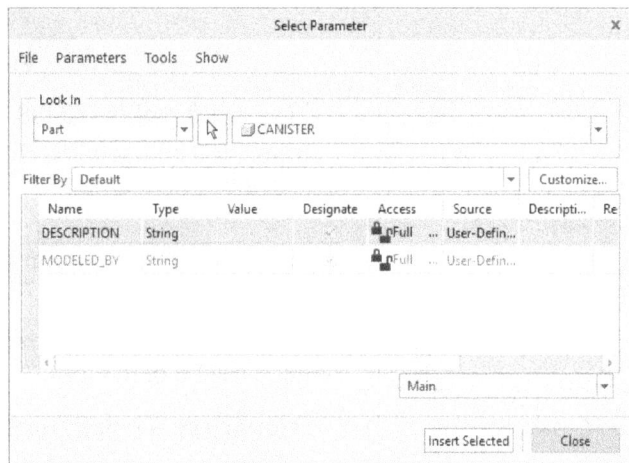

Figure 2–35

8. In the Look In drop-down list, select **Feature**.

9. In the Model Tree, select **SOLID** and click **Insert Selected**.

10. Type **-**.

11. Click [ ] (Insert Parameter Name).

12. In the Look In drop-down list, select **Feature**.

13. In the Model Tree, select **Cut** and click **Insert Selected**. The Relations editor displays as shown in Figure 2–36.

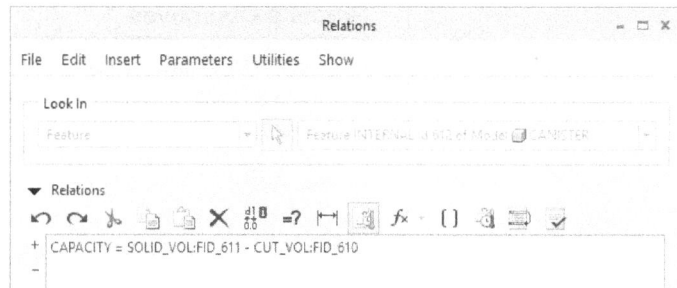

Figure 2–36

14. In the Relations dialog box, click ✅ (Verify) to verify the relation and click **OK**.

15. Click **OK** in the Relations dialog box.

16. Click ✔ (OK) to complete the Analysis feature.

Task 8 - Add the volume parameter to the Model Tree.

---

1. Add the **CAPACITY** feature parameter to the Model Tree. If required, refer to Task 5 for instructions on how to add this parameter. The calculated capacity of the canister is approximately 5.4 L.

Task 9 - Modify the location of the FILL datum.

---

1. Select the **FILL** datum plane and click ⬚ (Edit Dimensions) in the mini toolbar.

2. Change the offset dimension from *25* to **200**.

3. Regenerate the model. Note how the parameter values change in the Model Tree.

4. Restore the location of the **FILL** datum by modifying its offset value back to **25**. Regenerate the model.

5. In the Model Tree, click ⬚ ▾ (Settings)>**Reset Tree Settings>Reset Tree Settings**.

6. Save the model and erase it from memory.

Practice 2b

Analysis Features II

Practice Objectives

- Create a Measure Analysis feature.
- Create a Relation Analysis feature.
- Create a Model Analysis feature.

In this practice, you will create Analysis features in a flower vase model. These features are required by the designer to design and manufacture a stable model. The following information is required:

- The height of the flower vase. This will be calculated using a Measure Analysis feature.

- The amount of paint required to paint the outside surface area of the flower vase. This will be calculated using both a Measure and Relation Analysis feature.

- The location of the center of mass to help ensure the stability of the flower vase when it is used. This will be calculated using both a Model Analysis and Measure Analysis feature.

Using Analysis features in this way enables you to quickly and easily review the parameter values without having to recalculate them each time a design change is made.

Task 1 - Open the flower_vase.prt model.

1. Set the working directory to *Analysis_Features_II*.

2. Open **flower_vase.prt**.

3. Set the model display as follows:

- *(Datum Display Filters)*: Only ˣˣ (Point Display)

- *View* tab: (Point Tag Display)

- *(Spin Center)*: Off

- *(Display Style)*: (Shading With Edges)

The model displays as shown in Figure 2–37.

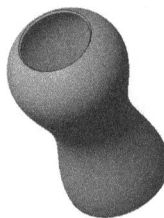

Figure 2–37

4. Select the *Tools* tab and use ⚐ (Model Player) to investigate the model.

Task 2 - Create an Analysis feature that measures the height of the model.

1. Create and place two datum points, the first at the bottom center of the vase and the second at the top center, as shown in Figure 2–38. To create these datum points, select the *Model* tab. In the Datum group, click ˣˣ (Point), then select the following:

Both datum points can be created within the same feature, or they can be created separately.

Shading turned off for clarity.

- Select the reference edge.
- Expand **On** in the *References* area of the dialog box.
- Select **Center** from the drop-down list.
- Click **New Point** and select the top edge.
- Click **OK**.

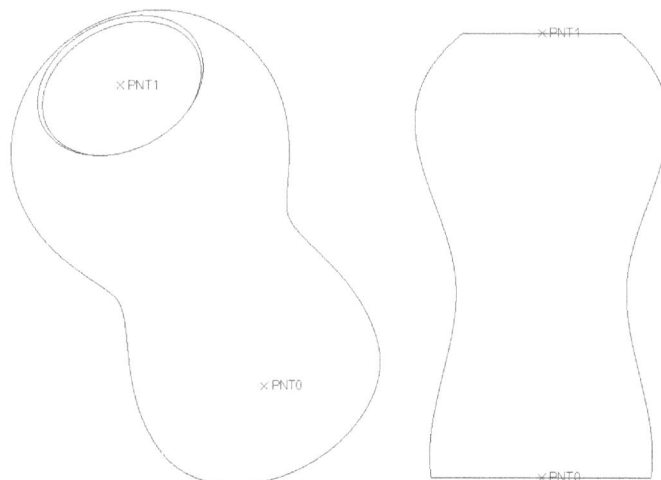

Figure 2–38

2. In the ribbon, select the *Analysis* tab.

3. In the Measure group, expand ⟋ (Measure) and select ⊓ (Distance).

4. The Measure dialog displays as shown in Figure 2–39.

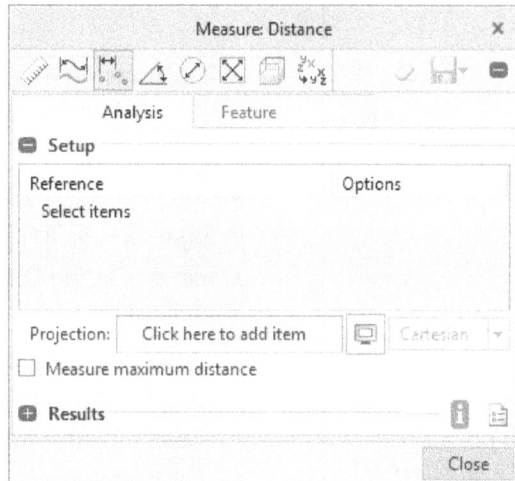

Figure 2–39

5. Select **PNT0**.

6. Press and hold <Ctrl> and select **PNT1**. Note that the vase part height is 270mm, as shown in Figure 2–40.

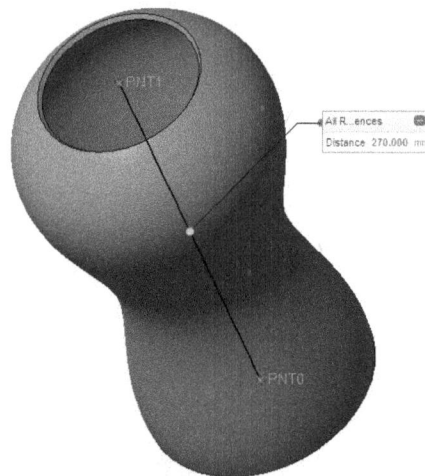

Figure 2–40

7. In the Measure: Distance dialog box, select the *Feature* tab.

8. Ensure that the **DISTANCE** parameter is selected.

9. Click 📑▾ (Save).

10. Ensure that **Make Feature** is selected, set the name to **HEIGHT**, and press <Enter>.

11. Click **Close** in the Measure: Volume dialog box.

Task 3 - Show feature parameters in the Model Tree.

1. In the Model Tree, click 🔧 ▼ (Settings)>**Tree Columns** from the drop-down list.

2. Select **Feat Params** from the Type drop-down list.

3. Set the parameter name to **DISTANCE** and select ≫ (Add Column).

4. Click **OK**.

5. The Model Tree shows the new parameter, as shown in Figure 2–41.

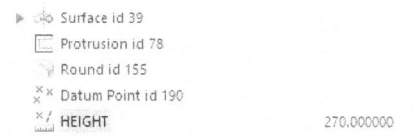

▶ Surface id 39
    Protrusion id 78
    Round id 155
ˣˣ Datum Point id 190
ˣ⁄ HEIGHT   270.000000

Figure 2–41

Task 4 - Create an Analysis feature that measures the surface area that is required to be painted.

1. In the Measure group in the ribbon, expand 📏 (Measure) and select ⊠ (Area).

2. Select one of the outside surfaces of the part. Note that the area is 119001mm2.

3. In the Measure: Distance dialog box, select the *Feature* tab.

   • Note that the **AREA** parameter will be created.

4. Click 💾▼ (Save).

5. Ensure that **Make Feature** is selected, set the name to **PAINT_AREA**, and press <Enter>.

6. Click **Close** in the Measure: Volume dialog box.The feature is added to the Model Tree.

7. Show the **AREA** parameter in the Model Tree.

Task 5 - Create an Analysis feature that uses the Model Analysis to find the center of mass for the model.

1. Click **File>Prepare>Model Properties**.

2. In the Model Properties dialog box, click **Change** in the Mass Properties line.

3. Ensure that the value for density is **1.00 e-9** and click **OK**.

4. Close the Mass Properties dialog box.

5. In the ribbon, in the Model Report group, click ⏚ (Mass Properties).

6. In the Mass Properties dialog box, click **Preview**.

7. The model mass properties display in the Results window, as shown in Figure 2–42.

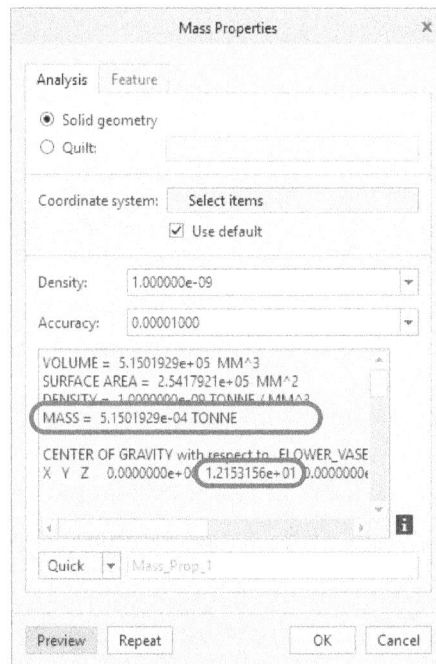

Figure 2–42

Note that the mass of the part is 0.5Kg and that its center of mass is located approximately 12 mm from default coordinate system in the Y-direction, as shown in Figure 2–43.

Shading turned off for clarity.

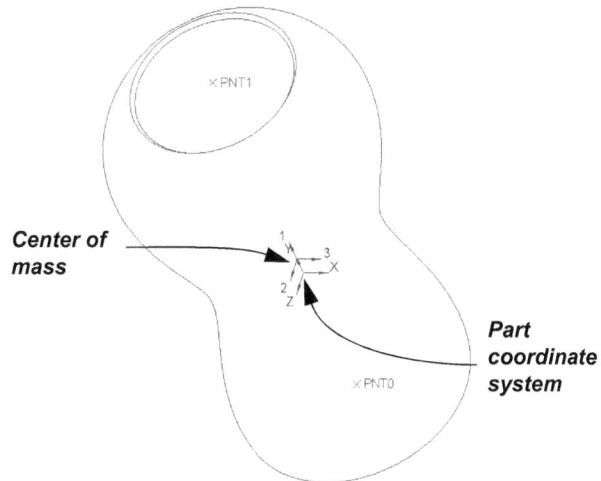

Center of mass

Part coordinate system

×PNT1

×PNT0

Figure 2–43

8. In the Quick drop-down list, select **Feature** and edit the name to **CENTER_MASS** and press <Enter>.

9. Select the *Feature* tab.

10. Remove the checkmark in the *Create* column next to the **VOLUME** parameter, so it is not created.

11. Add a checkmark in the *Create* column next to the **PNT_COG** parameter, as shown in Figure 2–44, to create it.

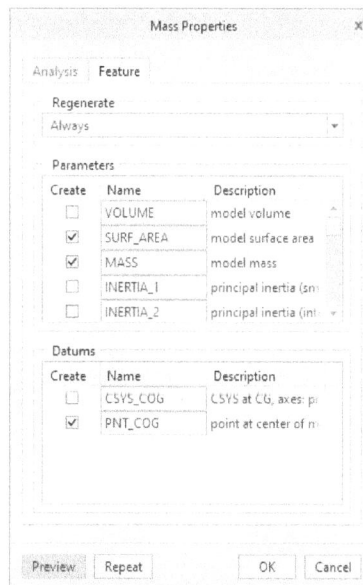

Figure 2–44

12. Select **OK** to complete the feature. The feature is added to the Model Tree and a point displays at the part's center of mass, as shown in Figure 2–45.

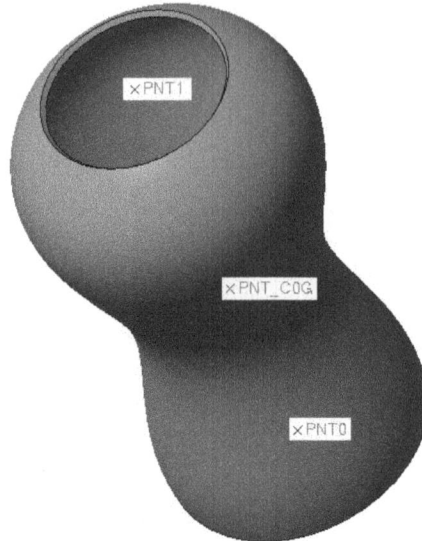

Figure 2–45

Task 6 - Create an Analysis feature that measures from the center of mass to the bottom of the flower_vase.

1. In the Measure group, expand (Measure) and select (Distance).

2. Select the point at the bottom of the model, **PNT0**.

3. Press and hold <Ctrl> and select **PNT_COG**.

4. The distance from the bottom to **PNT_COG** is 112.153mm.

5. In the Measure: Distance dialog box, click (Save).

6. Ensure that **Make Feature** is selected, set the name to **CENTER_TO_BOTTOM**, and press <Enter>.

7. Select the *Feature* tab.

8. Select the **DISTANCE** parameter, edit the name to **C_OF_G**, and press <Enter>.

9. Click **Close** in the Measure: Distance dialog box.

10. Show the **C_OF_G** feature parameters in the Model Tree.

Task 7 - Modify the part to ensure that the Analysis feature updates accordingly.

1. Increase the radius of the round (**feature id 155**) shown in Figure 2–46 to **35**. Note how the center of gravity changes. Reducing the center of mass below 1/3 of the overall height should ensure that the model remains stable when it is used.

A round size larger than 57 will cause the model to fail.

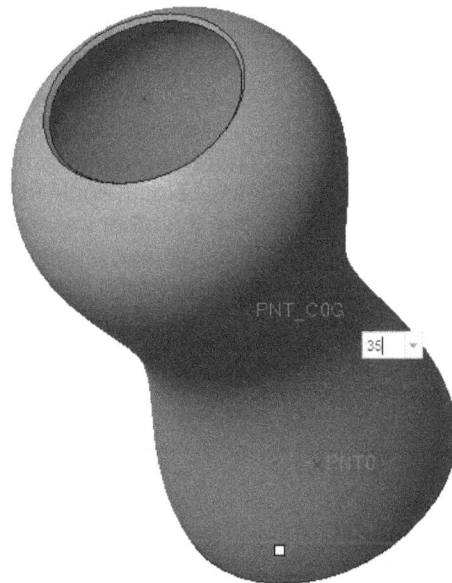

Figure 2–46

2. In the Model Tree, click 🔧 ▾ (Settings)>**Reset Tree Settings>Reset Tree Settings**.

3. Close the model and erase it from memory.

Practice 2c | User-Defined Analysis I

Practice Objectives

- Create a Field Point.
- Create a User-Defined Analysis.

In this practice, you will use a User-Defined Analysis (UDA) to determine the clearance between a model and its surrounding assembly components. The model analyzed is shown in Figure 2–47. The pipe connects two cold fluid containers in a top-level assembly. The underside of the pipe is surrounded by mechanical components, which produce a large amount of heat. These components are represented by the surface. The fluid must remain cool while traveling through the pipe and the heat from the other assembly components must dissipate. To achieve this goal, the pipe and components should always be separated by a minimum distance of 20 mm.

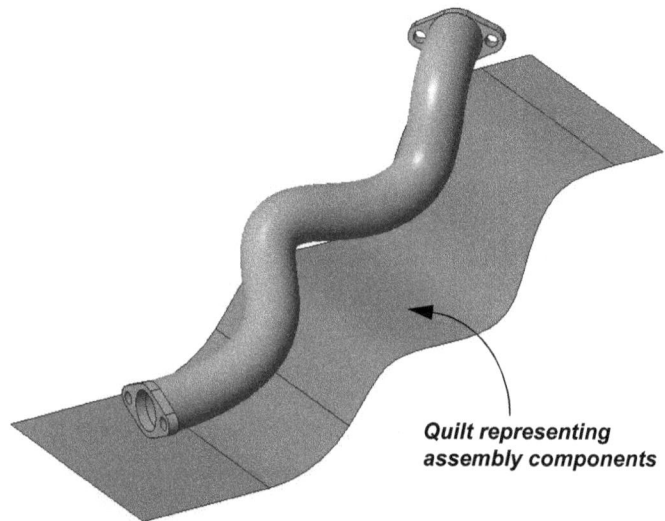

Quilt representing assembly components

Figure 2–47

Task 1 - Open the pipe.prt model.

1. Set the working directory to *User-Defined_Analysis_I*.

2. Open **pipe.prt**.

3. Set the model display as follows:

- *(Datum Display Filters)*: Only ⁙ (Point Display)

- *View* tab: ⁙ (Point Tag Display)

- ⟫ *(Spin Center)*: Off

- ▯ *(Display Style)*: ▭ (Shading With Edges)

Task 2 - Create a field point to measure from.

1. In the *Model* tab, expand ⁙ (Point) and select ⊡ (Field).

2. In the Selection Filter, select **Quilt**.

3. Select anywhere on the quilt (not a surface), as shown in Figure 2–48. The location does not matter because when it is used in the Analysis feature, it is permitted to move over the entire surface.

A field point is a special datum point feature that can be easily moved on the geometry on which it is placed. In this practice, the field point is constrained to the surface; however, no dimensions are rigidly constraining it to one location on the surface.

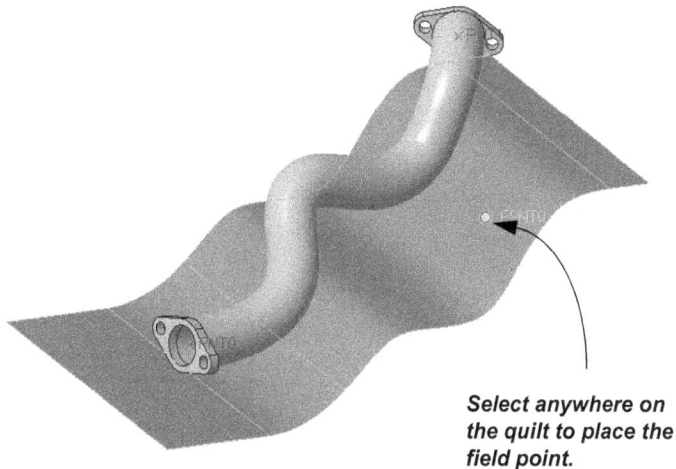

Select anywhere on the quilt to place the field point.

Figure 2–48

4. Click **OK** to complete the Field Datum Point.

Task 3 - Create a Measure Analysis feature.

1. Select the *Analysis* tab.

2. In the *Measure* group, expand ⟋ (Measure) and select ⊓ (Distance).

3. Select the field point **FPNT0**.

4. Press <Ctrl> and select the surface of the pipe.

5. The outer surface of the pipe is highlighted as shown in Figure 2–49. The resulting distance could be different than that shown, due to the placement of your field point.

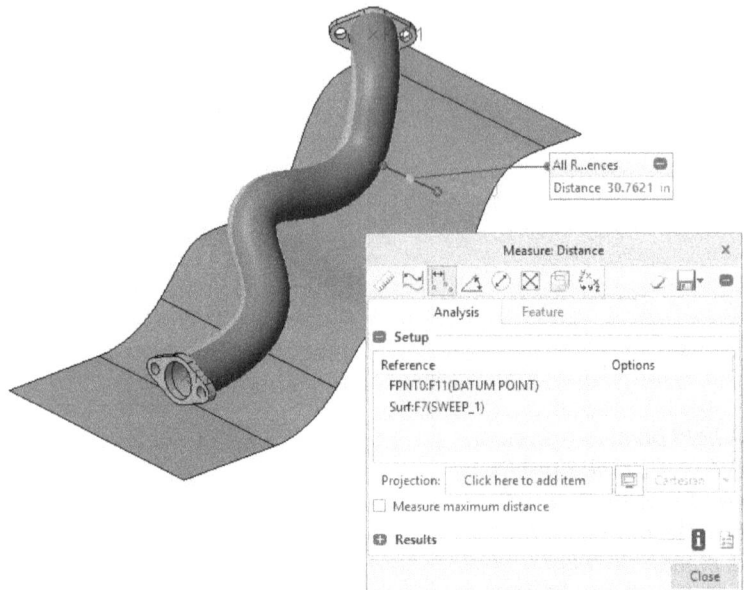

Figure 2–49

6. In the Measure: Distance dialog box, select the *Feature* tab.

7. Ensure that the **DISTANCE** parameter is selected for creation.

8. Click ▦▾ (Save).

9. Ensure that **Make Feature** is selected, set the name to **DISTANCE**, and press <Enter>.

10. Click **Close** in the Measure: Distance dialog box.

Task 4 - Create a local group.

1. In the Model Tree, select **FPNT0**, press <Ctrl>, and select **DISTANCE**.

2. Select ⬡ (Group) in the mini toolbar.

3. Right-click on the resulting Local group and select **Rename**.

4. Edit the name to **UDA** (after pressing <Enter> the name will read Group UDA).

Task 5 - Create a user-defined analysis.

1. In the *Custom* group in the ribbon, click ⚙ (User-Defined Analysis).

2. Note that **UDA** is selected in the Type drop-down list.

3. Accept all defaults in the *References* and *Calculation Settings* areas. The References default to those included in the UDA local group. The UDA calculates the values of the **DISTANCE** parameter. Since a field point was included in the group, this parameter is calculated for the entire field (or across the entire surface).

4. Click **Compute**. Once the analysis has completed, a fringe plot displays with a legend in the top left-hand corner of the screen. The *Results* area in the User Defined Analysis dialog box shows a minimum distance of approximately 10.38mm between the pipe and the surrounding assembly components. The fringe plot shown in Figure 2–50 indicates where this minimum occurs. This distance is lower than the 20 mm set by our design constraints; therefore, changes must be made to the design of the pipe.

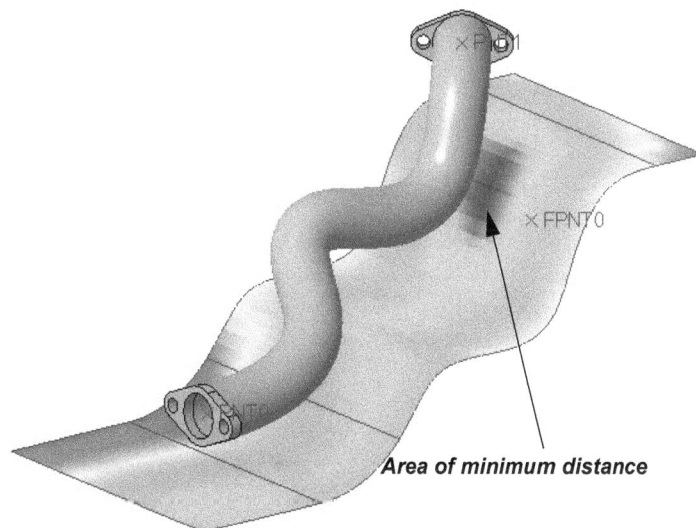

Area of minimum distance

Figure 2–50

5. Expand the *Saved Analyses* area. Set the name to **FIELD_DIST** and click 🖫 (Save) to save the analysis. By saving the analysis, this fringe plot can be shown on the model at any time without having to run the UDA again. By default, the fringe plot remains displayed. The display of the fringe can be controlled using the 👁 👁 icon.

   • Leave the results displayed for the remainder of the practice.

6. Close the User-Defined Analysis dialog box.

Task 6 - Modify the pipe feature.

1. Select the **Curve id79** feature from the Model Tree and select ↦ (Edit Dimensions) in the mini toolbar. The dimensions display as shown in Figure 2–51.

   • If the dimensions do not display, right-click **Curve id79** in the Model Tree and select ↦ (Show/Hide Sketch Dimensions). The datum curve is used as the trajectory for the swept pipe.

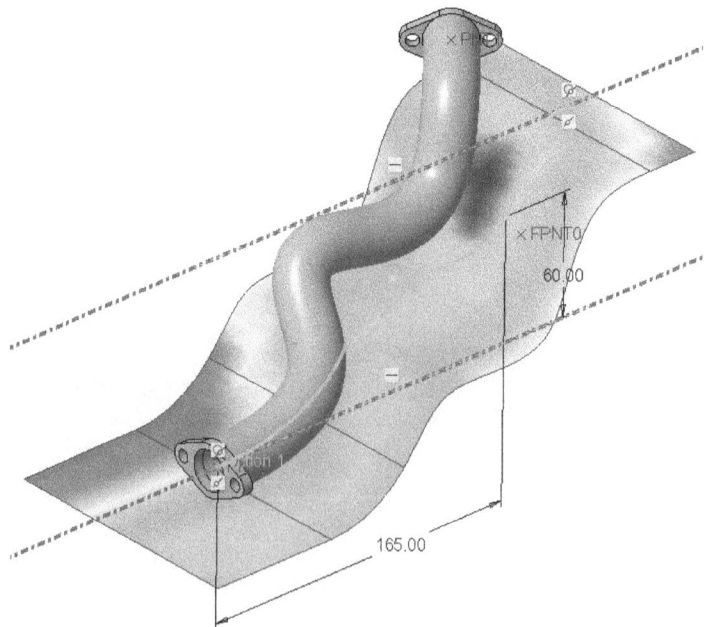

Figure 2–51

2. Change the 60 mm vertical dimension to **70** and the 165 mm horizontal dimension to **155**.

3. Regenerate the model. The pipe feature updates to its new location and the UDA is recalculated, as shown in Figure 2–52.

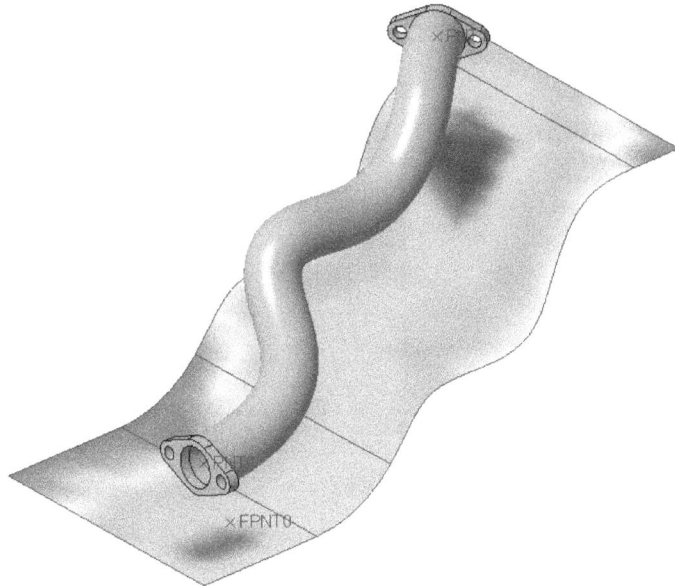

Figure 2–52

4. In the ribbon, select the *Analysis* tab.

5. Click ⬛ (User-Defined Analysis).

6. Expand the Saved Analysis area, select **FIELD_DIST** and click **Retrieve**.

7. Look at the Color Range window. The minimum value has changed to 23.3 mm. The design now meets the minimum distance constraint.

8. The exact minimum distance value can be obtained by opening the saved **FIELD_DIST** results. In the Custom group in the ribbon, click ⬛ (User-Defined Analysis) and expand the *Saved Analyses* area. Highlight the **FIELD_DIST** analysis and click **Retrieve**. The exact minimum distance is 23.314319 mm.

9. Save the model and erase it from memory.

Practice 2d

User-Defined Analysis II

Practice Objectives

- Create a Field Point.
- Create a User-Defined Analysis.

In this practice, you will use a User-Defined Analysis (UDA) to examine the cross-sectional area of internal surfaces of a model. The internal profile of the duct should vary evenly to deter turbulent flow.

Task 1 - Open the section_area model.

1. Set the working directory to *User-Defined_Analysis_II*.

2. Open **section_area.prt**.

3. Set the model display as follows:

- *(Datum Display Filters):* (Point Display), (Plane Display)

- *View tab:* (Point Tag Display)

- *(Spin Center):* Off

- *(Display Style):* (Shading With Edges)

Task 2 - Create a field point to measure from.

1. In the *Model* tab, expand (Point) and select (Field).

2. Select anywhere on the curve, as shown in Figure 2–53. The **FPNT0** point displays on the curve at the location where you have made the selection.

   Note that the location does not matter because when it is used in the Analysis feature, it is permitted to move over the entire length of the curve.

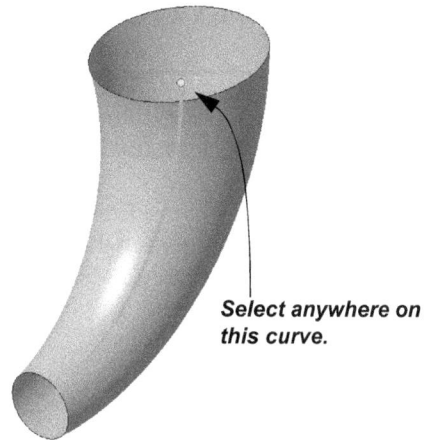

Select anywhere on this curve.

Figure 2–53

3. Click **OK** to complete the Field Datum Point.

Task 3 - Create a datum plane to be used to create a datum curve.

---

1. In the *Model* tab, click ▱ (Plane) to create a new datum plane.

2. Create the datum plane through **FPNT0** and normal to the curve on which **FPNT0** is located. The model displays as shown in Figure 2–54. If the Field Datum Point is still selected when you begin the creation of the datum plane, it is automatically selected for you. Press and hold <Ctrl> to select the datum curve to define the normal reference.

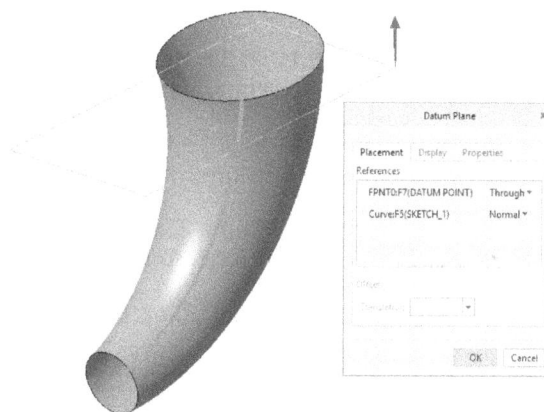

Figure 2–54

3. Click **OK** to complete the plane.

A field point is a special datum point feature that can be easily moved on the geometry on which it is placed. In this practice, the field point is constrained to the curve; however, no dimensions are rigidly constraining it to one location on the curve.

Task 4 - Create a datum curve at the intersection of the surface feature and DTM1.

1. Press and hold <Ctrl> and select **DTM1** and **Swept Blend 1** from the Model Tree.

2. In the Editing group, click ⌐ (Intersect) to create a datum curve at the intersection of these two references, as shown in Figure 2–55.

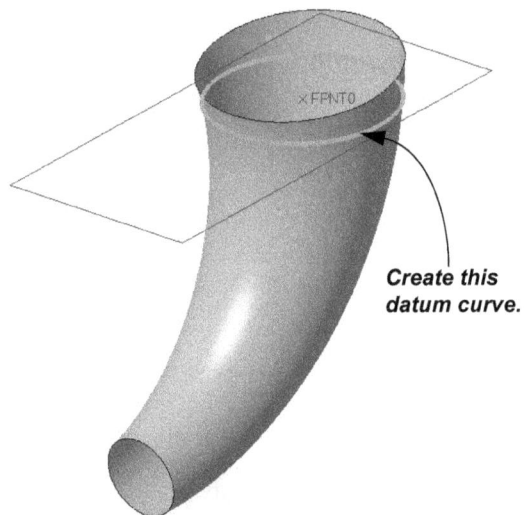

Create this datum curve.

Figure 2–55

Task 5 - Create a flat surface to represent the cross-sectional area of the model at the field point.

1. In the Surfaces group, click ⬚ (Fill) to create a flat surface that references the datum curve that was just created.

2. Right-click in the graphics window and select **Define Internal Sketch**.

3. In the Sketch dialog box, select **DTM1** as Sketch Plane and **FRONT** as the Top reference plane.

4. Click **Sketch**.

5. Right-click in the graphics window and select References.

6. Select **FPNT0** as a reference for the section.

7. Click **Close** in the References dialog box.

8. Click ☐ (Project) and select the curves created in Task 4 to define the section. The surface displays as shown in Figure 2–56.

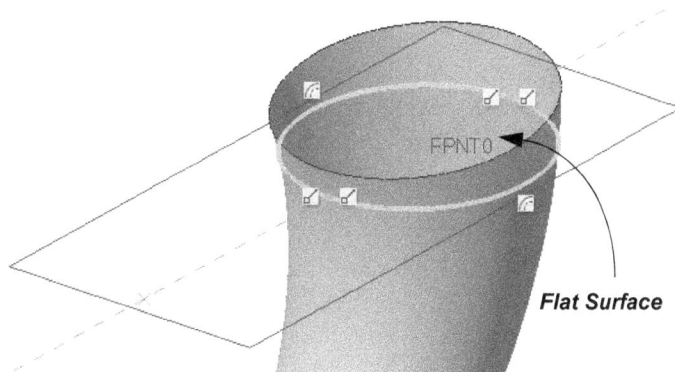

Figure 2–56

9. Click ✓ (OK)

10. Click ✓ (OK).

11. Toggle off the display of datum planes.

Task 6 - Create an Analysis feature to measure the area of the flat surface.

1. Select the *Analysis* tab.

2. In the Measure group, expand ⟋ (Measure) and select ⊠ (Area).

3. Select the Fill surface that you just created.

4. Click ⊟ (Save).

5. Ensure that **Make Feature** is selected, set the name to **FLAT_AREA**, and press <Enter>.

6. Click **Close** in the Measure: Area dialog box. The feature is added to the Model Tree.

7. Show the **AREA** parameter in the Model Tree.

Task 7 - Create a local group.

Press and hold <Shift> to select all features between the field point and the analysis feature.

1. Using the Model Tree, select all of the features between and including the field point, **FPNT0**, and the **FLAT_AREA** Analysis feature.

2. Click ⬤ (Group) in the mini toolbar.

3. Right-click on the Local group in the Model Tree and select **Rename**.

4. Edit the name to **section_area**.

Task 8 - Create a User-Defined Analysis feature to study the area at all points along the datum trajectory of the model geometry.

1. In the Custom group in the ribbon, click ⬤ (User-Defined Analysis).

   The User Defined Analysis dialog box displays as shown in Figure 2–57.

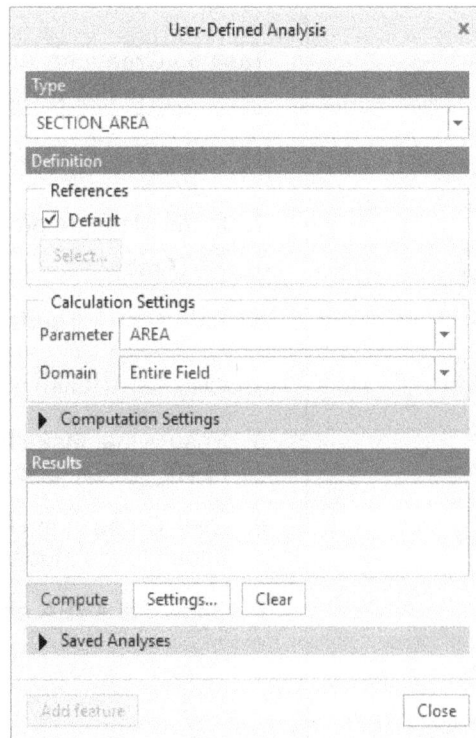

Figure 2–57

The Type drop-down list lists all UDA local groups in the model.

2. Ensure that **SECTION_AREA** is selected in the Type drop-down list.

3. Accept all defaults in the *References* area. The References options default to those included in the SECTION_AREA group. The SECTION_AREA group calculates values for the **AREA** parameter. Since a field point was included in the group, this parameter is calculated for the entire field.

4. Expand the *Computation Settings* area, as shown in Figure 2–58.

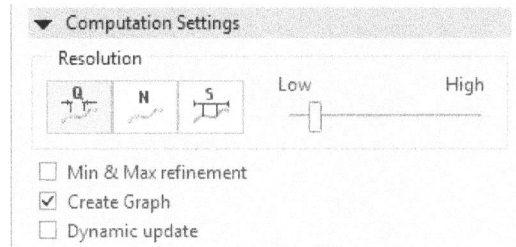

Figure 2–58

5. Drag the resolution quality slider to **High**.

6. Enable the **Min & Max refinement** option.

7. Clear the **Create Graph** option.

8. Select **Compute**. Once the analysis has been completed, it produces a porcupine plot of the surface area at each point along the model's trajectory, as shown in Figure 2–59. The porcupine plot displays the curvature progression along the trajectory. This shows that the flow in the duct is constant.

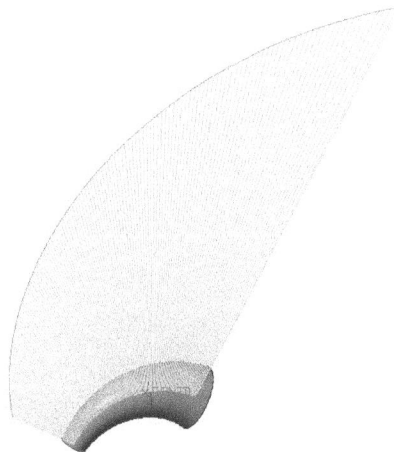

Figure 2–59

9. Clear the **Min & Max refinement** option.

10. Enable the **Create Graph** option.

11. Select **Compute**. Once the analysis has completed, a graph of the trajectory length against the sectional surface area is plotted, as shown in Figure 2–60.

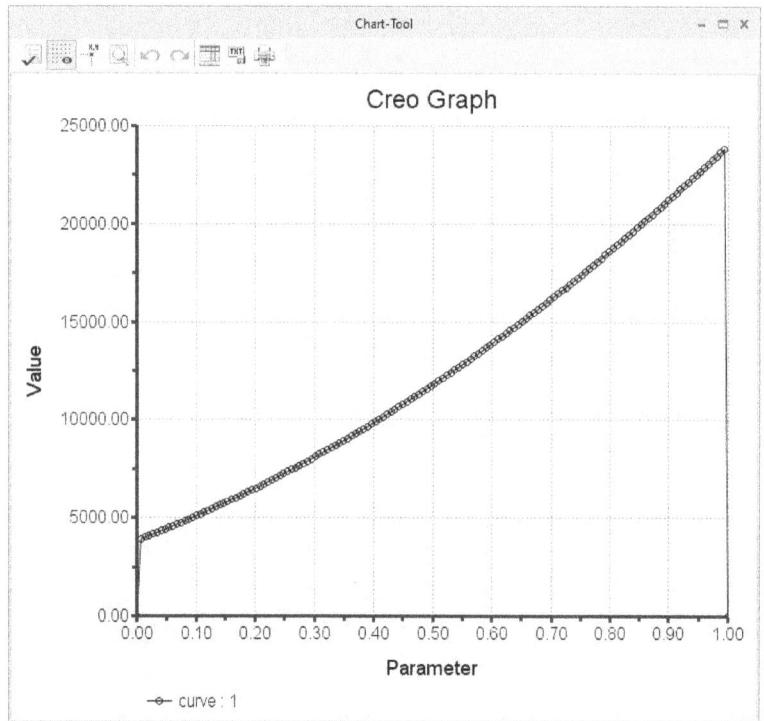

Figure 2–60

Task 9 - Customize the Chart.

1. In the Chart-Tool, click ✓ (Customize Graph). The Chart-Tool expands as shown in Figure 2–61.

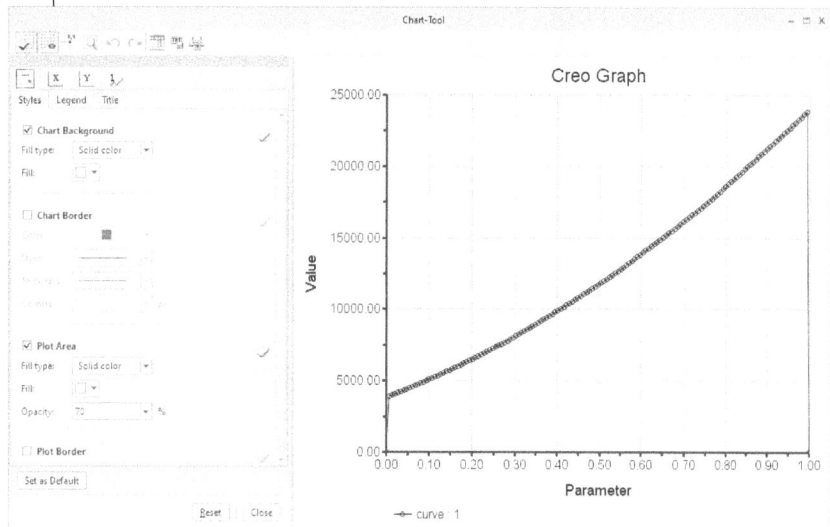

Figure 2–61

2. In the *Styles* tab, change the Fill type to **Gradient**.

3. Leave the first color swatch as white, then in the second swatch select the color **R: 28, G: 69, B: 135** as shown in Figure 2–62.

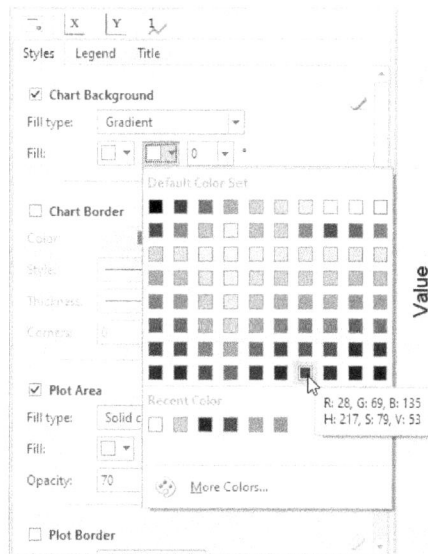

Figure 2–62

Edit the Fill angle to **-130**, and the chart updates as shown in Figure 2–63.

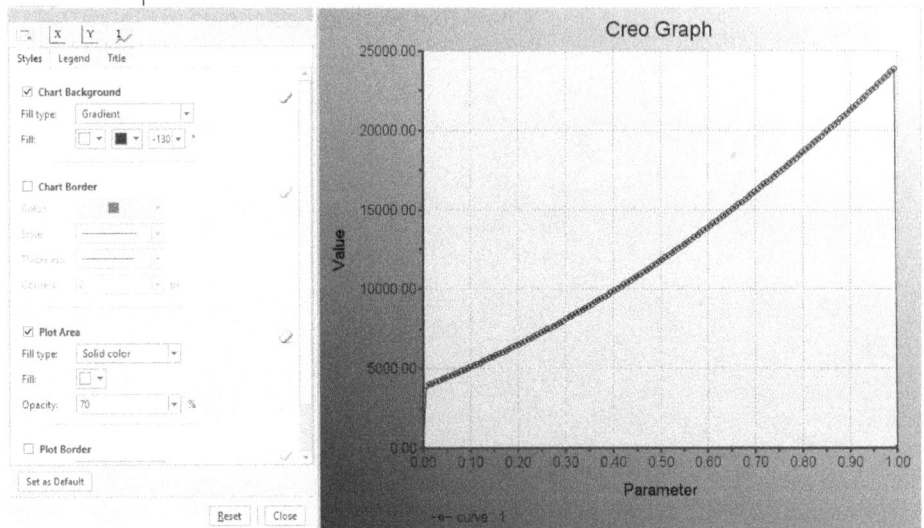

Figure 2–63

4. Select the *Legend* tab.

5. Remove the check mark next to Legend so the legend no longer displays on the chart.

6. Select the *Title* tab.

7. Click to remove the check next to Chart Title, then click to add it again.

8. The Text field activates. Change the title in the Text field to **Area vs Distance**.

9. Click the X (Format X-Axis) option.

10. Select the *Title* tab.

11. Click to remove the check next to X-axis Title, then click to add it again.

12. Change the Text field to **Distance**.

13. Change the Color to white.

14. Click the Y (Format Y-Axis) option.

15. Select the *Title* tab.

16. Click to remove the check next to Y-axis Title, then click to add it again.

17. Change the Text field to **Area**.

18. Change the Color to white.

*To make this the default chart appearance, in the customization panel of the Chart-Tool, click **Save as Default**. Note that if your changes are not saved as the default appearance, when a chart is closed and then displayed again, customizations will be reset to the standard defaults.*

19. Click **Close**. The charts updates as shown in Figure 2–64.

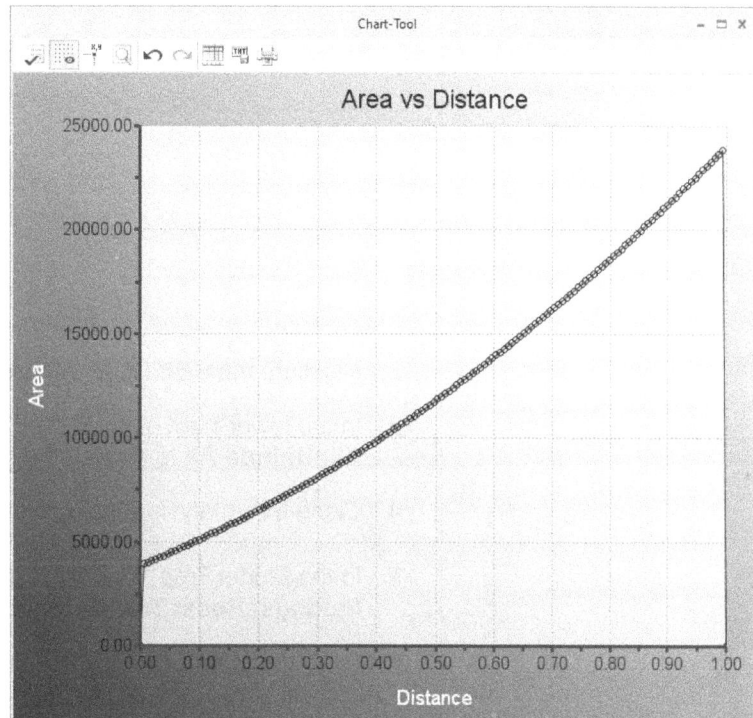

Figure 2–64

Task 10 - Save the analysis.

1. In the User-Defined Analysis dialog box, expand the *Saved Analyses* area. Set the name to **SECTION_AREA** and click ⊟ (Save). By saving the analysis, this porcupine plot can be shown on the model at any time without having to run the UDA again. By default, the graph remains displayed. The display of the plot and graph can be controlled using ⊙ ⊘.

2. Highlight the **SECTION_AREA** analysis and select ⊙ ⊘ to toggle the results display off.

3. Click **Close** to close the dialog box.

Task 11 - Display the SECTION_AREA saved analysis.

1. In the Manage group in the ribbon, click (Saved Analysis). The Analysis Display dialog box displays as shown in Figure 2–65.

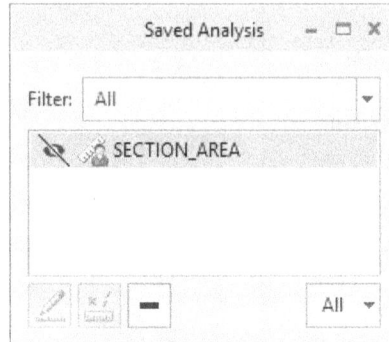

Figure 2–65

2. Highlight the **SECTION_AREA** analysis.

3. In the lower-right of the Saved Analysis dialog box, click **All>Unhide All** to display the graph and the porcupine plot.

4. Close the Analysis Display dialog box.

5. In the Model Tree, click ⫿ ▾ (Settings)>**Reset Tree Settings>Reset Tree Settings**.

6. Save the model and erase it from memory.

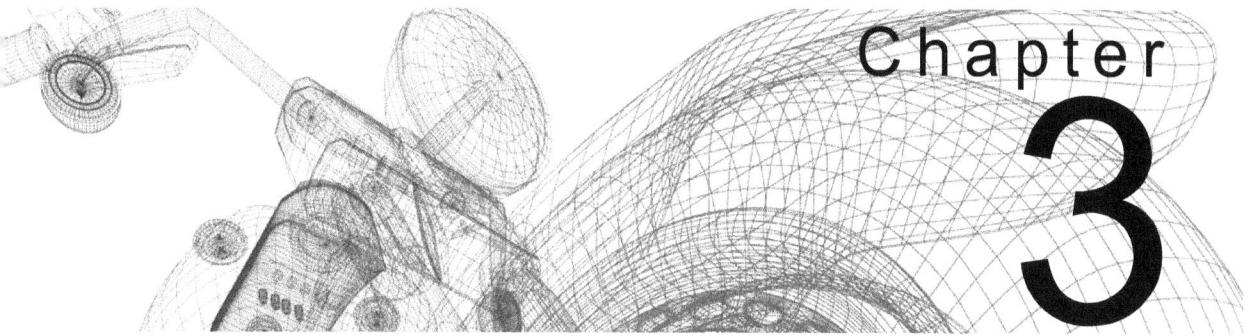

Behavioral Modeling Studies

Behavioral modeling studies enable you to test your design before manufacturing. You can assign various parameters and constraints that enable you to verify if your model reacts as intended. This chapter introduces sensitivity, feasibility, and optimization analyses.

Learning Objectives in This Chapter

- Understand how a Sensitivity Analysis shows the way in which a design parameter reacts when a design variable is changed over a specified range.
- Learn how to use a Feasibility analysis to adjust design variables to meet specific design constraints.
- Understand how to use an Optimization analysis to adjust the design variables to meet a specific goal.

3.1 Sensitivity Analysis

A Sensitivity Analysis shows how a design parameter reacts when a design variable is changed over a specified range. This analysis provides insight to an ideal start value for design variables when running a Feasibility or Optimization study. To run an analysis, in the *Analysis* tab, in the *Design Study* group, click ⬚ (Sensitivity Analysis).

Example:

The design variable for the container shown in Figure 3–1 is the thickness of the shell feature.

10.00 O_THICK

Figure 3–1

The Sensitivity Analysis dialog box is shown in Figure 3–2.

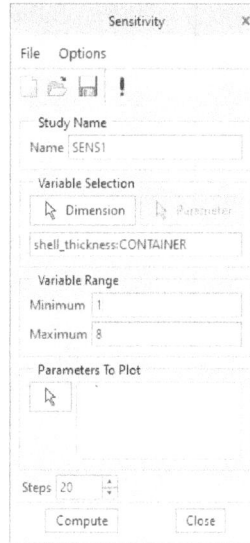

Figure 3–2

The elements in a Sensitivity Analysis are described as follows:

Element	Description
Study Name	Enter the name of the sensitivity analysis.
Variable Selection	Define the dimension or model parameter to be analyzed. Only one variable can be changed per sensitivity analysis.
Variable Range	Specify the upper and lower range for the variable.
Parameters to Plot	Select the design parameters to plot against the design variable. More than one design parameter can be selected by pressing and holding <Shift> while selecting the parameters. Each parameter is shown on a separate plot.
Steps	Specify the number of steps for the analysis.

To generate the data, the system modifies the design variable in equal increments between the minimum and maximum value for the number of steps specified. At each modification, the model is regenerated and the value of the design parameter is stored and plotted.

The results of a Sensitivity analysis comparing the shell thickness to a design parameter for the model's solid volume are shown in Figure 3–3.

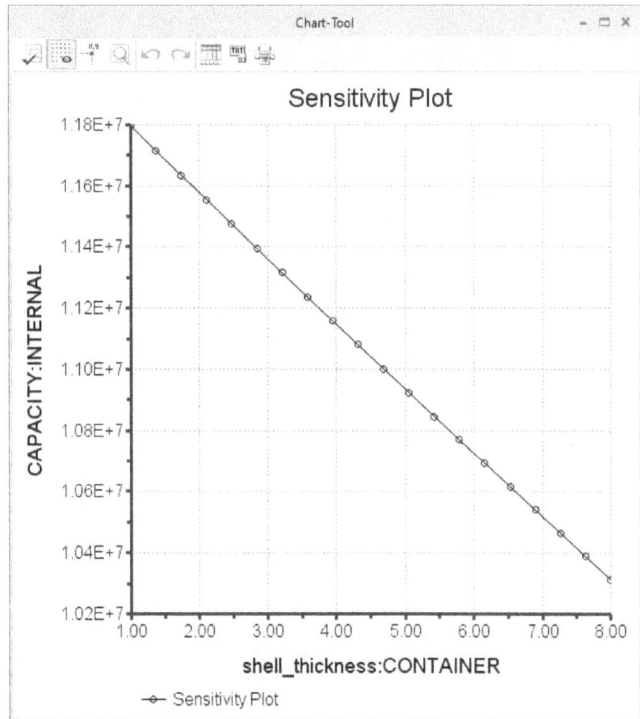

Figure 3–3

The graph begins at a wall thickness of 1.00 and makes 20 sensitivity passes to increase the thickness to 8.00. The graph shows, as expected, that an increase in shell thickness decreases the model's capacity. If the goal of your optimization is to minimize mass, an ideal start point for the shell thickness would be a low value.

3.2 Feasibility and Optimization Analyses

Feasibility

A Feasibility analysis adjusts design variables to meet specific design constraints. It tests if a feasible solution exists, given the range in which the system can adjust the design variables. If more than one parameter is varied, many solutions can exist. A Feasibility analysis stops after the first successful solution.

Design constraints have specific values. The constraint can be greater than or equal to (>=), or equal to (=) or less than (<) its current value or it can be a user-specified value.

Example:

The design constraint on the container shown in Figure 3–4 is that it must be able to hold exactly 10 L of water.

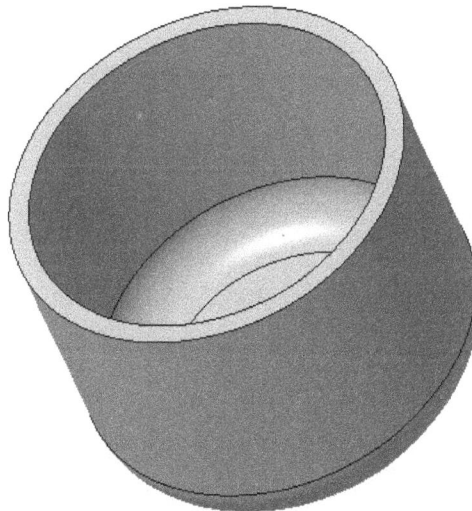

Figure 3–4

To achieve this, you can vary the design variables shown in Figure 3–5 using the minimum and maximum limits listed below.

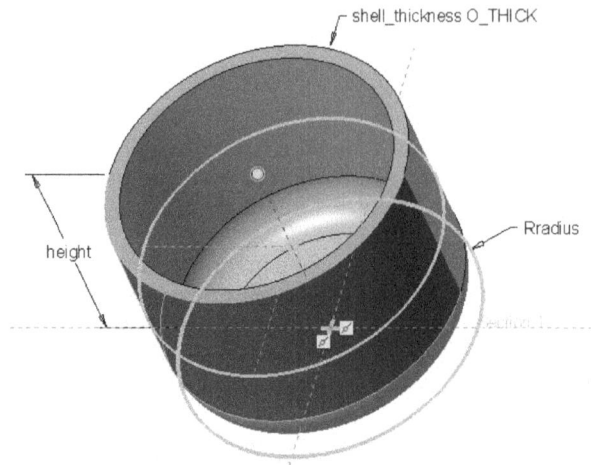

Figure 3–5

	Current Value	Minimum Value	Maximum Value
Shell_Thickness	10	2	20
Radius	100	50	300
Height	150	100	600

The Feasibility analysis determined that by modifying the dimensions to those shown in Figure 3–6, the capacity is exactly 10 L.

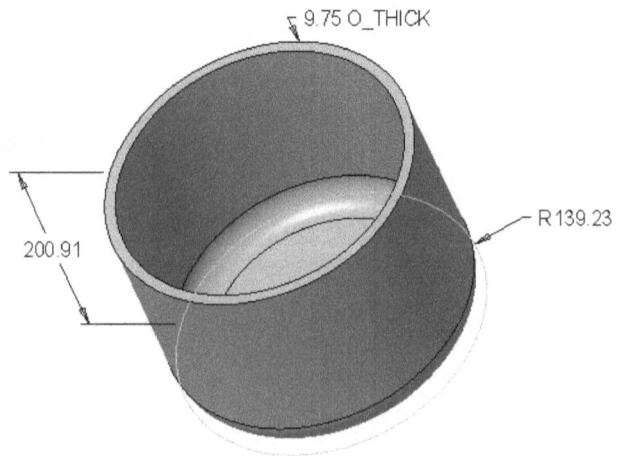

Figure 3–6

Optimization

An optimization analysis starts by adjusting the design variables to meet specific design constraints. It then makes successive passes and changes the design variables to meet a specific goal. It optimizes the model with respect to this goal while maintaining the design constraints.

A goal does not have a specific value. Goals either minimize or maximize a design parameter. It continues to improve the design until it converges on a user-specified percentage. For each pass taken, the system compares the current value of the goal to the value from the last pass. If the difference between the two values is within the convergence percentage, then the analysis is considered successful and stops. In the end, the part may not be truly optimized; the calculations stop once convergence is met, which can actually converge at a local minimum. The Multi-Objective Design Study finds the true minimum. (This topic is discussed in more detail in a later chapter.

Example:

A new design criteria has been set for the container used in the feasibility study. The container must hold exactly 10 L of water, but it must also be as light as possible. You can optimize the design to minimize mass while maintaining the original design constraint. Figure 3–7 shows the graph output of the optimization study.

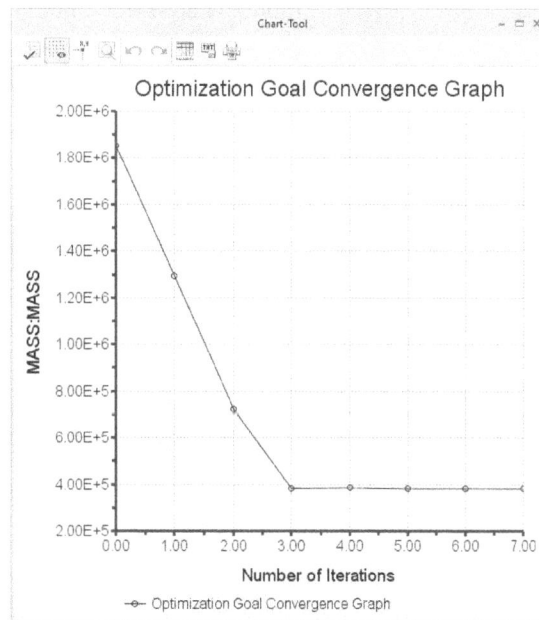

Figure 3–7

The optimization was able to reduce the weight of the container by more than 80% while still maintaining a capacity of 10 L.

Figure 3–8 shows the optimized model.

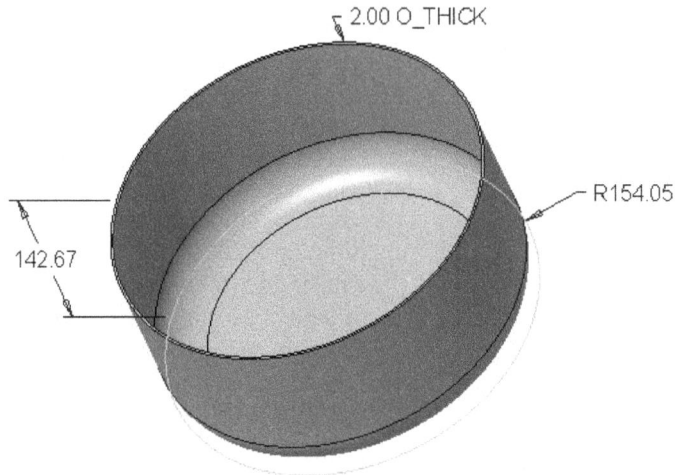

Figure 3–8

An optimization feature can be created once a study has been completed successfully. In doing so, you create a feature reflecting the settings for the optimization study. Each time the model is regenerated, the study is run and a newly optimized model is created. Once the study has completed, you can create the optimization feature by clicking ⊟ (Save Design Study) in the Optimization/Feasibility dialog box.

Both the Feasibility and Optimization studies are performed using the same dialog box. In the Design Study group, click

⚲ (Feasibility/Optimization) to open the Optimization/Feasibility dialog box shown in Figure 3–9.

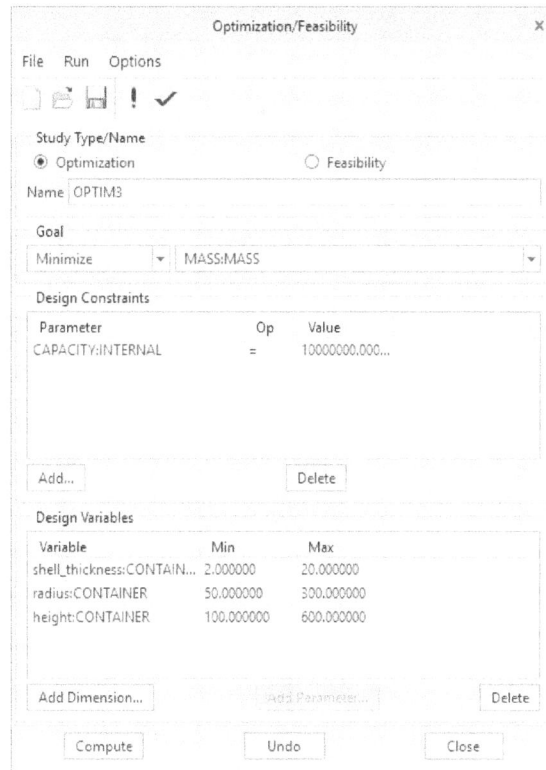

Figure 3–9

The elements required for the creation of a Feasibility or Optimization Study are described as follows:

Element	Description
Study Type/Name	Select the type of study to perform (Feasibility or Optimization) and enter a name for the study.
Goal (Optimization Studies only)	Select the optimization goal and the design parameter to optimize. The optimization criteria include. • **Minimize** • **Maximize** • **Minimize Abs Val** • **Maximize Abs Val** Only one design parameter can be selected per Optimization Study.

Design Constraints	Add one or more design parameters to optimize a specific value. The Design Constraint dialog box shown below enables you to select the parameter, its operator, and the design constraint value.

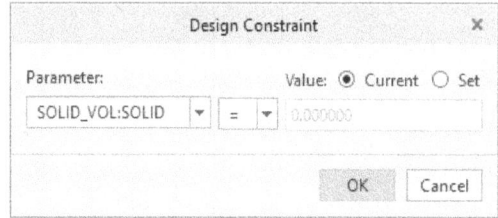

Design Constraint	✕
Parameter:	Value: ⦿ Current ○ Set
SOLID_VOL:SOLID ▾ = ▾ 0.000000	
	OK Cancel

Design Variables	Add dimensions or parameters that can be modified to achieve the design constraints and goal. Each variable requires a minimum and maximum value between which the design study can make modifications. Only include variables that have a significant effect on the design constraints or goal. Additional design variables increases the study run time. The use of the sensitivity study before hand helps determine which variables should be added.

A feasibility and optimization analysis can be customized by clicking an option in the **Options** menu in the Optimization/ Feasibility dialog box. These options are described as follows:

Option	Description
Preferences	Enables you to customize the creation of graphs and how the study is run.
	The *Graphs* tab enables you to select which result graphs are created. Contains various options.
	The *Run* tab enables you to set convergence criteria and limit the number of iterations for the optimization analysis. By selecting **Animate model**, the model regenerates at each iteration.

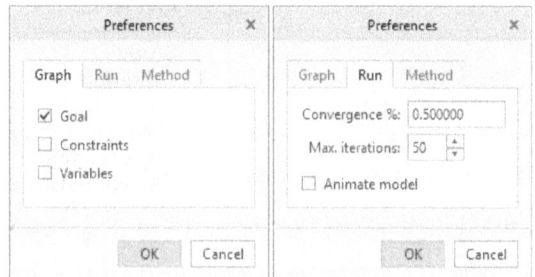

Preferences	✕
Graph Run Method	
☑ Goal	
☐ Constraints	
☐ Variables	
	OK Cancel

Preferences	✕
Graph Run Method	
Convergence %: 0.500000	
Max. iterations: 50	
☐ Animate model	
	OK Cancel

The *Method* tab enables you to select the optimization method.

- **GDP** - Use the standard algorithm (gradient-based) to optimize the model using the current model conditions as the starting point.

- **MDS** - Use the multi-objective design studies algorithm to determine the optimum starting point for the optimization. You can specify the number of starting points to compute in the *Max. Iterations* field. After the number of experiments has been filled, Behavioral Modeling uses a Paretto capability to identify the best candidates of the populated space. The best candidates are the starting points of the gradient-based optimization. This method has a higher chance of finding the overall optimum design within the design parameters and dimensions.

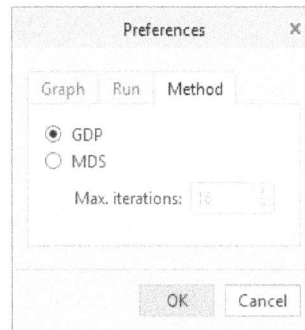

| | Default Range | Enables you to control the default minimum and maximum values assigned to the design variables. |

Default Range — Enables you to control the default minimum and maximum values assigned to the design variables.

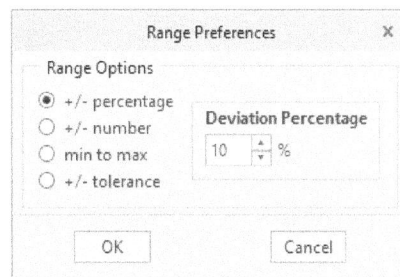

Practice 3a

Sensitivity Analysis

Practice Objective

- Set up and run a sensitivity analysis.

In this practice, you will work on a simple layout of an engine's power take-off belt system. You will create a sensitivity analysis to graph how the length of the belt and contact angle are affected by moving the location of a pulley.

Task 1 - Open the drive_train part.

1. Set the working directory to *Sensitivity_Analysis*.

2. Open **drive_train.prt**.

3. Set the model display as follows:

- $\overset{x/}{\not{\wedge}}$ *(Datum Display Filters)*: All Off

- $\not{\sim}$ *(Spin Center)*: Off

- $\Box$ *(Display Style)*: $\Box$ (Shading With Edges)

The model displays as shown in Figure 3–10.

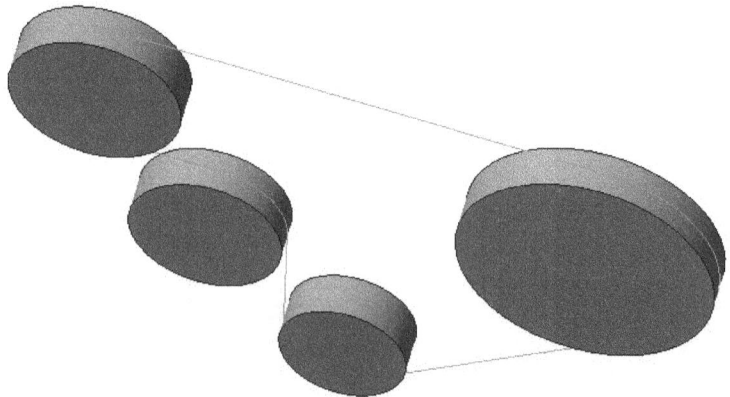

Figure 3–10

4. Investigate the model. The model is a simple layout of an engine belt system. The protrusions representing the drive, air conditioning (**AC**), power steering (**power_steer**), and the idler pulleys have been renamed for easy identification in the Model Tree. A datum curve (**BELT**) has been included to represent the belt in the system.

5. In the In-graphics toolbar, expand 📷 (Saved Orientations) and select **FRONT**.

6. Double-click on the belt datum curve directly on the model. The dimension used to create the feature displays.

7. Select the *Tools* tab and in the Model Intent group, click ⅟ₓ (Switch Dimensions) to show the dimension as a symbolic value.

8. Select the Idler pulley in the Model Tree. The dimensions associated with this feature are shown.

Figure 3–11 displays the dimension symbols for both features. This functionality is not currently available in Creo Parametric. When a feature is edited, all other dimensions are cleared from the screen.

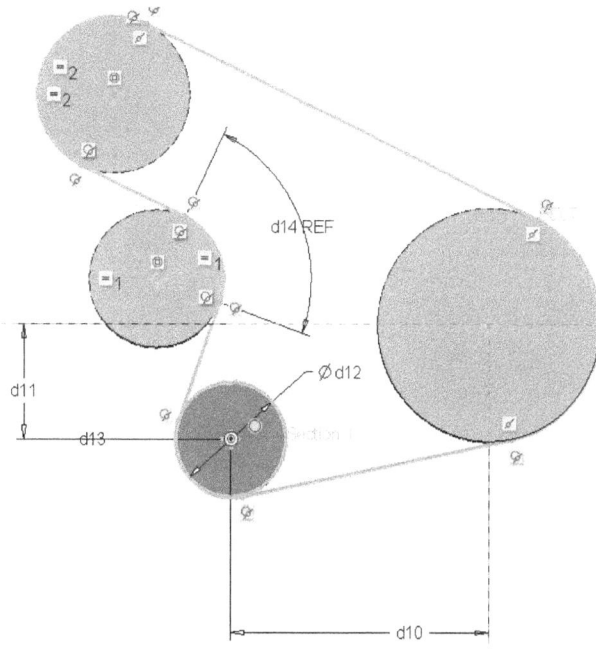

Figure 3–11

In the sensitivity analysis, review the results when modifying:

- The position of the idler pulley (dimension **d10**) on the overall belt length.
- The contact angle (dimension **d14**) with the power steering pulley. Note that the final design requires a contact angle of at least 120 degrees.

Task 2 - Create an Analysis feature to measure the length of the belt.

1. Select the *Analysis* tab.

2. In the Measure group, expand (Measure) and select (Length).

3. Right-click on the belt until the entire curve is highlights, then select it. The curve length should be 1135.97.

4. In the Measure: Length dialog box, select the *Feature* tab and note that the **LENGTH** parameter is selected for creation.

5. Click (Save), ensure that **Make Feature** is selected, and edit the name to **BELT_LENGTH** and press <Enter>.

6. Click **Close**.

Task 3 - Create an Analysis feature that calculates the contact angle.

1. In the Manage group in the ribbon, click (Analysis).

2. In the Name field of the ANALYSIS dialog box, enter **CONTACT_ANGLE** and press <Enter>.

3. Select **Relation** as the analysis type.

4. Click **Next**. The Relations dialog box displays to enter the relation.

5. Enter the following relation:

   CONTACT = d14

6. Click ☑ (Verify) to verify the relation and click **OK**.

7. Click **OK** to close the Relations dialog box.

8. Click ✓ (OK) to complete the Analysis feature.

Task 4 - Run a model sensitivity analysis.

1. In the Design Study group, click ▣ (Sensitivity Analysis). The Sensitivity dialog box displays.

2. In the Sensitivity dialog box, leave the default name for the analysis.

3. Click **Dimension** and select dimension **d10** shown in Figure 3–12.

If the dimension no longer displays on the screen, double-click on the feature in the model or in the Model Tree.

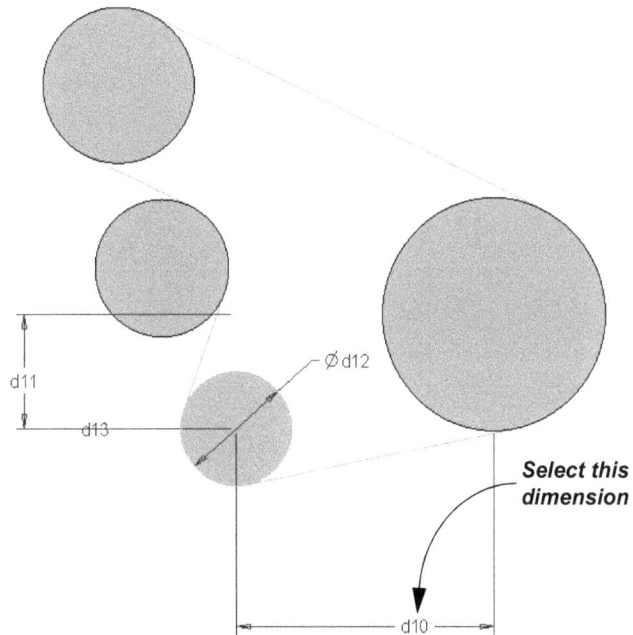

Figure 3–12

4. Enter **175** and **350** as the minimum and maximum *Variable Ranges*, respectively.

To select multiple parameters at one time, press and hold <Ctrl>.

5. In the *Parameters To Plot* area, click ⌖ (Select) and select both the **belt_length** and **contact_angle** parameters.

6. Click **OK**. The Sensitivity dialog box displays as shown in Figure 3–13.

Figure 3–13

7. Click **Compute** to run the analysis. Two graphs display, showing how the belt length and contact angle change as dimension **d10** increases from *175* to *350*. These graphs are shown in Figure 3–14 and Figure 3–15.

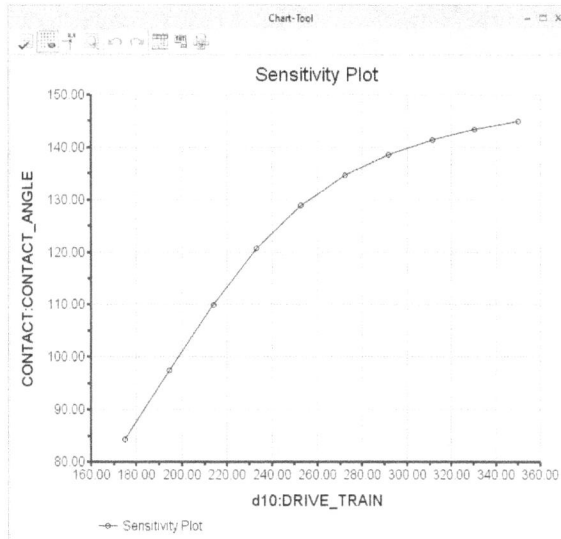

Figure 3–14

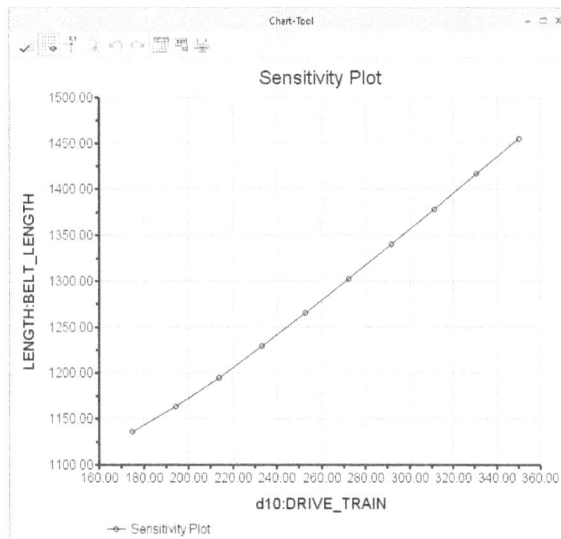

Figure 3–15

- What value must dimension **d10** be to achieve the design goal of having a minimum contact angle of 120 degrees? What should the belt length be?

By saving this design study, you can recall and rerun it without having to set it up again.

8. Save the design study.

9. Close the Sensitivity dialog box.

10. Close the model and erase it from memory.

Practice 3b | Optimization Analysis

Practice Objectives

- Create and run an optimization analysis.
- Update the model.

In this practice, you will continue to work with the canister model that you analyzed in the earlier practice. You will optimize the model with respect to the volume parameter to ensure that the fluid capacity of the canister is exactly 4L.

Task 1 - Open the canister.prt part model.

1. Set the working directory to *Optimization_Analysis*.

2. Open **canister_final1.prt**.

3. Set the model display as follows:

- *ⁿ/ᵢ₊ (Datum Display Filters)*: Only ⌷ (Plane Display)
- *View* tab: ⌷ (Plane Tag Display)
- ⟩• *(Spin Center)*: Off
- ⌷. *(Display Style)*: ⌷ (Shading With Edges)

There are three analysis features in this model:

- **SOLID -** This model analysis feature calculates the **SOLID_VOL** parameter. This is the volume of the canister before the cut feature is added.
- **CUT -** This model analysis feature calculates the **CUT_VOL** parameter. This is the volume of the canister after the cut feature is added.
- **INTERNAL -** This relation analysis feature calculates the **CAPACITY** parameter. The relation subtracts **CUT_VOL** from **SOLID_VOL** to get the fluid capacity of the canister.

Task 2 - Review the values for the capacity and thickness parameters.

1. Determine the current capacity of the canister. In the Model Tree, right-click on the **INTERNAL** analysis feature and select **Information>Feature Information**. The Creo Parametric browser opens.

2. Scroll to the bottom of the browser. The **CAPACITY** parameter is listed with a current value of approximately 5.4 L.

3. Close the browser.

4. Display the **CAPACITY** parameter in the Model Tree.

   To change the capacity of the canister, you modify the overall height or wall thickness of the canister. The thickness is controlled by a model parameter called **THICKNESS**.

5. Double-click on the inside surface of the cannister. The wall thickness is approximately 4.27 mm.

6. Click anywhere on the screen.

Task 3 - Create an analysis feature for the model's mass.

1. Select the *Analysis* tab.

2. In the Model Report group, click ⬚ (Mass Properties).

3. In the Quick drop-down list, select **Feature** and edit the name to **Mass**.

4. Click **Preview**. The system calculates the model mass properties based on a default density of 1.

5. Select the *Feature* tab.

6. In the *Parameters* area, remove the checkmark next to the **VOLUME** and **SURF_AREA** parameters so that they are not created.

7. Ensure that **MASS** is selected for creation.

8. Click **OK** to complete the feature.

9. Add the **MASS** parameter to the Model Tree display.

Task 4 - Optimize the model.

Design Consideration

A feasibility analysis tests the model to see if the design variables specified enable the study to meet the design constraints. For example, does changing the thickness of the canister wall between 3 mm and 6mm create a capacity of 4 L? If so, the model is regenerated to provide the first feasible solution found.

An optimization analysis runs a feasibility analysis as its first step. It then continues to change the design parameters to meet a specific goal. Minimizing the mass of the model is an example of a goal. The study continues to change the design variables over several optimization passes until it reaches an optimized value (determined by a convergence percentage), or until it runs out of passes.

In this example, the optimization analysis uses the values listed below:

	Parameter	Setting	
Goal	Mass	Minimize	
Design Constraints	Capacity	4 L	
Design Variables	Wall Thickness	2	10
	Height (d0)	300	600

1. In the Design Study group, click 🔍 (Feasibility/Optimization). The **Optimization** option is selected by default.

2. In the *Goal* area, select **Minimize** and **MASS:MASS** from the drop-down lists.

3. In the *Design Constraints* area, click **Add**. The Design Constraint dialog box displays.

4. Select the **CAPACITY:INTERNAL** parameter, as shown in Figure 3–16. The required capacity is 4,000,000 mm^3 or 4 L.

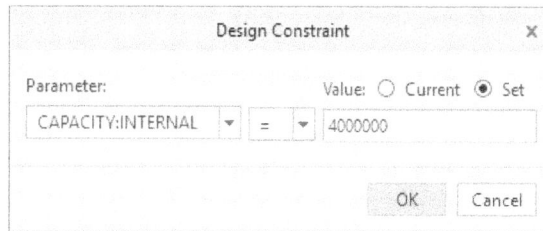

Figure 3–16

5. Click **OK**. The design constraint is added to the Optimization/Feasibility dialog box.

6. Click **Cancel** to close the Design Constraint dialog box.

7. In the *Design Variables* area, click **Add Dimension**. Select **Revolve 1** in the Model Tree and select the **400 mm** dimension, as shown in Figure 3–17.

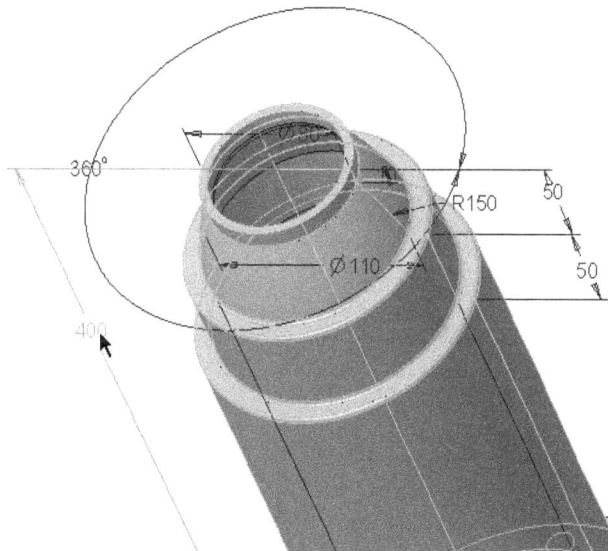

Figure 3–17

8. Click **Add Parameter**. The Select Parameter dialog box displays.

9. Select **THICKNESS:CANISTER_FINAL1** and click **OK**.

10. Click **Cancel** to close the Select Parameter dialog box.

11. Select each of the *Min* and *Max* cells for each parameter and set their values as shown in Figure 3–18.

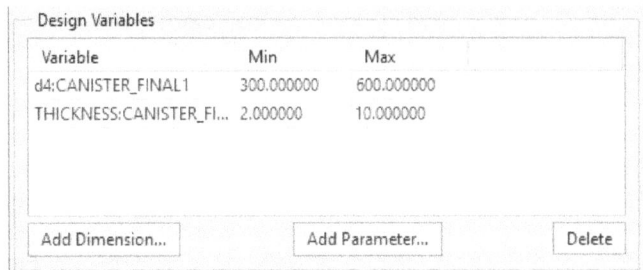

Design Variables

Variable	Min	Max
d4:CANISTER_FINAL1	300.000000	600.000000
THICKNESS:CANISTER_FI...	2.000000	10.000000

Add Dimension...	Add Parameter...	Delete

Figure 3–18

12. Click **Compute**. The optimization analysis begins and a graph displays, which updates the status of the optimization goal, **MASS**, with each pass of the study. Once complete, the phrase "The part was successfully optimized." displays in the message area. Figure 3–19 shows an optimized graph whose mass was reduced by over 40% using the optimization study.

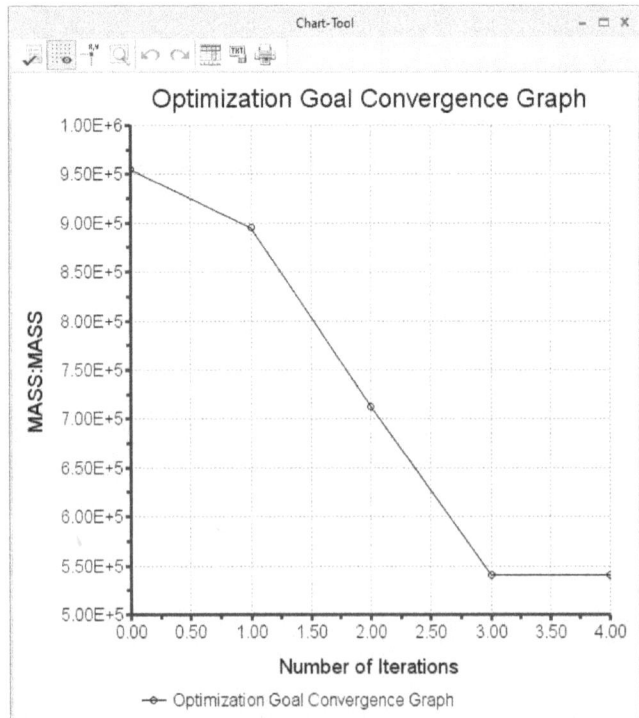

Figure 3–19

13. In the Optimization/Feasibility dialog box, select **Close** to keep the optimized values. The Confirm Model Change dialog box displays as shown in Figure 3–20.

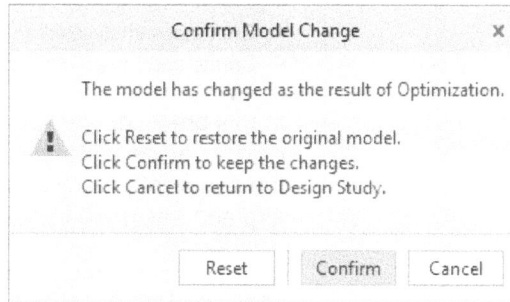

Confirm Model Change ✕

The model has changed as the result of Optimization.

⚠ Click Reset to restore the original model.
Click Confirm to keep the changes.
Click Cancel to return to Design Study.

| Reset | Confirm | Cancel |

Figure 3–20

14. Select **Confirm** to keep the changes. The model displays as shown in Figure 3–21. The height of the model is 300mm and the thickness is 2.75mm.

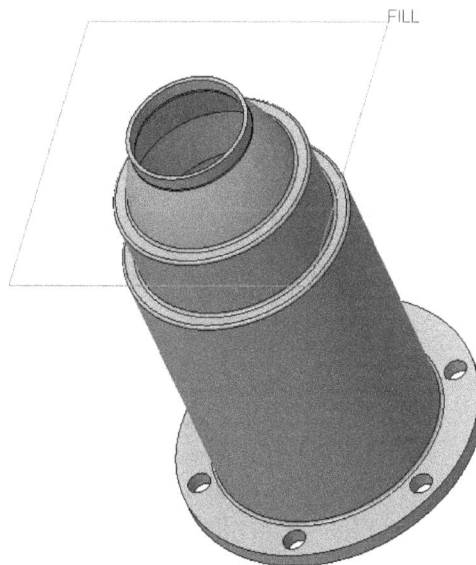

Figure 3–21

15. In the Model Tree, click 🔧 ▾ (Settings)>**Reset Tree Settings**>**Reset Tree Settings**.

16. Close the model and erase it from memory.

Practice 3c	# Assembly Optimization

Practice Objectives

- Create assembly level analysis features.
- Create and run an optimization study.

In this practice, you will optimize a floor plan layout for a large room used as a storage area in a large airplane. The position of the center of gravity of the room is important to ensure that the airplane has good handling and is correctly balanced.

The center of gravity of the entire airplane lies at the intersection of the **CENTER_HORIZ** and **CENTER_VERT** datum planes. You will optimize the model to ensure that the center of gravity of the room also lies at the intersection of these two planes. You will then minimize the mass of the room to conserve fuel.

Task 1 - Open the floor_plan assembly model.

1. Set the working directory to *Assembly_Optimization.*

2. Open **floor_plan.asm**.

3. Set the model display as follows:

    - ⁤ (*Datum Display Filters*): (Point Display), (Csys Display)

    - (*Spin Center*): Off

    - (*Display Style*): (Shading With Edges)

4. Use the Model Tree to investigate the assembly components. The assembly consists of a floor model, two water cabinets, and three part cabinets. All five cabinets are assembled to the floor model using datum points. The points were created on curves using the **Length Ratio** option. The location of the cabinets can be modified by changing the length ratio value for each point.

Task 2 - Create a model analysis feature to create a mass parameter and a datum point at the center of gravity.

1. Select the *Analysis* tab.

2. In the Model Report group, click (Mass Properties).

3. In the Mass Properties dialog box, click **Preview**.

4. Select **Feature** from the Quick drop-down list.

5. Edit the name to **COFG**.

6. Select the *Feature* tab.

7. Do not create the **VOLUME** or **SURF_AREA** parameter.

8. Create the **MASS** parameter.

9. In the *Datums* area, enable **CSYS_COG**. Edit the name to **COG**.

10. Click **OK**. The COG coordinate system display on the model, as shown in Figure 3–22. The COG does not match the center of gravity of the airplane; therefore, an optimization study is required.

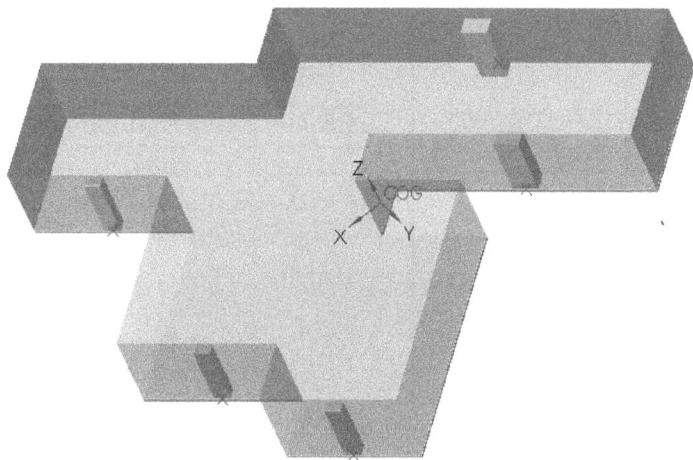

Figure 3–22

Task 3 - Create two measurement analysis features that measure the distance between the center of gravity for the room to the center of gravity for the airplane.

1. In the In-graphics toolbar, select ⟑ (Plane Display).

2. In the Measure group, expand ✎ (Measure) and select ⊓. (Distance).

3. Press and hold <Ctrl> and select the COG coordinate system and the **CENTER_HORIZ** datum plane. The distance is 612.677mm.

4. Select the *Feature* tab.

5. Edit the name of the *DISTANCE* parameter to **HORIZ**. Press <Enter> after changing the name.

6. Click 🖫▾ (Save), ensure that **Make Feature** is selected, and set the name to **DIST_HORIZ**.

7. Click **Close** to complete the feature.

8. Repeat the previous steps to create an additional measure analysis feature. Add the resulting parameter to the model and set the name to **VERT**. Set the name of the analysis feature to **DIST_VERT**. This feature measures the distance between the COG coordinate system and the **CENTER_VERT** datum plane.

Task 4 - Create an optimization study.

To select the water cabinet dimensions, expand **water_cabinet.prt,** *double-click on the protrusion, and select the dimensions. Do the same for the* **parts_cabinet** *components. To select the datum point dimension symbols, expand* **floor.prt** *in the Model Tree, click on* **Datum Point id 469,** *and select the dimensions.*

1. In the Design Study group, click ◪ (Feasibility/Optimization). The **Optimization** option is enabled by default.

2. Set the goal for the **MASS:COFG** parameter **Minimize.**

3. In the *Design Constraints* area, click **Add**. Set the **HORIZ** and **VERT** parameters equal to zero.

4. In the *Design Variables* field, add the dimensions, and edit the *Min* and *Max* values specified in the table below. Use Figure 3–23 to locate the dimensions.

Dimension	Minimum	Maximum
d0:WATER_CABINET	200	1000
d1:WATER_CABINET	200	1000

d0:PARTS_CABINET	200	1000
d1:PARTS_CABINET	200	1000
d68:FLOOR	0.2	0.8
d76:FLOOR	0.2	0.8
d83:FLOOR	0.2	0.8
d82:FLOOR	0.2	0.8
d85:FLOOR	0.2	0.8

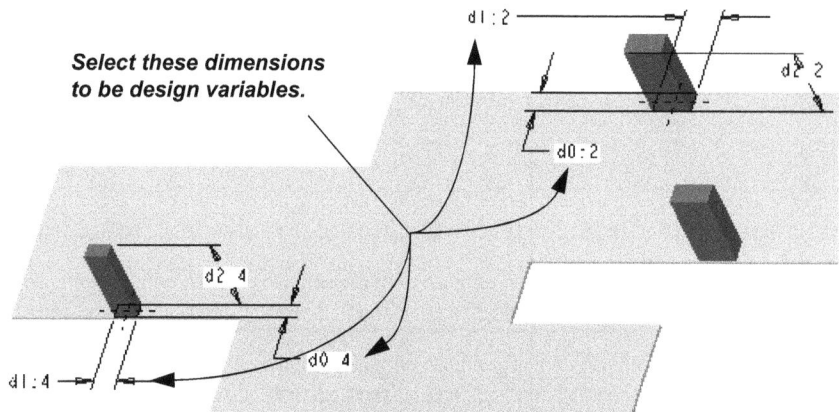

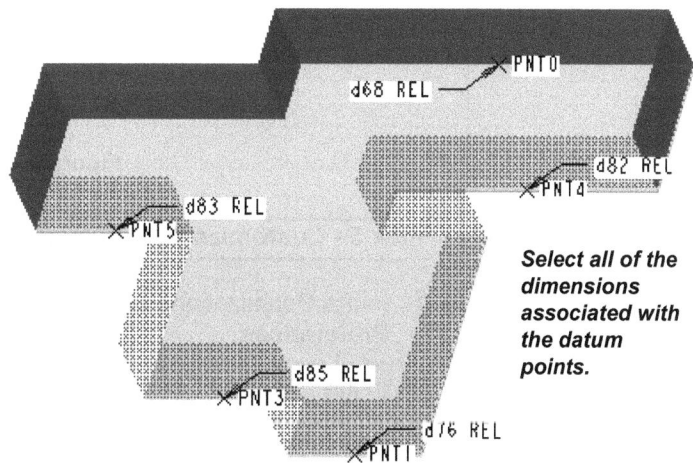

Select these dimensions to be design variables.

Select all of the dimensions associated with the datum points.

Figure 3–23

The Optimization/Feasibility dialog box displays as shown in Figure 3–24.

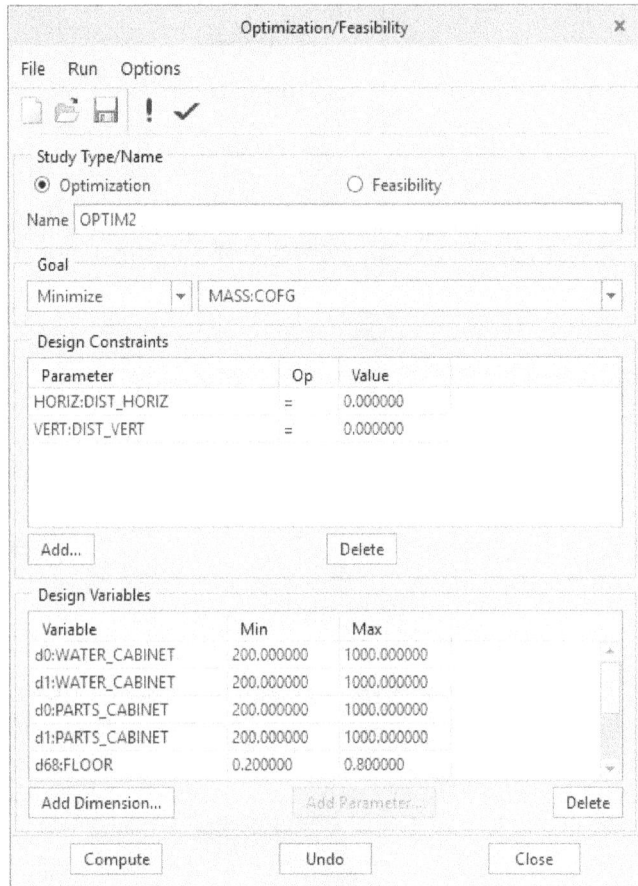

Figure 3–24

Task 5 - Customize the optimization study.

1. In the Optimization/Feasibility dialog box, click **Options> Preferences**.

2. In the *Graph* tab, select **Goal** and **Constraints**.

3. Select the *Run* tab and set the *Max Iterations* value to **10**.

4. In the Preferences dialog box, click **OK**.

5. Click **Compute** to begin the analysis. Convergence graphs for **HORIZ**, **VERT** (two design constraints) and **MASS** (the goal) display, and update with each pass. The graph for the **MASS** goal is shown in Figure 3–25.

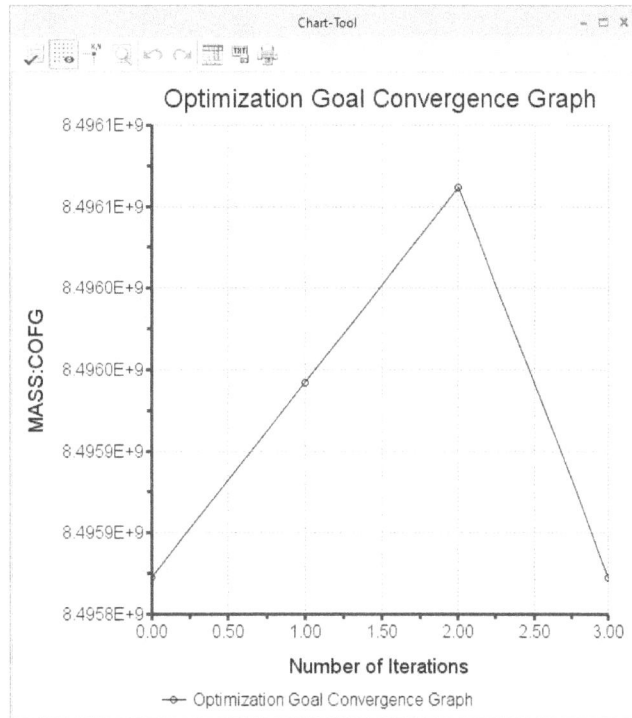

Figure 3–25

- Was the system able to minimize the mass of the model while still maintaining the design constraints? The message window reads "The part was successfully optimized."

Note that the design constraints were met, as shown in the graphs for the **HORIZ** and **VERT** parameters. With the optimized model, the position of the center of gravity is located at the intersection of the **CENTER_HORIZ** and **CENTER_VERT** datum planes.

Task 6 - Update the assembly.

1. In the Optimization/Feasibility dialog box, select **Close**.

2. Select **Confirm** to update the model. The optimized model displays as shown in Figure 3–26 and Figure 3–27. Note the new positions of the water and part cabinets.

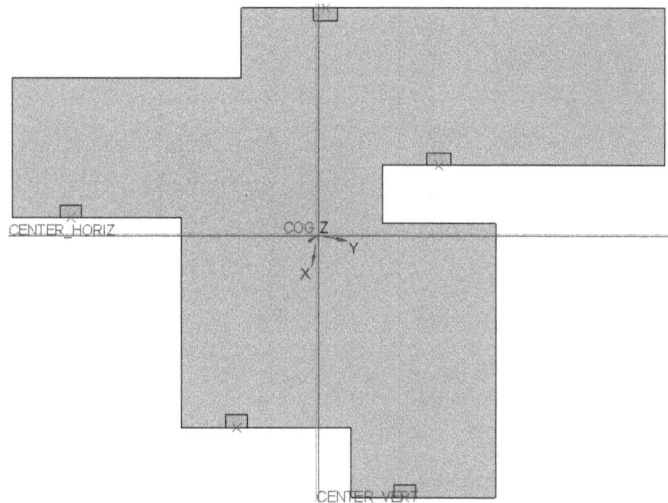

Figure 3–26

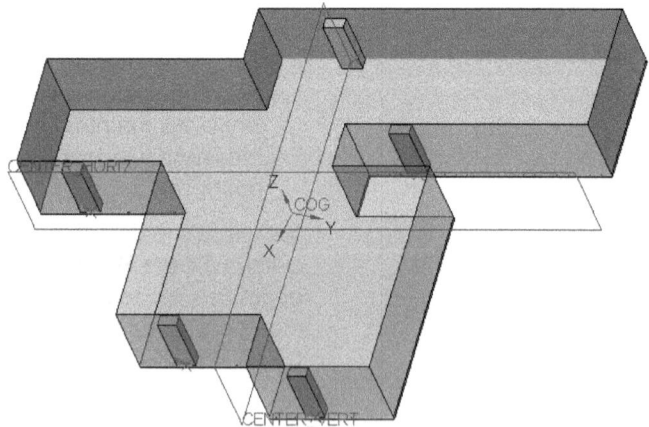

Figure 3–27

3. Close the assembly and erase it from memory.

Multi-Objective Design Studies

A Multi-Objective Design Study takes a different approach to finding an optimized solution for a design problem. A Feasibility or Optimization study checks the design parameter for each variation of the design variable. It continues to do this until the parameter meets the required design constraints. The Multi-Objective Design Study reports all values of the design parameters across a variation of the design variables. The design variables are changed within their minimum and maximum bounds in an attempt to capture all variations of the model that can possibly occur. Therefore, the Multi-Objective Design Study provides access to all permutations and variations of the model within the bounds of the design variables.

Learning Objectives in This Chapter

- Understand how Multi-Objective Design Studies are used to modify dimensions and parameters while attempting to achieve a design goal.
- Create a Multi-Objective Design Study.

4.1 Multi-Objective Design Study Methods

A Multi-Objective Design Study (MODS) enables you to find optimal solutions using multiple design goals. A multi-objective design assists you in finding an optimal range of variables for use in extracting optimal solutions. If there is more than one optimal solution, you are presented with the results so you can decide on the most appropriate the solution.

The data is stored in a master table, which lists each of the records or experiments calculated in the design study. To find the correct solution to the design problem, data is derived from the table by comparing it to design constraints that you have specified. You can specify any number of constraints to reduce the number of records down to one optimized solution.

There are two methods of deriving the optimized solution from the master table: **Constraint** and **Pareto**.

Constraint Derivation

This method allows a design constraint to be specific for any of the goals. Any records that fall out of these constraints are removed. The constraint method is accessed by selecting the **Constraint** option, as shown in Figure 4–1.

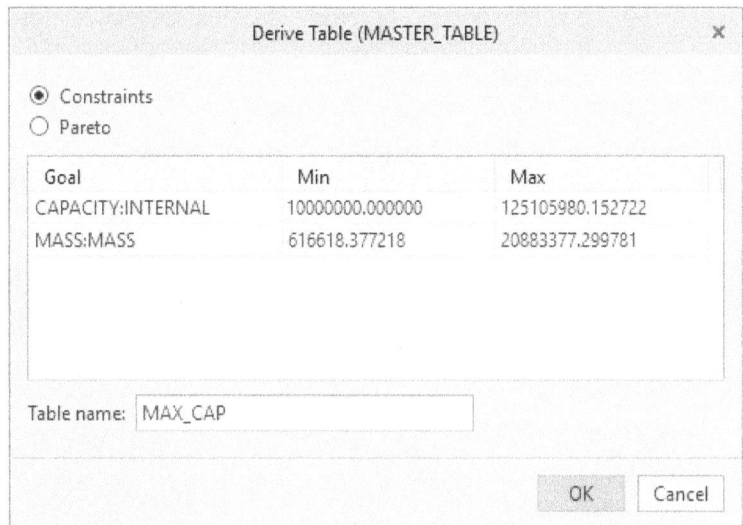

Derive Table (MASTER_TABLE)			
◉ Constraints			
○ Pareto			
Goal	Min	Max	
CAPACITY:INTERNAL	10000000.000000	125105980.152722	
MASS:MASS	616618.377218	20883377.299781	

Table name: MAX_CAP

OK   Cancel

Figure 4–1

Pareto Derivation

This method works only with minimums and maximums, rather than with constraints. If only one goal is selected to derive a table, it finds the global min/max and one solution is obtained. If more than one goal is selected, the table can have more than one solution. None of these remaining designs are necessarily better than the other. The study trades one goal at the expense of the other goal. The solutions not found in this derived table show no improvement in either of the goals and are thus excluded. Select **Pareto**, as shown in Figure 4–2. Each goal can be **Excluded**, **Minimized**, or **Maximized** using the drop-down list in the *Options* column.

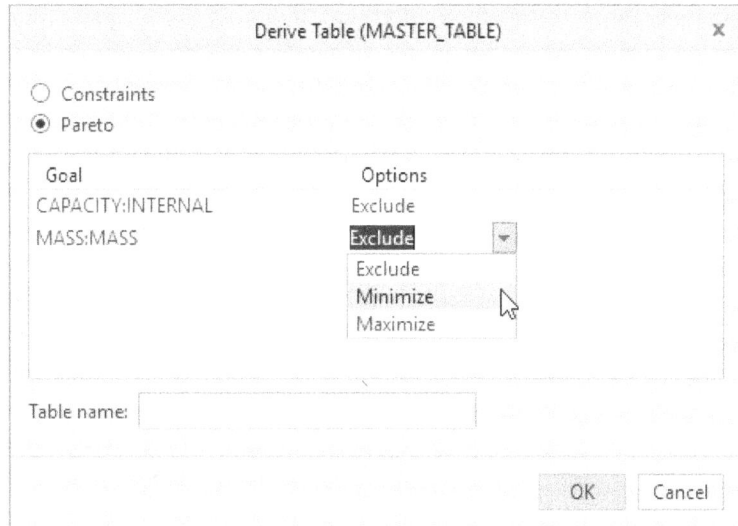

Figure 4–2

4.2 Multi-Objective Design Studies

How To: Create a Multi-Objective Design Study

1. In the *Analysis* tab, expand (Feasibility/Optimization) and select (Multi-Objective Design Study).
2. Click (New Design Study) and enter a name for the study.
3. Click (Setup Master Table) to create the master table.
4. You can select one of two options when selecting the sampling method to be used for the study: **Automatic** (default) and **Manual**.
   - The **Automatic** method evenly distributes experiments between specified minimum and maximum design variables. The Master Table for this option is shown in Figure 4–3. Click (Add Dimension) and (Add Parameter) to specify the design variables and enter their minimum and maximum limits. Click **Select Goals** to define the goals of the study.

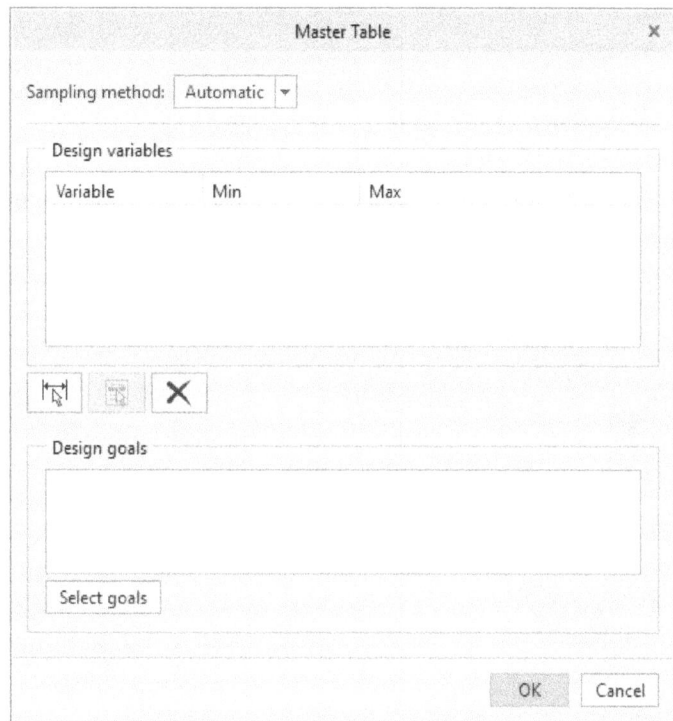

Figure 4–3

- The **Manual** method enables you to perform experiments using a table of values. You can enter values manually or import them from a file. The Master Table for this option is shown in Figure 4–4. To run experiments on all of the combinations of design variables, select **All combination** in the *Run Experiments On* area. To set the number of experiments as the number of rows that are defining the design variables, select **One per row**.

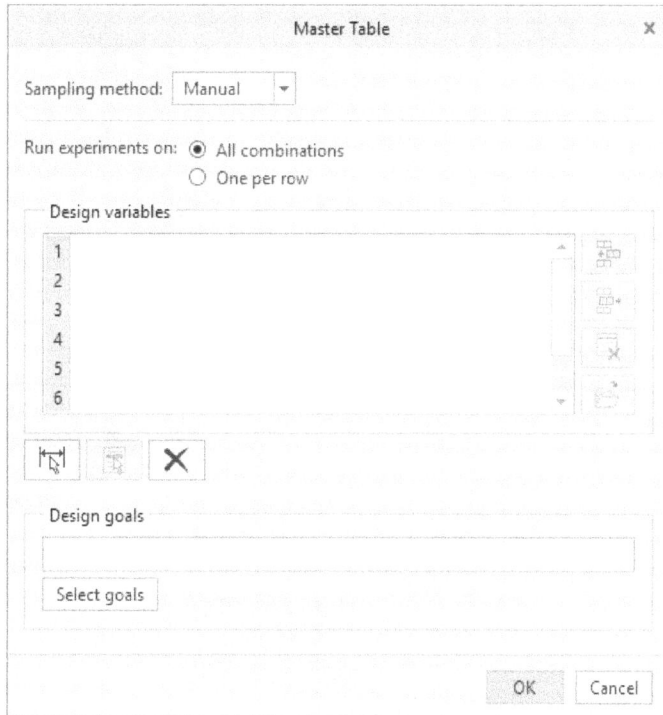

Figure 4–4

Results are more accurate and the run time longer with a higher number of experiments.

5. In the Multi-Objective Design Study dialog box, click
   ! (Compute Master Table) to run the study.

6. Specify the number of experiments to create. This is the number of records that will be calculated and listed in the master table.

7. Click 🗗 (Derive New Table) to derive further solutions from the results. Use the **Constraints** or the **Pareto** method to derive the optimized solution from the data.

Example:

Using the container shown in Figure 4–5, you can perform a Multi-Objective Design Study to optimize the model with respect to two goals: *capacity* and *mass*.

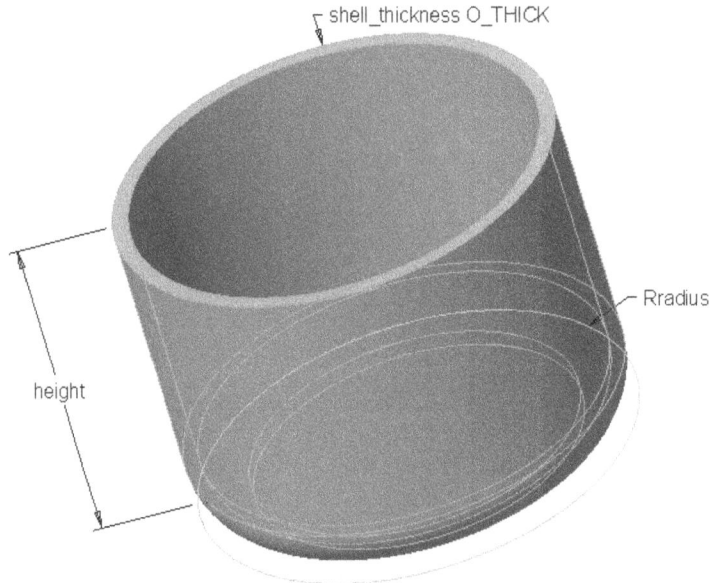

shell_thickness O_THICK

Rradius

height

Figure 4–5

The **shell_thickness**, **height**, and **radius** design variables are added to the Master Table using the following *minimum* and *maximum* values:

	Current Value	Minimum Value	Maximum Value
Shell_Thickness	10	2	20
Radius	100	50	300
Height	150	100	600

The design goals added are mass and capacity (a relation analysis which calculates the inner capacity of the container). The Master Table dialog box is shown in Figure 4–6.

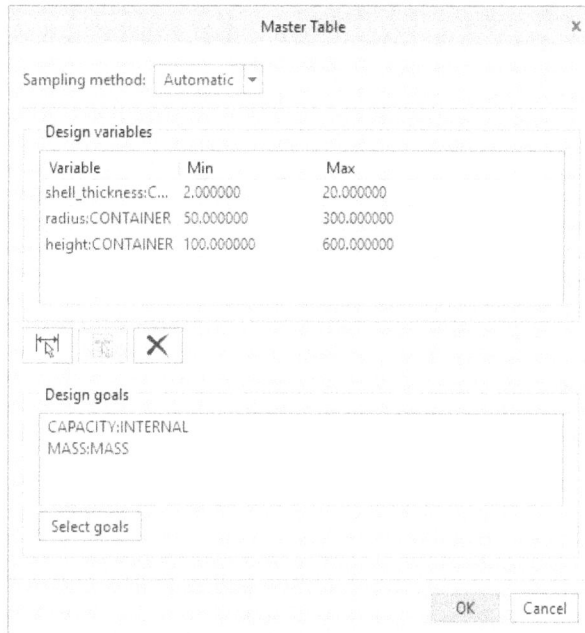

Figure 4–6

By clicking ! (Compute Master Table) and specifying 100 experiments, the master table data is generated. Figure 4–7 shows a subset of the 100 records that were produced.

Table Data

Name: MASTER_TABLE Records: 100

Record #	CAPACITY:INTE...	MASS:MASS
0	28521027.494563	4876772.462357
1	13534972.358540	5178488.384505
2	36382993.237389	3108853.521239
3	22996935.246690	3557238.859350
4	28550261.232075	7891035.295352
5	3940677.001170	1897612.415656
6	68108286.967029	3395667.297099
7	11738024.061978	1278692.561396
8	87948553.018458	13548791.691539
9	2472992.267689	2589725.848786

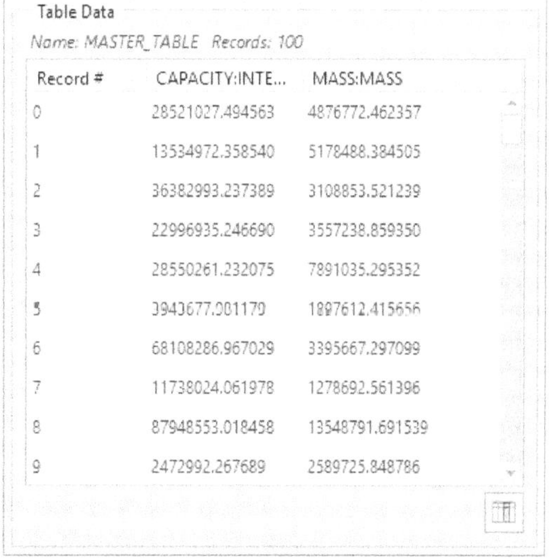

Figure 4–7

To find the optimized solution from all this data, design constraints are applied by clicking ⬚ (Derive New Table). Two derivations are used. The first design constraint is to remove all records with a capacity less than 10L. This can be done using a **Constraint** derivation, as shown in Figure 4–8, where the *minimum* for the **CAPACITY** parameter is set to **10 L**.

Derive Table (MASTER_TABLE)		✕

⦿ Constraints
○ Pareto

Goal	Min	Max
CAPACITY:INTERNAL	10000000.000000	125105980.152722
MASS:MASS	616618.377218	20883377.299781

Table name: MAX_CAP

OK   Cancel

Figure 4–8

A number of records still meet this constraint. The second design criteria is to minimize mass. The **Pareto** derivation, shown in Figure 4–9, was used to select the record with the minimum mass. This derivation is performed on the reduced records to ensure that the 10L capacity constraint is met while still minimizing the mass.

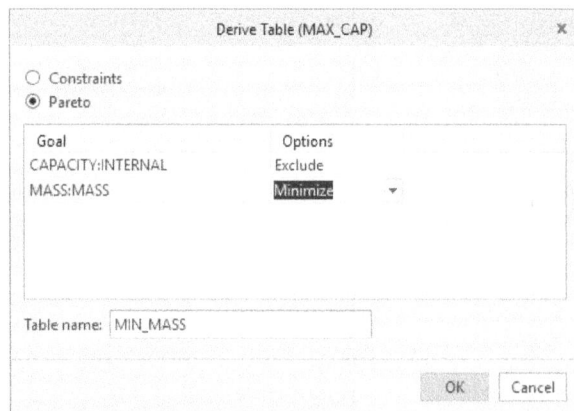

Derive Table (MAX_CAP)		✕

○ Constraints
⦿ Pareto

Goal	Options
CAPACITY:INTERNAL	Exclude
MASS:MASS	Minimize ▾

Table name: MIN_MASS

OK   Cancel

Figure 4–9

A single, optimized record is the result. The model can be shown in its optimized state by right-clicking the remaining record and selecting **Show Model**. The optimized model is shown in Figure 4–10.

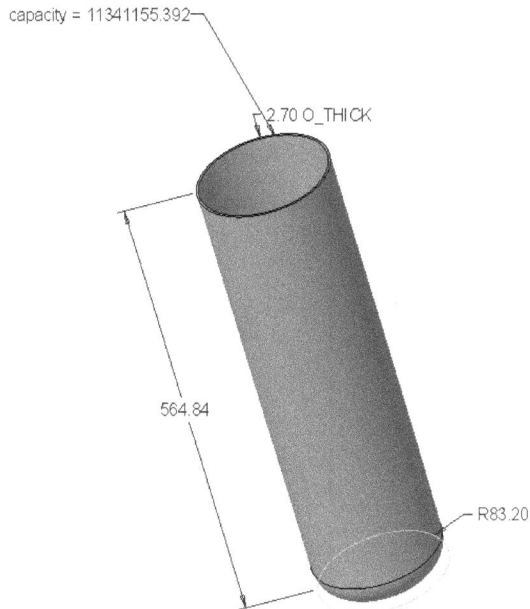

Figure 4–10

This solution differs from that found using the Optimization Study. This is because the design constraints were selected using different methods. The previous solution exists in the Master Tables records and can be extracted using different derivations. The resulting Multi-Objective Design Study dialog box is shown in Figure 4–11.

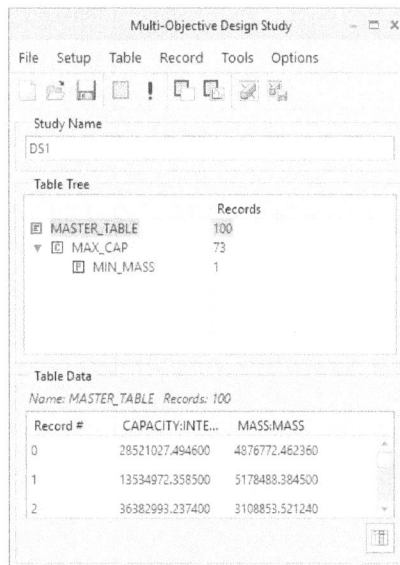

Figure 4–11

The elements of the Multi-Objective Design Study dialog box are described as follows:

Element	Description
Study Name	Specifies the name for the study.
Table Tree	Lists the tables and derivations in the study. Select the active table from the table tree when creating or modifying a derivation. The number of records contained in each table is listed in the right-hand column.
Table Data	Lists all records for the selected table. The records are listed in numeric order and provide values for all design goals and variables.

The buttons in the Multi-Objective Design Study dialog box are described as follows:

Button	Description
	Creates a new Multi-Objective Design Study.
	Opens an existing Multi-Objective Design Study.
	Saves the current Multi-Objective Design Study.
	Creates a Master Table. Selecting this button opens the Master Table dialog box.
	Runs the Multi-Objective Design Study. Once selected, you must enter the number of experiments (records) to be created.
	Opens the Derive dialog box, which enables you to find an optimized record from the table data.
	Creates a graph of the table data. Selecting this button opens the Graph dialog box. A single variable or goal must be selected for each axis.
	Shows the regenerated model based on the parameters of the selected record.
	Saves a copy of the model with the parameter values of the selected record.

Practice 4a | # Heat Sink Model

Practice Objectives

- Create and run a multi-objective design study.
- Derive optimized designs from the study.

Heat sinks are used to dissipate heat from electronic parts and small motors. In this practice, you will apply the behavioral modeling techniques to a heat sink model to meet the following four objectives:

- Minimize the mass of the heat sink.

- Maximize the surface area of the heat sink to dissipate heat.

- Determine the ratio of fin height to base thickness to accommodate manufacturing.

- Determine the ratio of fin height to heat sink width to locate the device on the part.

The results of each of these objectives can conflict with one another. You will use a multi-objective design study to provide design options.

Task 1 - Open the part heat_sink.prt

1. Set the working directory to *Heat_Sink*.

2. Open **heat_sink.prt**.

3. Set the model display as follows:

- *(Datum Display Filters)*: All Off

- *(Spin Center)*: Off

- *(Display Style)*: (Shading With Edges)

The model units are mmNs. The heat sink material density is 1e-008 tonne/mm^3.

The model displays as shown in Figure 4–12.

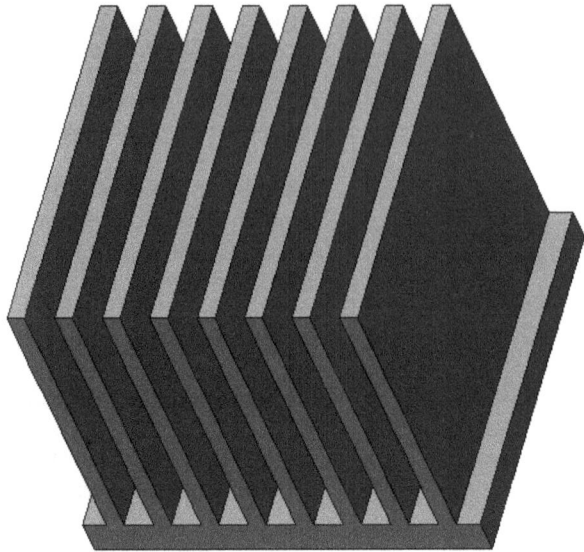

Figure 4–12

Task 2 - Create an analysis feature for the model's mass.

1. Create a Mass Properties analysis feature and set the name to **MASS_PART**.

2. Click **Preview**. The heat sink properties display in the result area as shown in Figure 4–13.

The part mass is 120g = 0.26lb.

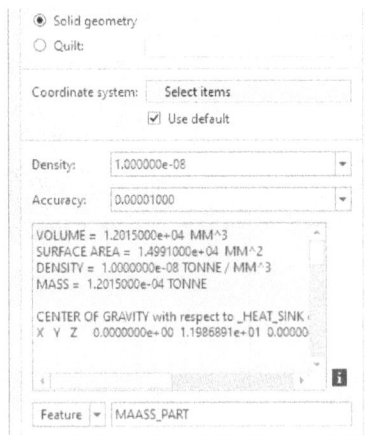

Figure 4–13

3. Select the *Feature* tab.

4. Remove the checkmark next to **VOLUME** and **SURF_AREA** in the *Parameters* area so that only **MASS** is created.

5. Edit the model mass parameter name to **HS_MASS** and press <Enter>.

6. Click **OK** to complete the feature.

Task 3 - Create a Measure analysis feature to measure the surface area of one of the fins.

---

1. In the Measure group, expand ✎ (Measure) and select ⊠ (Area).

2. In the Measure: Area dialog box, click ⊕ (Expand The Dialog) if required, to display the *Analysis* and *Feature* tabs.

3. Select the surface shown in Figure 4–14. The surface area (750) should display.

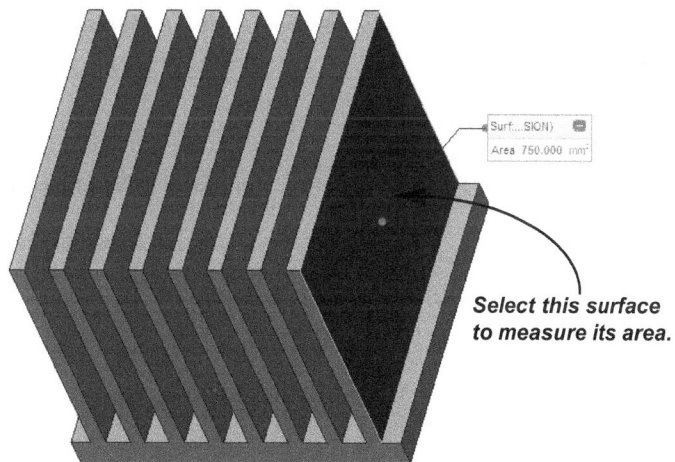

Select this surface to measure its area.

Figure 4–14

4. Select the *Feature* tab. Note that the **AREA** parameter is selected for creation.

5. Click 🖫▾ (Save. Ensure that **Make Feature** is selected, set the name to **SURFACE_AREA**, and press <Enter>.

6. Click **Close** to complete the analysis feature.

Task 4 - Create a Relation analysis feature to calculate the height ratio.

1. In the Manage group, click ⁞ (Analysis).

2. Edit the name to **HEIGHT_RATIO** and press <Enter>.

3. In the *Type* area, select **Relation**.

4. Click **Next**.

5. Double-click on the model to display all the dimensions.

6. Enter the following relation in the relation editor:

    HEIGHT = (FIN_HEIGHT/BASE_THICK)

As an alternative to entering the symbol, click ⊢⊣ (Display Specified Dimension) and select the dimension directly on the model. The dimension symbol is automatically added at the point where the cursor was located.

7. Click ☑ (Verify) to verify the relation and select **OK**.

8. Click **OK** in the Relations dialog box.

9. Click ✔ (OK) to complete the analysis feature.

Task 5 - Create a Relation analysis feature to calculate the width ratio.

1. In the Manage group, click ⁞ (Analysis).

2. Edit the name to **WIDTH_RATIO** and press <Enter>.

3. In the *Type* area, select **Relation**.

4. Click **Next**.

5. Enter the following relation in the relation editor:

    WIDTH = (FIN_HEIGHT/BASE_THICK)

If the dimensions that were shown in the previous analysis feature were cleared, you can double-click on the model once you are in the Relations dialog box to display them again.

6. Click ☑ (Verify) to verify the relation and click **OK**.

7. In the Relations dialog box, click **OK**.

8. Click ✔ (OK) to complete the analysis feature.

Task 6 - Create a Relation analysis feature to calculate the total area of the heat sink.

1. In the Manage group, click ⁞ (Analysis).

2. Edit the name to **TOTAL_AREA** and press <Enter>.

3. In the *Type* area, select **Relation**.

4. Click **Next**.

The smaller surfaces on each fin have not been included because their area is much smaller relative to the larger surface areas.

5. Enter the following relation in the relation editor.

   TOTAL_SURFACE=16*(AREA:FID_SURFACE_AREA)

6. Click ☑ (Verify) to verify the relation and click **OK**.

7. In the Relations dialog box, click **OK**.

8. Click ✓ (OK) to complete the analysis feature.

Task 7 - Create a Multi-Objective Design Study.

1. Select the *Tools* tab and click ⅟ₓ (Switch Dimensions).

2. Select the *Analysis* tab.

3. In the Design Study group, expand ✎ (Feasibility/ Optimization) and select ⚙ (Multi-Objective Design Study). The Multi-Objective Design Study dialog box displays as shown in Figure 4–15.

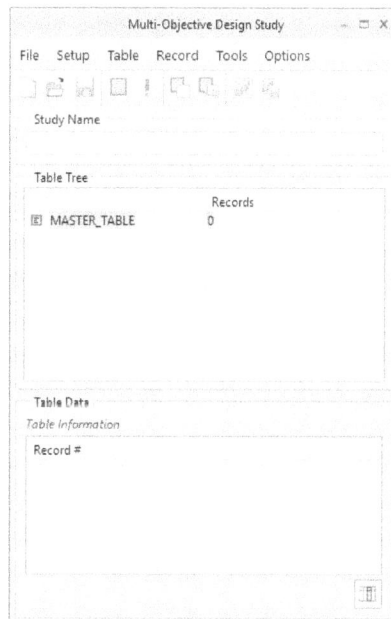

Figure 4–15

4. Click ▢ (New Design Study) to create a new design study.

5. Edit the Study name to **HEAT_SINK** and press <Enter>.

6. Click ▥ (Setup Master Table) to create a Master Table. The Master Table dialog box displays as shown in Figure 4–16.

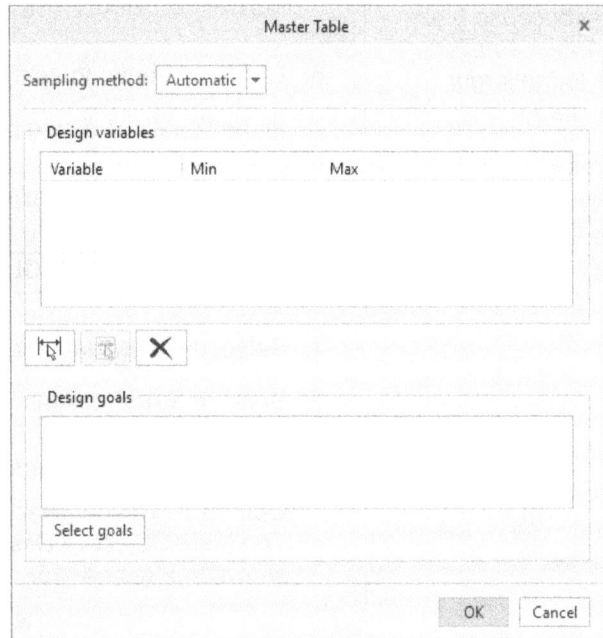

Master Table	×

Sampling method: Automatic ▼

Design variables

Variable	Min	Max

▨ ▧ ✕

Design goals

Select goals

OK   Cancel

Figure 4–16

7. Click **Select Goals**. The Select Parameters dialog box displays as shown in Figure 4–17.

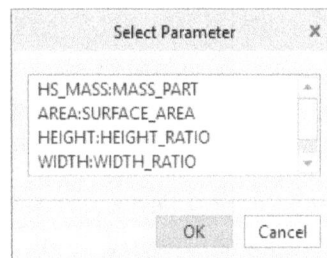

Select Parameter	×

HS_MASS:MASS_PART
AREA:SURFACE_AREA
HEIGHT:HEIGHT_RATIO
WIDTH:WIDTH_RATIO

OK   Cancel

Figure 4–17

8. Press and hold <Ctrl> and select all the parameters in the Parameters dialog box. Click **OK**. The parameters display in the *Design goals* area of the Master Table dialog box.

9. Click ⌐⌐ (Add Dimension).

10. Select the first fin on the model and select the **FIN_HEIGHT** and **FIN_WIDTH** dimensions. Additionally, select the base and select **BASE_WIDTH** and **BASE_THICK** dimensions. Refer to Figure 4–18 to locate the dimensions. Press the middle mouse button to stop selecting dimensions.

*Model displayed in **No Hidden** mode for clarity.*

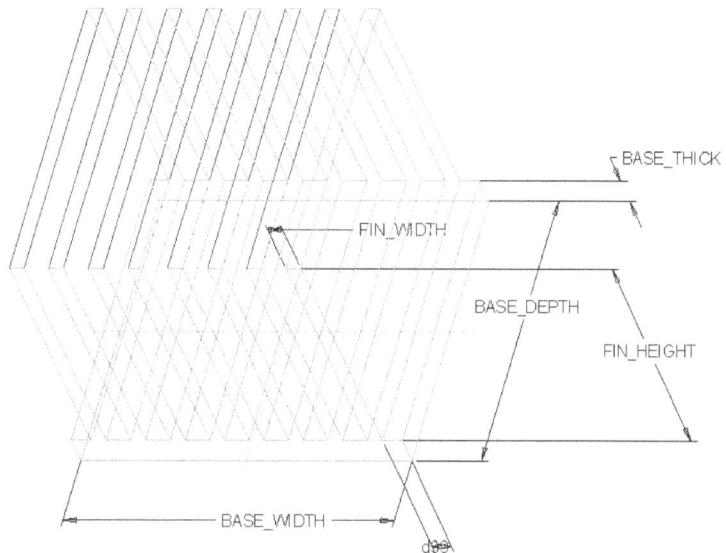

Figure 4–18

11. Select the Min and Max cells for each dimension in the Master Table dialog box. Enter the following values:

Dimension	Minimum	Maximum
FIN_HEIGHT	20	30
FIN_WIDTH	1.2	1.9
BASE_THICK	2	4
BASE_WIDTH	25	35

Note that the variables will be listed in the order in which you selected them, so be careful when entering the Min and Max values.

The Master Table dialog box displays as shown in Figure 4–19.

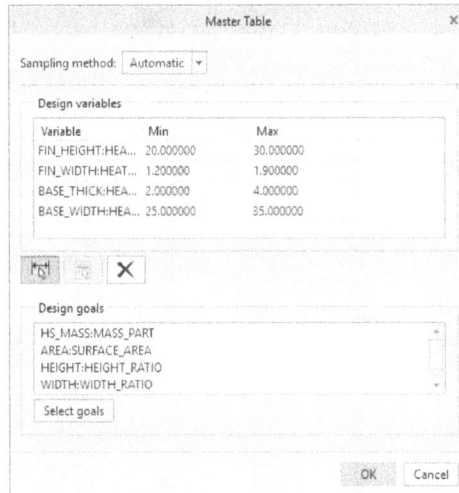

Figure 4–19

12. Click **OK** to close the Master Table dialog box.

Alternatively, you can click Setup>Compute/Expand to start the design study.

13. Click ! (Compute Master Table) to start the design study.

14. Enter **100** as the number of experiments to generate. Once complete, the Multi-Objective Design Study dialog box displays as shown in Figure 4–20.

Figure 4–20

Task 8 - Derive a solution from the results.

Design Consideration

The Multi-Objective Design Study done in the previous task shows that 100 different solutions exist for each design goal selected. The solutions were obtained by varying the design variables within their limits and recalculating the value of each parameter. Which record is the correct answer? Remember that you have multiple objectives. Focus on the total surface area. Using the Derive dialog box, you can find the record that provides the largest total surface area.

1. Click ⬚ (Derive New Table). The Derive Table dialog box displays as shown in Figure 4–21.

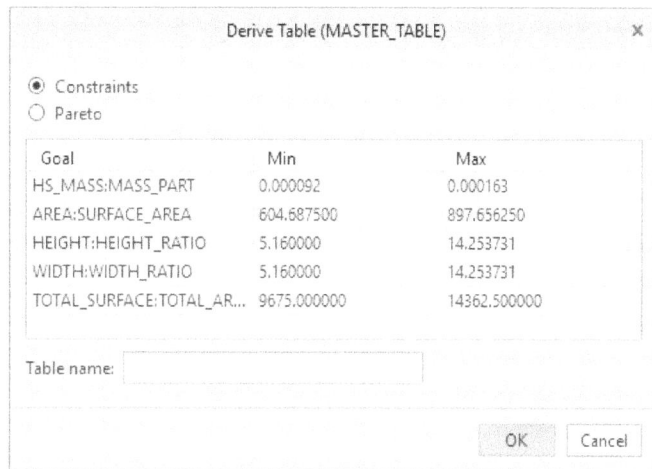

Derive Table (MASTER_TABLE)			×
⦿ Constraints			
○ Pareto			

Goal	Min	Max
HS_MASS:MASS_PART	0.000092	0.000163
AREA:SURFACE_AREA	604.687500	897.656250
HEIGHT:HEIGHT_RATIO	5.160000	14.253731
WIDTH:WIDTH_RATIO	5.160000	14.253731
TOTAL_SURFACE:TOTAL_AR...	9675.000000	14362.500000

Table name: _____

OK   Cancel

Figure 4–21

2. Select **Pareto**.

3. Select the **Exclude** cell adjacent to the **TOTAL_SURFACE** parameter.

4. Select **Maximize** from the drop-down list. The Derive Table dialog box displays as shown in Figure 4–22.

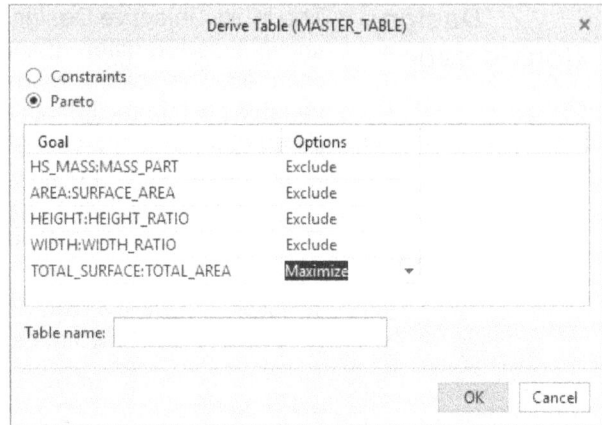

Figure 4–22

5. Set the table name to **TOTAL_AREA** and press <Enter>.

6. Click **OK**. The Multi-Objective Design Study dialog box displays as shown in Figure 4–23.

A single record exists in the Table Data field. This record is the derived version of the model with the largest total surface area.

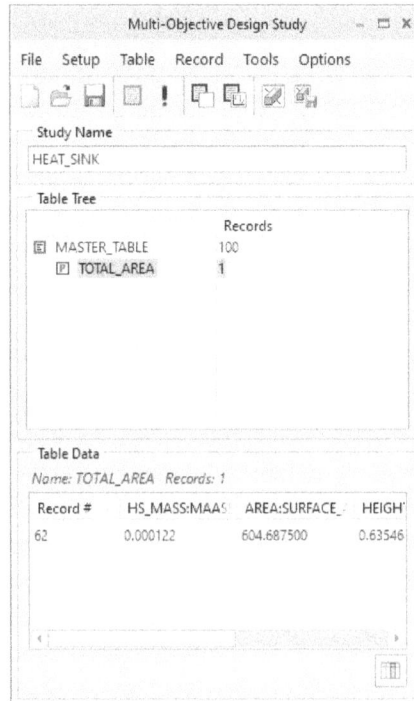

Figure 4–23

Task 9 - Create a second derivation.

1. Select the Master Table in the *Table Tree* area.

2. Create a second derived table to Minimize the model's mass.

3. Review the records in more detail using the INFORMATION WINDOW.

Task 10 - (Optional) Create two additional derivations.

1. Create a derivation to minimize the fin height to the base thickness ratio (**HEIGHT**). Compare this to the resulting weight of the models.

2. Create a derivation to minimize the fin height to the base width ratio (**WIDTH**). Compare this to the resulting weight of the models.

Task 11 - Save all design studies.

1. In the Multi-Objective Design Study dialog box, click ⊟ (Save Design Study) to save all of the design studies.

2. Close the dialog box.

3. Close the part and erase it from memory.

Practice 4b

Floor Plan Model

Practice Objectives

- Create and run a Multi-Objective Design Study.
- Derive optimized designs from the study.

In this practice, you will use the **floor_plan** model from a previous practice. You now have two conflicting objectives for the design of the floor plan. You will need to minimize the mass of the assembly while maximizing the storage capacity of the cabinets. It has been determined that the storage capacity constraint is your primary objective. A multi-objective design study will be used to provide a series of options for the final design.

Task 1 - Open the floor_plan_final assembly.

1. Set the working directory to *Floor_Plan*.

2. Open **floor_plan_final.asm** from the *completed_models* directory.

3. Set the model display as follows:

    - ⅍ *(Datum Display Filters)*: ↳ (Csys Display) and
      ⎏ (Plane Display) only

    - ⅃ *(Spin Center)*: Off

    - ⬚ *(Display Style)*: ⬡ (Shading With Edges)

    The model displays as shown in Figure 4–24.

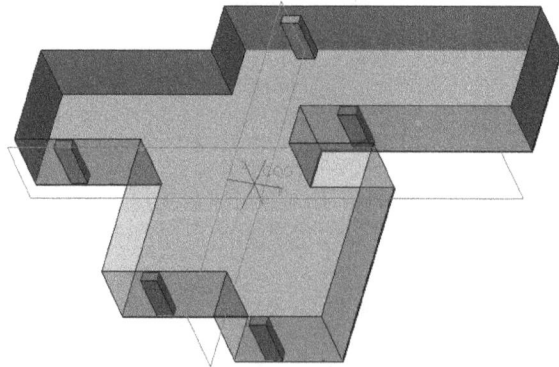

Figure 4–24

To determine the capacity of the cabinets, you must create a model analysis feature in each individual model. The parameters developed from these features can then be used in the top-level assembly.

Task 2 - Create an analysis feature in water_cabinet.prt.

1. Select **WATER_CABINET_FINAL.PRT** in the Model Tree and click (Open).

2. Select the *Analysis* tab.

3. In the Measure group, expand (Measure) and select (Volume).

4. In the Measure: Volume dialog box, click (Save), ensure that **Make Feature** is selected, set the name to **WATER_VOL** and press <Enter>.

5. Select the *Feature* tab.

6. Create the **VOLUME** parameter.

7. Click **Close** to complete the feature.

8. Close the part window.

9. Open **PARTS_CABINET_FINAL.PRT**.

10. Select the *Analysis* tab.

11. In the Measure group, expand (Measure) and select (Volume).

12. In the Measure: Volume dialog box, click (Save), ensure that **Make Feature** is selected, set the name to **PARTS_VOL**, and press <Enter>.

13. Select the *Feature* tab.

14. Create the **VOLUME** parameter.

15. Click **Close** to complete the feature.

16. Close the part window.

Task 3 - Create relation analysis features.

Design Consideration

In this task, you create three relation analysis features. The first analysis calculates the total water cabinet volume; the second analysis calculates the total parts cabinet volume; the third analysis sums the two of these together.

1. If not already active, set **floor_plan_final.asm** as the active model.

2. Select the *Analysis* tab.

3. In the *Manage* group, click ✕⁄ (Analysis).

4. Edit the name to **WATER** and press <Enter>.

5. Select **Relation**.

6. Click **Next**.

7. Click **Show>Session ID>Part** and select **water_cabinet_final**. The session id displays in the message window. Click **Part** and select the **parts_cabinet_final** component. These values are used in upcoming relations.

The part level **water_vol** *parameter is multiplied by two since two components exist in the assembly*

8. Enter the following relation in the relation editor. Enter the session id for **water_cabinet** in place of the # symbol in the relation.

   WATER_VOL = 2*(VOLUME:FID_WATER_VOL:#)

9. Click ✓ (Verify) to verify the relation and click **OK**.

10. Click **OK** in the Relations dialog box.

11. Click ✔ (OK) to complete the analysis feature.

12. Create a second Relation analysis feature and set the name to **PARTS**.

13. Click **Next**.

14. Enter the following relation in the relation editor. Enter the session id for **parts_cabinet** in place of the # symbol in the relation

   PARTS_VOL = 3*(VOLUME:FID_PARTS_VOL:#)

15. Click ✓ (Verify) to verify the relation and click **OK**.

16. Click **OK** in the Relations dialog box.

17. Click ✓ (OK) to complete the analysis feature.

18. Create a third Relation analysis feature named **TOTAL_VOL**.

19. Click **Next**.

20. Enter the following relation in the relation editor.

    TOTAL_VOL = WATER_VOL:FID_WATER +
    PARTS_VOL:FID_PARTS

21. Click ☑ (Verify) to verify the relation and click **OK**.

22. Click **OK** in the Relations dialog box.

23. Click ✓ (OK) to complete the analysis feature.

Task 4 - Create a Multi-Objective Design Study.

---

1. Select the *Tools* tab and click ⅟₅ (Switch Dimensions).

2. In the *Design Study* group, expand ⚲ (Feasibility/
   Optimization) and select ⚼ (Multi-Objective Design Study).

3. Click ▢ (New Design Study) to create a new design study.
   Accept the default name.

4. Click ▦ (Setup Master Table) to create the Master Table.

5. Click ⌖ (Add Dimension). Add the following dimensions and *Min* and *Max* values. Use Figure 4–25 to locate the dimensions.

Dimension	Minimum	Maximum
d0:WATER_CABINET_FINAL	200	1000
d1:WATER_CABINET_FINAL	200	1000
d2:WATER_CABINET_FINAL	300	1500
d0:PARTS_CABINET_FINAL	200	1000
d1:PARTS_CABINET_FINAL	200	1000
d2:PARTS_CABINET_FINAL	300	1500

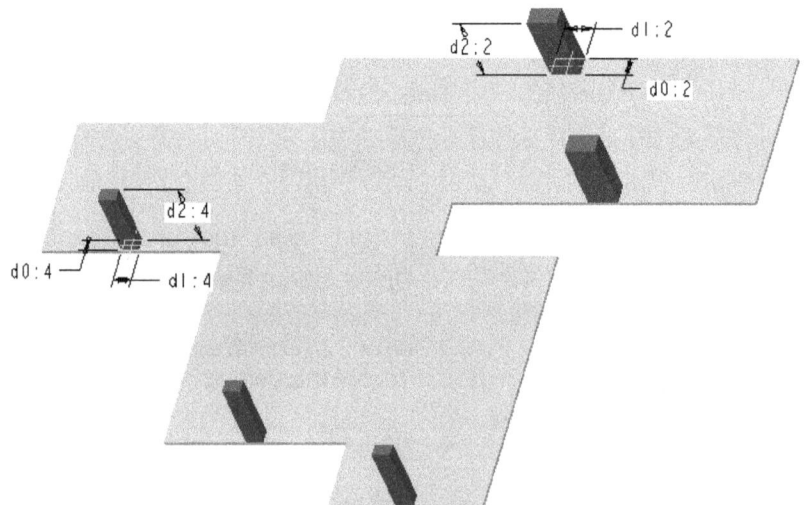

Figure 4–25

6. Click **Select Goals**. The Parameter Selection dialog box displays. Select the following parameters:

- **MASS:COFG**
- **WATER_VOL:WATER**
- **PARTS_VOL:PARTS**
- **TOTAL_VOL:TOTAL_VOL**

7. Click **OK** when complete. The Master Table dialog box displays as shown in Figure 4–26.

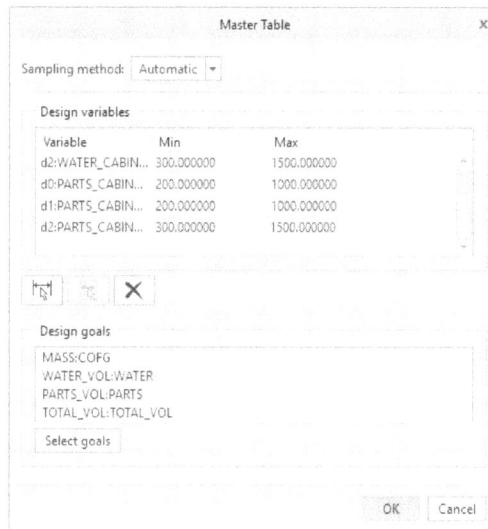

Figure 4–26

8. Click **OK**.

9. Click ! (Compute Master Table) to start the design study.

10. Enter **100** for the number of experiments to generate. The system runs through each experiment.

Task 5 - Derive a solution from the results.

Design Consideration

Based on the analysis done in the previous task, 100 different solutions exist for each design goal selected. The solutions were obtained by varying the design variables within their limits, and by recalculating the value of each parameter. Which record is the correct answer? Remember that you have multiple objectives. Focus in on mass. Using the Derive dialog box, you can find the record that provides the lowest mass.

1. Click ⌷ (Derive New Table). The Derive Table dialog box displays.

2. Select **Pareto**.

3. Select the **Exclude** cell, adjacent to the **MASS:COFG** parameter.

4. Select **Minimize** from the drop-down list.

5. Set the table name to **MIN_MASS**. The Derive Table dialog box displays as shown in Figure 4–27.

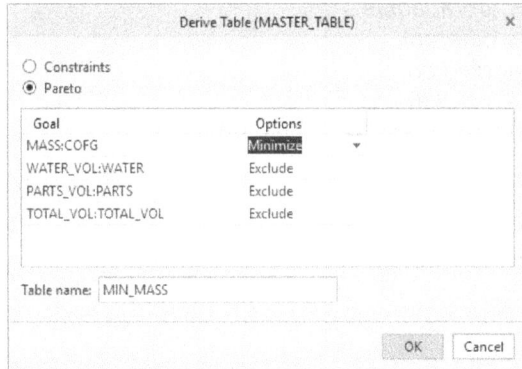

Figure 4–27

6. Click **OK**. A single record exists in the *Table Tree* area. This is the derived version of the model with the least mass. It can be viewed in more detail by clicking **Table>Show Data**. The record displays as shown in Figure 4–28.

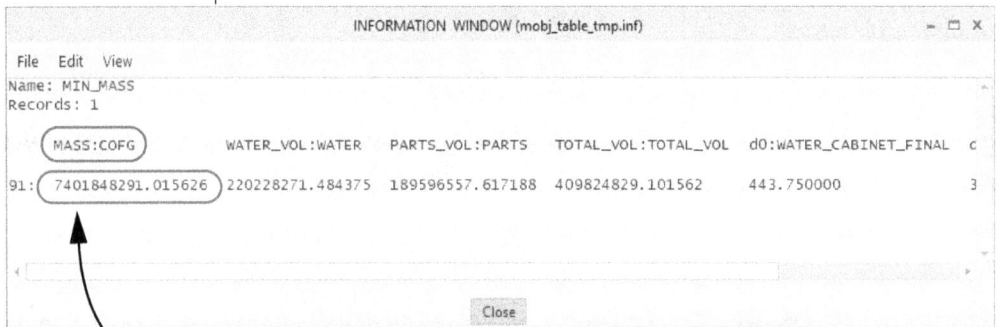

Derived minimum mass

Figure 4–28

You can continue to create several derivations of the table data and look at each version of the model. You can now focus in on your design constraints. The design requires a minimum of 800 L of water storage and 1,000 L of parts storage.

7. Create a second derivation. Highlight the Master Table in the *Table Tree* field and click ⬚ (Derive New Table).

8. Name the table **MAX_STOR**. Enter table data shown in Figure 4–29 for the **WATER_VOL** and **PARTS_VOL**. The derivation provides a list of all data that meets the design requirements of 800 L of water and 1,000 L of parts storage.

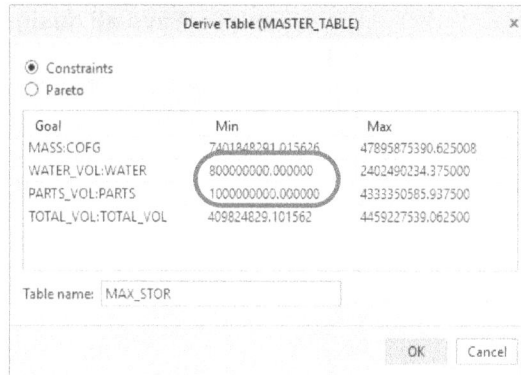

Figure 4–29

9. Click **OK**. There are a total of 10 records which meet these design constraints. Since our primary objective has been satisfied, you can create a further derivation based on mass.

10. Highlight **MAX_STOR** in the *Table Tree* area. Click (Derive New Table).

11. Set the table name to **MIN_MASS_MAX_STOR**.

12. Use the **Pareto** method and in the MASS:COFG drop-down list, select **Minimize**.

13. Click **OK**.

14. The solution to the design problem is shown in the *Table Data* area. Select the record in the *Table Data* area, right-click, and select **Show Model**. The assembly displays in a sub-window, as shown in Figure 4–30. Close the sub-window.

*This model can also be saved to a new model name by selecting the record, right-clicking, and selecting **Save Model**.*

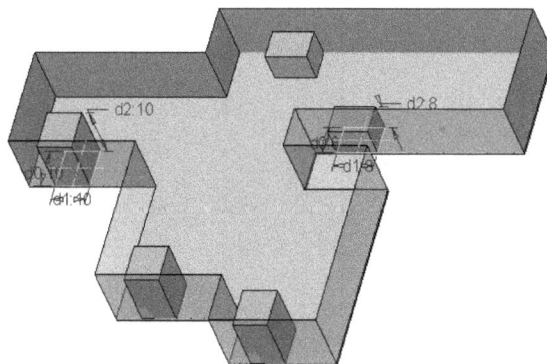

Figure 4–30

Task 6 - Save all design studies.

1. In the Multi-Objective Design Study dialog box, click
    ▣ (Save Design Study) to save all of the design studies.

2. Close the dialog box.

3. Close the assembly and erase it from memory.

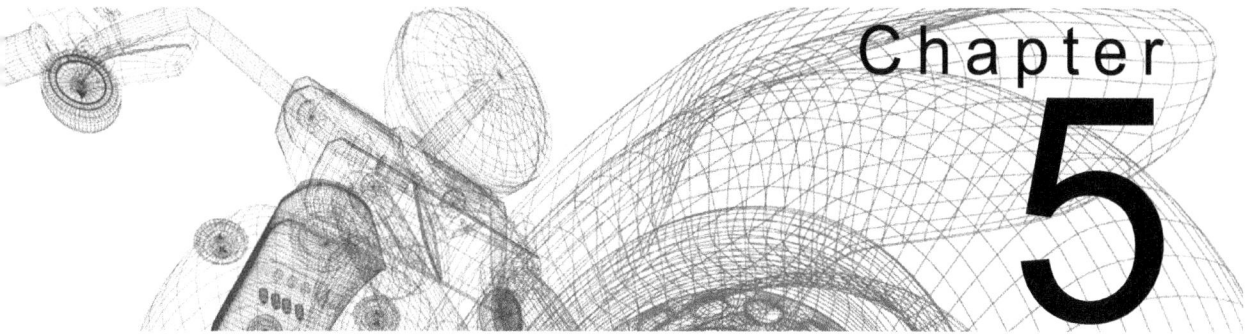

Graph Matching

A Datum Graph feature can be used to associate a graphical XY function to part geometry. Through relations, it can be used to control geometry. The graph feature must display before the feature it controls in the feature list.

Learning Objectives in This Chapter

- Understand how to use a datum graph to associate a graphical XY function to part geometry.
- Learn how to use Behavioral Modeling to compare two graphs to determine the differences in distributions of one parameter along the other parameter.
- Recognize the four methods available for comparing graphs.

5.1 Datum Graphs

A Datum Graph feature can be used to associate a graphical XY function to part geometry. Through relations, it can be used to control geometry. The graph feature must display before the feature it controls in the feature list.

To define a datum graph, in the *Model* tab, in the **Datum** group, select **Graph**. Enter a name for the graph and press <Enter>. Creo Parametric places you in the *Sketch* tab. Figure 5–1 shows an example of a datum graph sketch. This graph can be used in a relation to create the model shown in Figure 5–2.

Datum graphs must have only one x value for each y value.

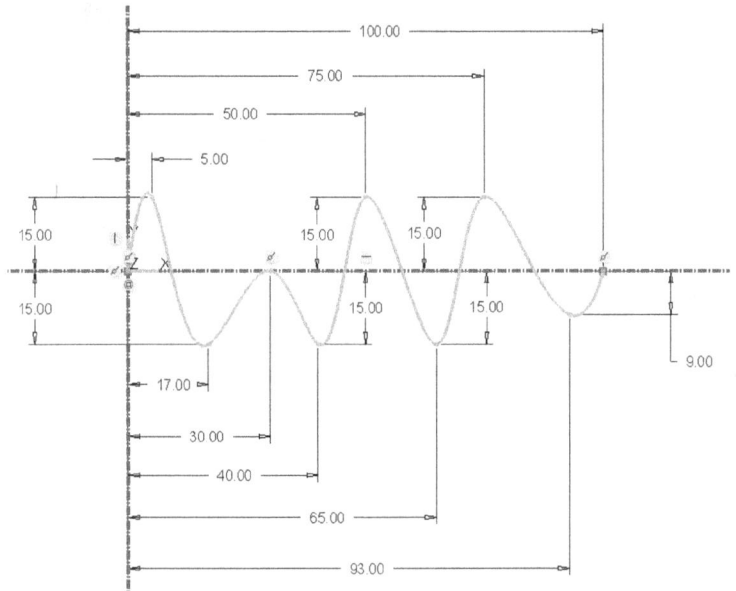

Figure 5–1

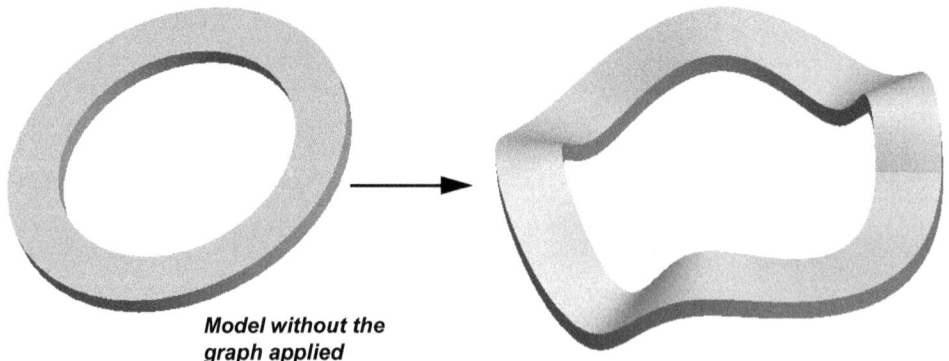

Model without the graph applied

Figure 5–2

Datum Graph sketches require the following geometry:

- Coordinate system

- Sketched entities to represent the function

- Dimensioning scheme that captures your design intent

- Horizontal and vertical centerlines (recommended)

A datum graph is stored with the model and can be used in any relation. The syntax used to reference the datum graph in a relation is as follows:

evalgraph ("graph_name", x)

Where:

evalgraph = A system-defined parameter that recognizes a datum graph feature is being referenced

graph_name = The name of the graph referenced in the relation.

x = The value along the x-axis for which the y value is returned

Consider the example in Figure 5–3. The figure shows a model before and after a relation referencing a datum graph was written.

Before Relation:

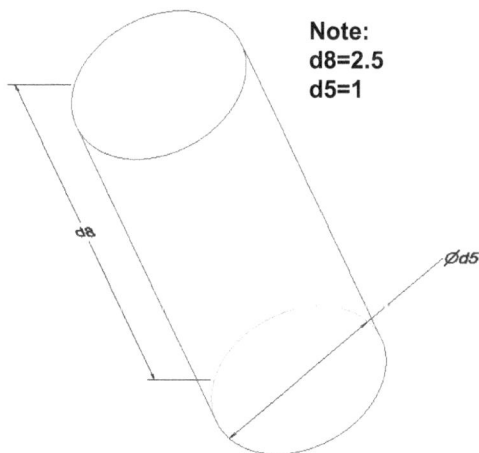

Note:
d8=2.5
d5=1

After Relation:

Relation: d5 = evalgraph ("diameter",7)

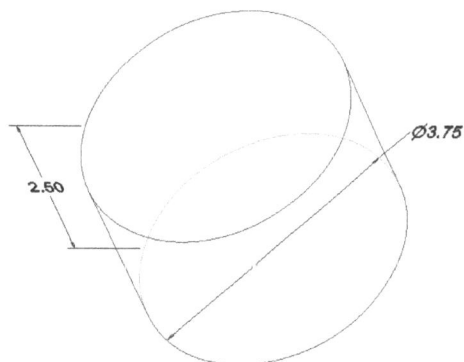

2.50

⌀3.75

d8

⌀d5

(Refer to Figure 5–4 to verify the value for d5 at x=7 is 3.75.)

Figure 5–3

The referenced datum graph is shown in Figure 5–4.

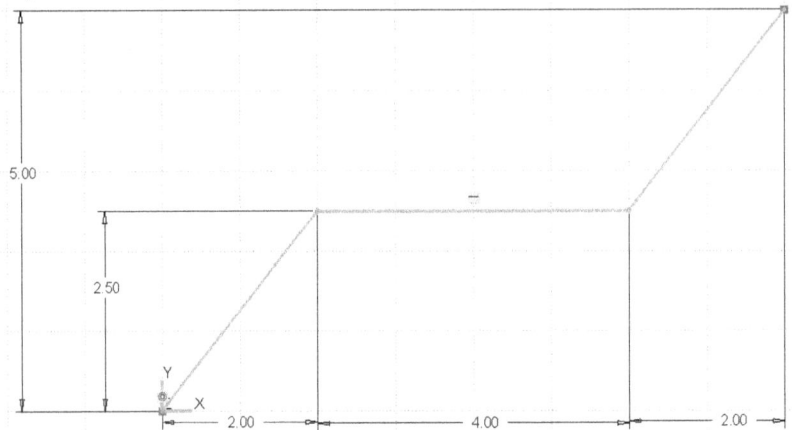

Figure 5–4

A relation can also include functions that are performed on the evalgraph portion of the relation, d5 = evalgraph ("diameter",7) * 2, or it can use the trajpar parameter.

5.2 Comparing Datum Graphs

Using Behavioral Modeling, you can compare two graphs to determine the differences in distributions of one parameter along the other parameter.

For example, the duct shown in Figure 5–5 is created as a variable section sweep and uses the graph shown in Figure 5–6 to drive the geometry along the trajectory.

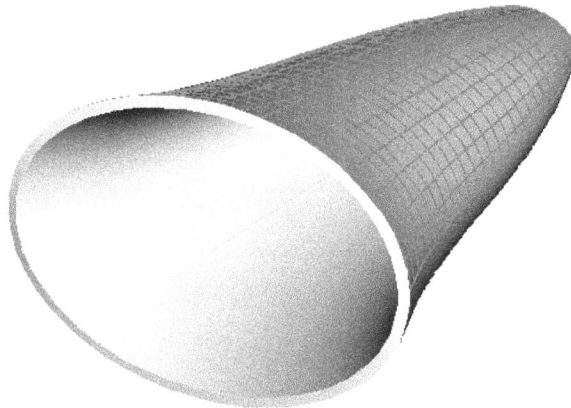

Figure 5–5

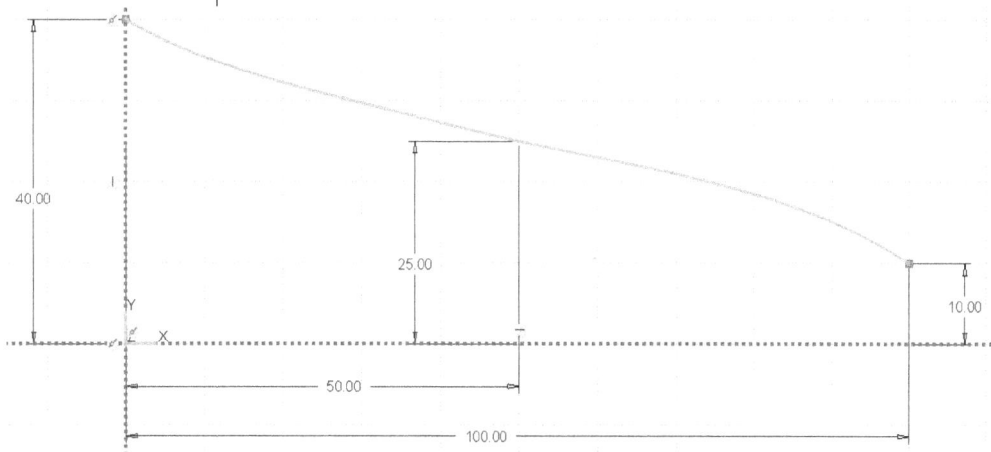

Figure 5–6

Using the compare graph functionality, you can compare the distribution of the first graph to a second graph. Once this is accomplished, you can use this parameter in Behavioral Modeler to optimize the difference and obtain the most desirable distribution.

For example, the first graph is compared with the graph shown in Figure 5–7 to obtain the graphs shown in Figure 5–8.

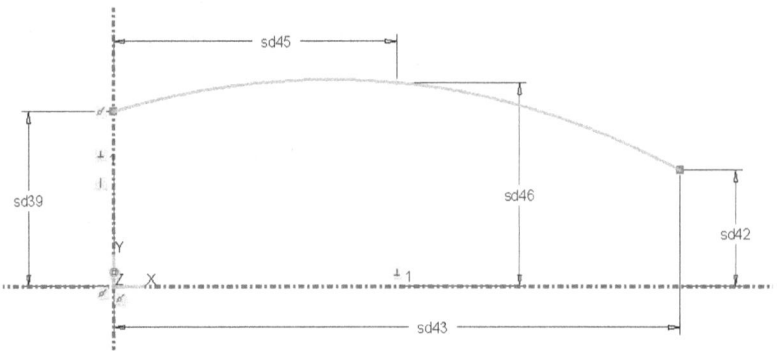

Figure 5–7

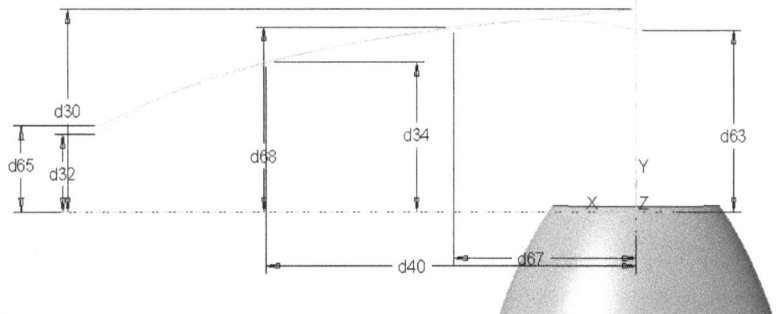

Figure 5–8

The geometry of the model updates to reflect the optimized results, as shown in Figure 5–9.

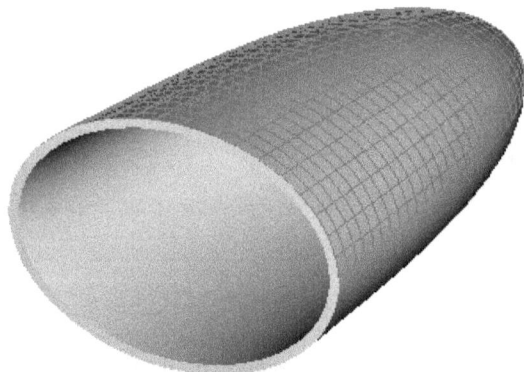

Figure 5–9

5.3 Graph Matching

Datum Graphs can be compared using one of four methods. These methods are described as follows:

Type	Based on Formula	What it measures
lone	L1norm of f(t)-g(t)=$\int$|f(t)-g(t)|dt -∞<t<∞	Measures the area between f(t) and g(t).
ltwo	L2norm of f(t)-g(t)=sqrt($\int$(f(t)-g(t))^2dt -∞<t<∞	Where f(t)-g(t) is a measure of the error, larger values of the error have more weight on L2 norm.
linf	L∞ norm of f(t)-g(t)=maxf(t)-g(t) -∞<t<∞	Measures the maximum error between two functions.
area	integral of f(t)-g(t)=$\int$(f(t)-g(t))dt -∞<t<∞	Measures the signed area between f(t) and g(t).

The types are based on the concept of the norm of a vector that has been extended to functions. It assumes a function as an n-dimensional vector (where n= ∞).

How To: Match Two Datum Graph Features

1. Create both Datum Graph features in the model. The graphs must exist before the analysis feature that compares them.
2. Create a Relation analysis feature that compares the two graphs. The syntax used in the relation determines the comparison method. Add the relation using the following syntax:
   relation_name = comparegraphs("graph1", "graph2", "type", left_bound_1, right_bound_1, left_bound_2, right_bound_2)

   The relation components are described as follows:

Components	Description
relation_name	Name of the relation.
graph1	Name of first datum graph.
graph2	Name of second datum graph.
left_bound_1	Left boundaries of the first datum graph.
right_bound_1	Right boundaries of the first datum graph.
left_bound_2	Left boundaries of the second datum graph.
right_bound_2	Right boundaries of the second datum graph.
type	Comparison method (e.g., lone, ltwo, linf, area).

When adding the relation, you are permitted some flexibility. You can specify all seven components in the relation; however, you can also create the relation using either of the following methods:

- Specify the "names" only - Creo Parametric uses the lone comparison method and compares over the entire length of the graph. For example:

  RELATION=comparegraphs("GRAPH1", "GRAPH2")

- Specify the "names" and "type" only - Creo Parametric uses the specified comparison method over the entire length of the graph. For example:

  RELATION=comparegraphs("GRAPH1", "GRAPH2", "area")

3. As the final step in comparing the graphs, run an optimization study to minimize the difference.

Practice 5a

Using Graph Features

Practice Objective

- Review how a graph feature can be used to create geometry.

In this practice, you will use a graph feature to create some model geometry. The purpose of this practice is to review how graph features are used to create geometry.

Design Consideration

The completed model is shown in Figure 5–10.

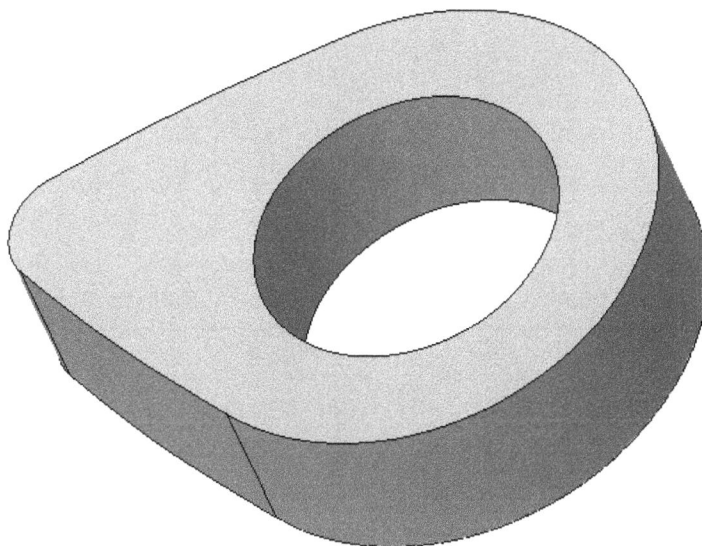

Figure 5–10

The geometry of the cam will be created using a sweep with a variable section, where the section is controlled by a circular curve as shown in Figure 5–11 and the graph feature shown in Figure 5–12.

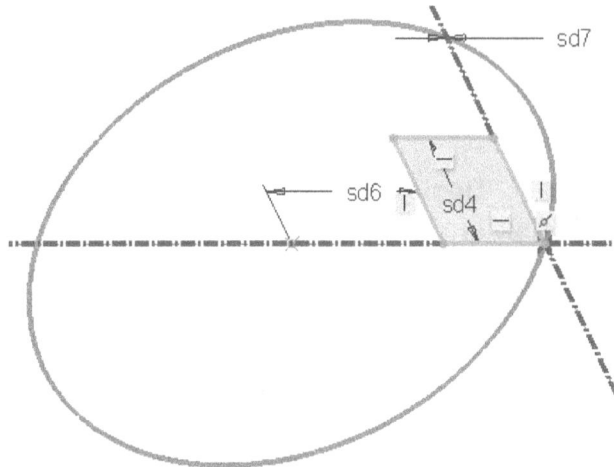

Figure 5–11

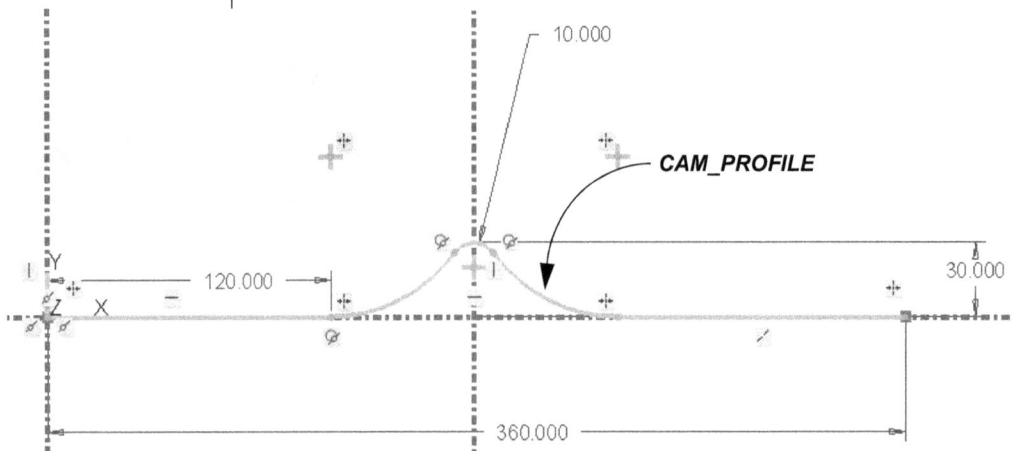

Figure 5–12

As the cam profile sweeps around the circular center, the width of the geometry is driven by the following relation:

$$sd7 = evalgraph("cam\_profile", trajpar*360)/10$$

Trajpar is a trajectory parameter that varies between 0 and 1 as the section is swept from the beginning to the end of the trajectory.

The trajpar*360 portion of the relation obtains corresponding values from the graph for X-coordinates of 0 to 360 degrees.

Task 1 - Open the cam_graph part and review the existing graph feature.

1. Set the working directory to *Using_Graph_Features*.
2. Open **cam_graph.prt**.
3. Set the model display as follows:
   - *(Datum Display Filters)*: All On
   - *(Spin Center)*: Off
   - *(Display Style)*: (Shading With Edges)
4. In the Model Tree, select **SWEEP_CIRCLE** and click (Show) in the mini toolbar. The part displays as shown in Figure 5–13.

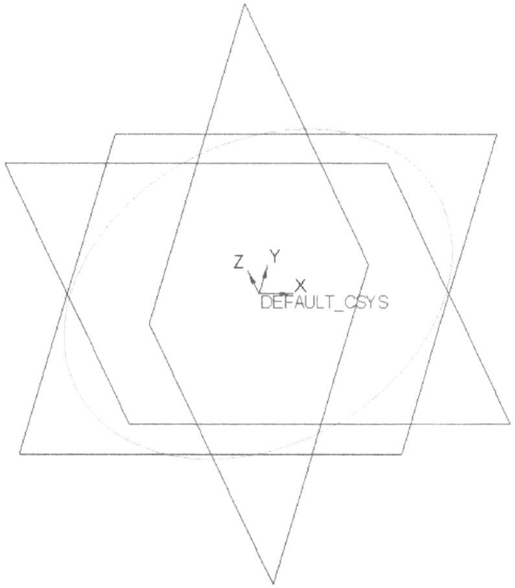

Figure 5–13

5. Toggle off the display of datum entities.

Note that the sketch below includes a coordinate system. The width of the cam is controlled by the height of the graph through the full 360 degree range.

6. In the Model Tree, select **CAM_PROFILE** and select (Edit Definition) in the mini toolbar.
7. In the **REDEFINE** menu in the Menu Manager, click **Done** to edit the Section.

8. Press <Enter> to accept the graph name. The sketch of the graph displays as shown in Figure 5–14.

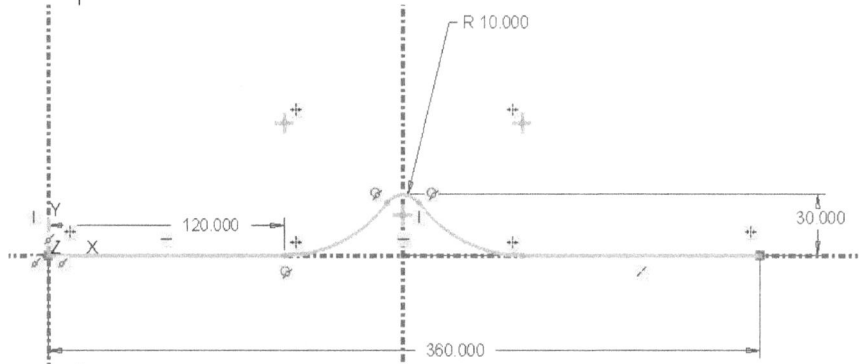

Figure 5–14

9. Click ✕ (Cancel) to exit Sketcher.

10. Click **Yes** if prompted to confirm.

Task 2 - Create a sweep to establish the cam geometry.

---

1. In the *Model* tab of the ribbon, click ✎ (Sweep).

2. Select the circular curve as the trajectory.

3. In the *Sweep* dashboard, click ✍ (Variable Section) and then click ✎ (Create or Edit Section).

4. Create and dimension the sketch shown in Figure 5–15.

   • Initially, sketch the rectangle so it extends past the vertical centerline, then add the dimension and edit it to **0.00**.

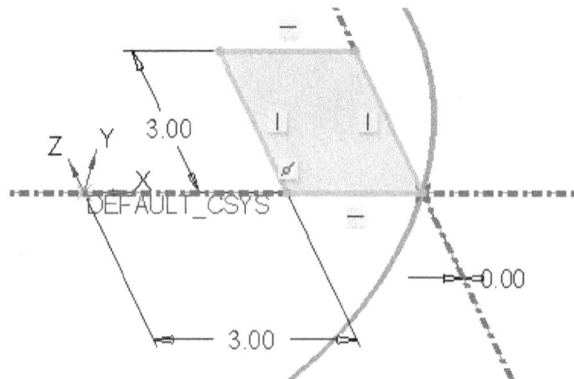

Figure 5–15

5. Select the *Tools* tab and click ⬚ (Switch Dimensions).

6. Take note of the symbol for the 0.00 dimension. In the image shown in Figure 5–16, the symbolic name is **sd7**.

- Depending on how you created the sketch, the symbolic name may be different on your system. For the remaining steps, use the symbolic name from your sketch.

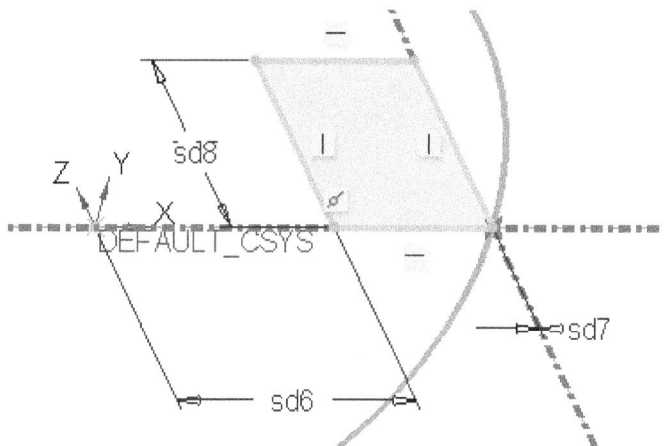

Figure 5–16

7. Ensure that the *Sketch* tab is active in the ribbon.

8. Click ✓ (OK) to complete the sketch.

9. Click ✓ (OK) to complete the sweep. The resulting geometry is shown in Figure 5–17.

The model is not yet controlled by the graph feature.

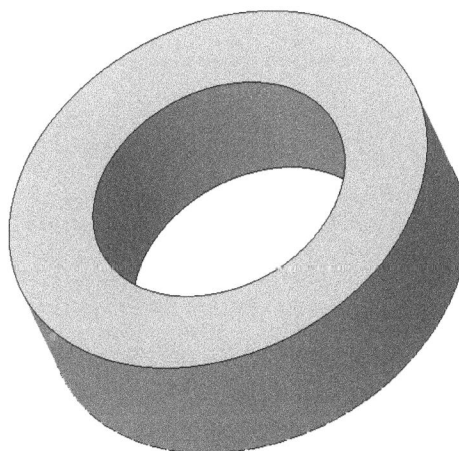

Figure 5–17

10. Select the *Tools* tab and click d= (Relations).

11. In the Relations dialog box, select **Section** from the Look In drop-down list.

12. Select **Sweep 1** in the Model Tree.

13. Select **sd7** (your number may differ), as shown in Figure 5–18.

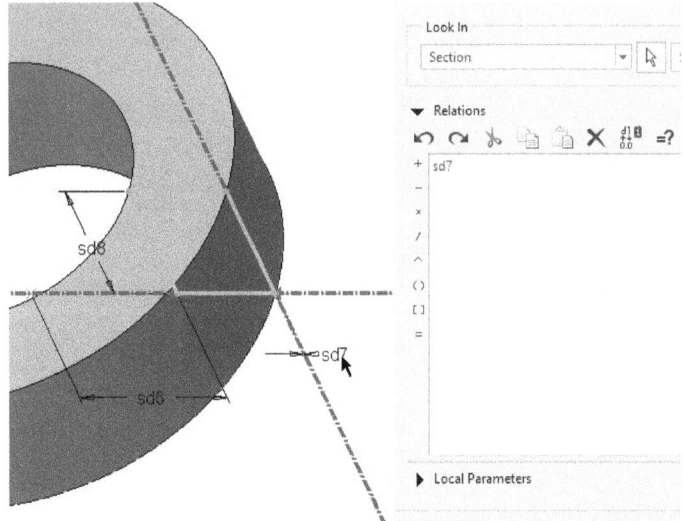

Figure 5–18

14. Type in the rest of the relation as shown in Figure 5–19.

The relation is created as a Section relation because it has to be regenerated as the sketch itself is regenerating.

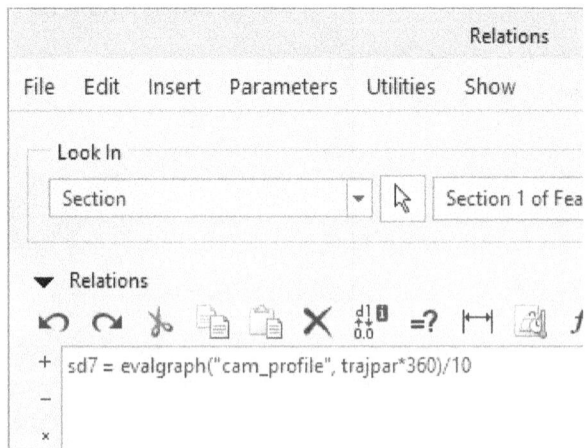

Figure 5–19

15. In the Relations dialog box, click ✔ (Verify) and click **OK**.

16. Click **OK** in the Relations dialog box.

17. If required, click (Regenerate) in the Quick Access toolbar. The model updates as shown in Figure 5–20.

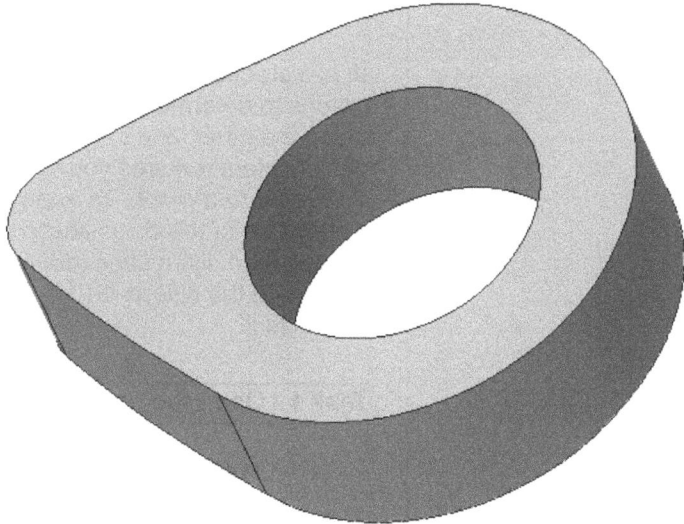

Figure 5–20

18. Close the part and erase it from memory.

| Practice 5b | # Comparing Graphs |

Practice Objectives

- Compare two graphs.
- Optimize the distribution one along the other.

In this practice, you will use BMX functionality to compare two graphs to determine the difference in the distribution of one along the other, and to obtain the optimized distribution. The design intent requires you to change the cross-section of a duct according to a graph. To analyze it, you will compare the actual distribution of the cross-section along the length of the duct to the required distribution (defined by a graph). Once you have measured the difference, you will run the optimization study to minimize it.

Task 1 - Open the graph_matching part.

1. Set the working directory to *Comparing_Graphs*.

2. Open **graph_matching.prt**. The part displays as shown in Figure 5–21. The mesh has been added to help show the depth and shape of the model. The model represents a duct used to control air flow.

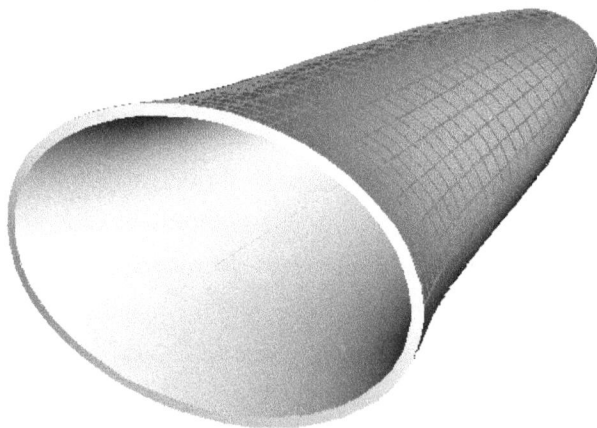

Figure 5–21

Design Consideration

The outside surface of the model is constructed as a variable section sweep with the section, as shown in Figure 5–22.

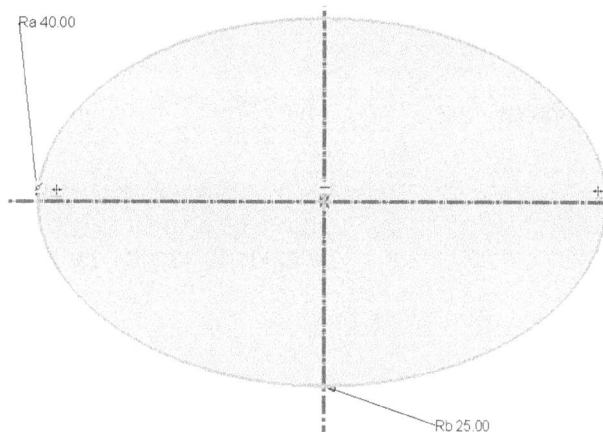

Ra 40.00

Rb 25.00

Figure 5–22

The minor radius (Rb) of the section is 0.625 of major radius (Ra. The Ra dimension (sd5) of the model is driven by a relation that references the graph feature, **GRAPH1**. This graph is shown in Figure 5–23.

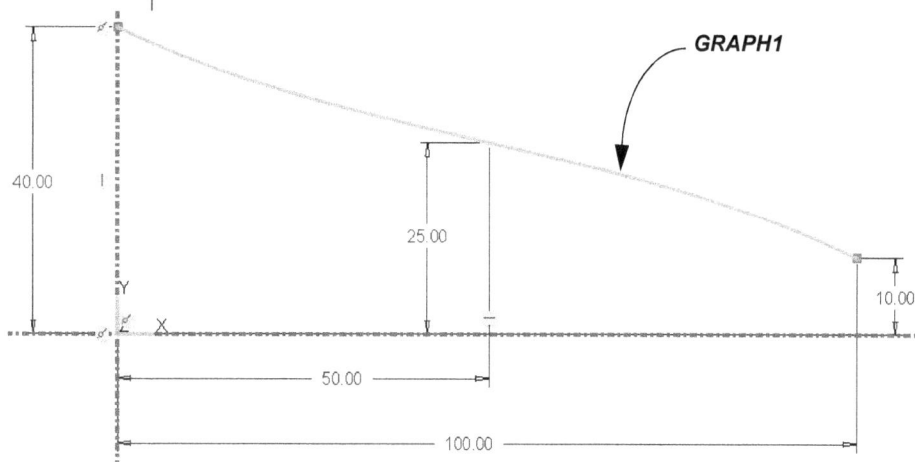

GRAPH1

40.00

25.00

10.00

50.00

100.00

Figure 5–23

The relations used for both Ra (**sd5**) and Rb (**sd6**) as the section moves along the trajectory are shown in Figure 5–24.

Trajpar is a trajectory parameter that varies between 0 and 1 as the section is swept from the beginning to the end of the trajectory.

sd5=evalgraph("graph1",trajpar*100)
sd6=(sd5*.625)

Figure 5–24

The trajpar*100 portion of the relation obtains corresponding values from the graph for X-coordinates of 0 to 100.

To control the air flow through the model, the shape of the duct should be compared to the second graph feature, **GRAPH2**. This graph is shown in Figure 5–25.

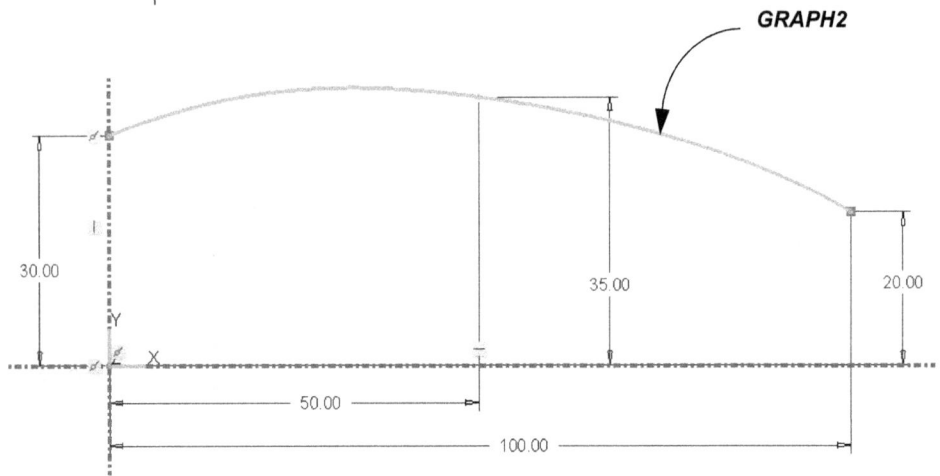

Figure 5–25

Task 2 - Create a relation analysis feature.

1. Set the model display as follows:

    *   ⁺⁄₊ *(Datum Display Filters)*: All Off
    *   ⊱ *(Spin Center)*: Off
    *   ⬜ *(Display Style)*: ⬜ (Shading With Edges)

2. Select the *Analysis* tab.

3. Click ×⁄ (Analysis) and create a **Relation** analysis feature and set the name to **COMPARE_GRAPH**.

4. In the ANALYSIS dialog box, click **Next**.

5. Enter the following relation in the relation editor:

    RELATION = comparegraphs("GRAPH1", "GRAPH2")

Creo Parametric uses all values along the entire length of the graph.

6. Click ✅ (Verify) to verify the relation and click **OK**.

7. Click **OK** in the Relations dialog box.

8. Click ✓ (OK) to complete the analysis feature.

Task 3 - Create an optimization study.

1. In the Design Study group, click ◈ (Feasibility/Optimization).

2. In the *Goal* area, select **Minimize** and **RELATION:COMPARE_GRAPH** from the drop-down lists.

3. In the *Design Variables* area, click **Add Dimensions**.

4. Orient the model to the saved **Back** view. Select **GRAPH1** in the Model Tree. Select the graph dimensions listed in the following table.

5. Repaint the main window. Select **GRAPH2** in the Model Tree. Select the graph dimensions listed in the following table. Refer to Figure 5–26 and Figure 5–27 to locate the dimensions.

	Dimension	Minimum	Maximum
	d32	10	20
Graph 1	d34	25	35
	d30	30	40
	d40	25	75
	d65	10	20
Graph 2	d68	25	35
	d63	30	40
	d67	25	75

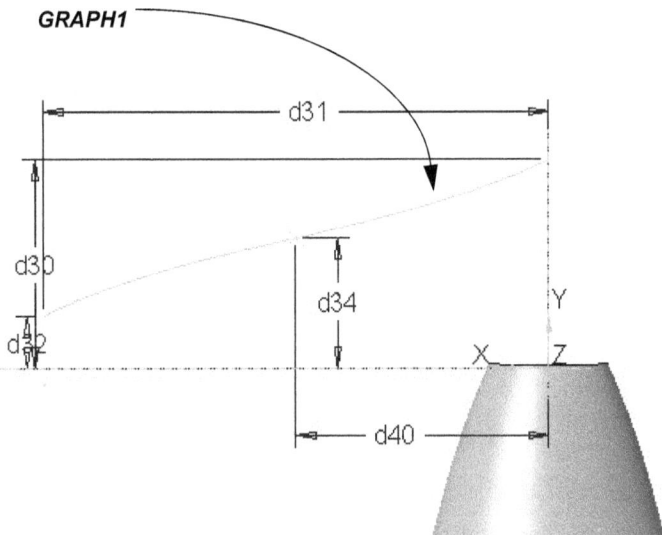

Figure 5–26

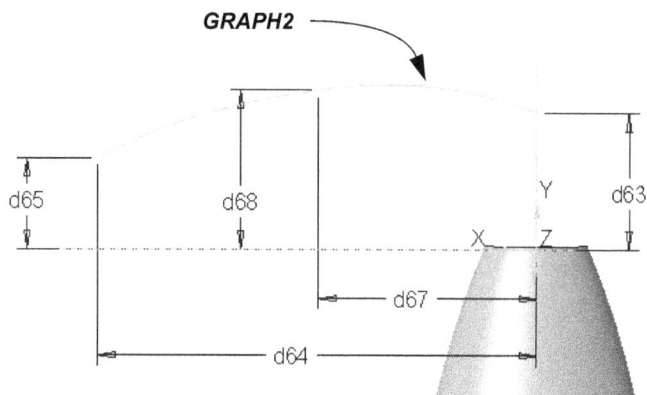

Figure 5–27

6. Middle-click once you have selected all dimensions.

7. Modify the *Min* and *Max* values as shown in the table in Step 5.

8. In the Optimization/Feasibility dialog box, click **Options>Preferences** and ensure that the **Goal** option is selected in the Preferences dialog box.

9. In the Preferences dialog box, select the *Run* tab. Enter **10** in the *Convergence %* field.

10. Click **OK**. The Optimization/Feasibility dialog box displays as shown in Figure 5–28.

Your variables may display in a different order, depending on how you selected them.

Figure 5–28

11. Click **Compute**. An optimization graph displays in the GRAPH WINDOW, as shown in Figure 5–29.

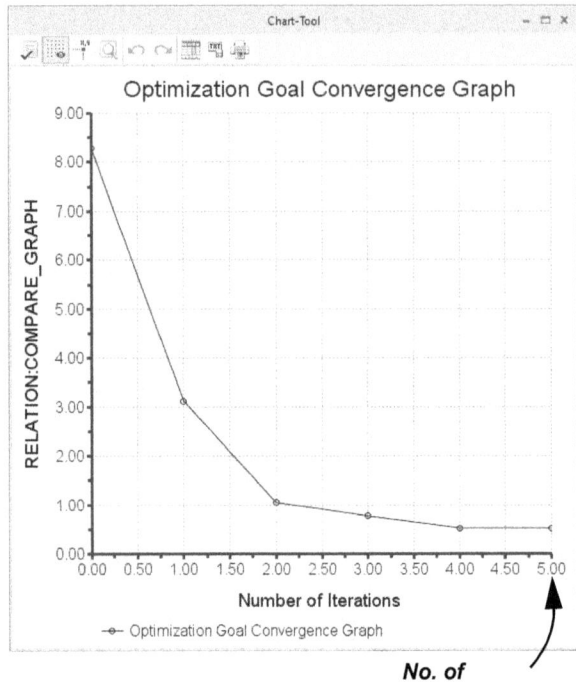

Figure 5–29

Note that the analysis is completed in five steps. The optimized graph displays on the model as shown in Figure 5–30. This graph shows the best fit result based on the optimization of the selected dimensions in **GRAPH1** and **GRAPH2**. The optimization was done using the lone type of comparison.

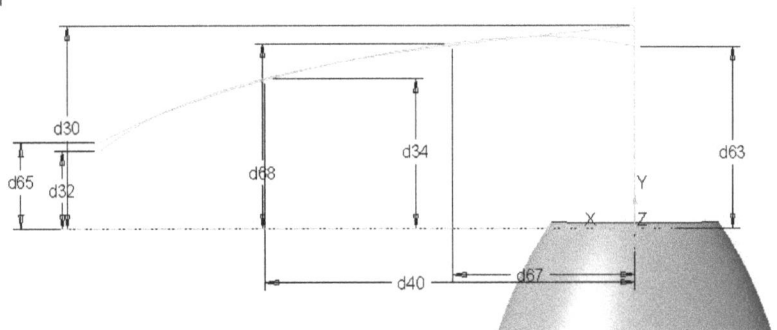

Figure 5–30

12. In the Optimization/Feasibility dialog box, click ▦ (Save Design Study).

13. Click **Close** and **Confirm** to keep the model changes.

14. Reorient the model as shown in Figure 5–31.

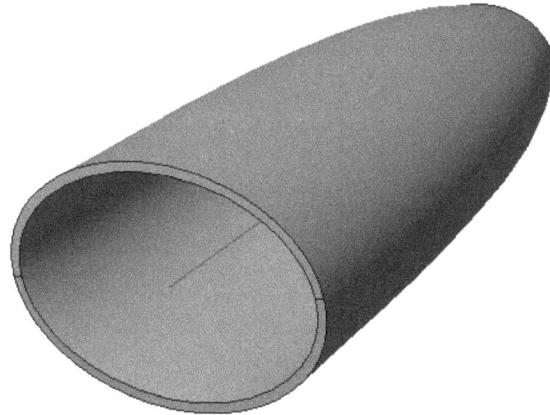

Figure 5–31

15. Close the part and erase it from memory.

Excel Analysis

Microsoft Excel is an application that many companies use to perform calculations
for their designs. BMX enables this design tool to be integrated directly into the
Creo Parametric model so that the model conforms to the design requirements.
This integration is accomplished using an Excel Analysis analysis feature that
references an external Excel file to make calculations. Once an Excel
spreadsheet is created, it can be easily referenced by multiple models.

Learning Objectives in This Chapter

- Create an Excel Analysis Feature.
- Recognize the difference between an Excel Analysis and an Excel Analysis Feature.
- Learn where Excel Files are stored.
- Review Config.pro options related to Excel Analyses.

6.1 Running Excel Analyses

Create an Excel Analysis Feature

How To: Create an Excel Analysis Feature

1. In the *Analysis* tab, in the Manage group, click $\times^{/}_{\underline{\ldots}}$ (Analysis). The ANALYSIS dialog box displays.
2. Type a new name for the analysis feature and press the <Enter> key.
3. In the *Type* area, select **Excel Analysis**.
4. Select an option from the *RegenRequest* area to define the regeneration option for the analysis feature.
5. Click **Next**. The Excel Analysis dialog box displays as shown in Figure 6–1.

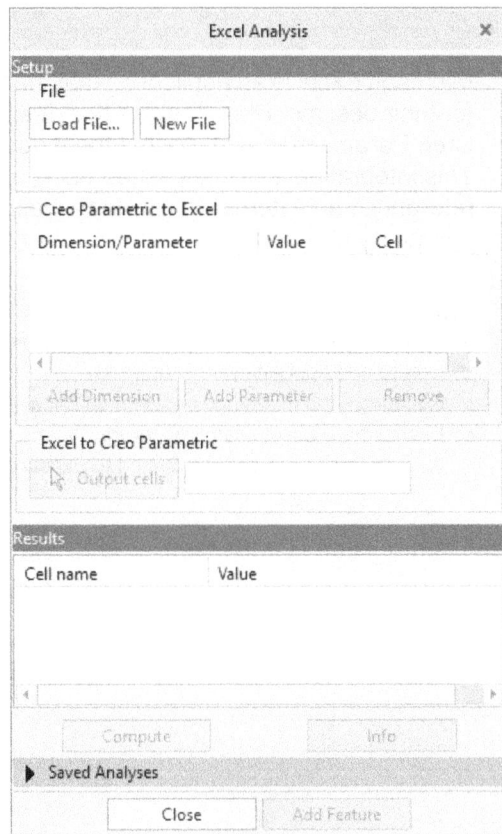

Figure 6–1

6. Click **Load File** and select the Excel file to be referenced. If an existing Excel file does not exist, click **New File** to create a new one. The Excel application displays in the background.

Use the window buttons on the bottom of the screen to switch between Excel and Creo Parametric if they do not activate automatically.

7. Select **Add Dimension** or **Add Parameter** to specify input settings (dimensions or parameters) for the feature. These input settings indicate the values that are referenced to the Excel data. As each input setting is selected, you must select a corresponding cell in the Excel spreadsheet. After each dimension or parameter and corresponding cell are selected, click **Done Sel**. Continue this procedure until all the required dimensions and parameters have been selected and cells have been assigned. Figure 6–2 shows an example of a list of Input Settings and their associated cell references.

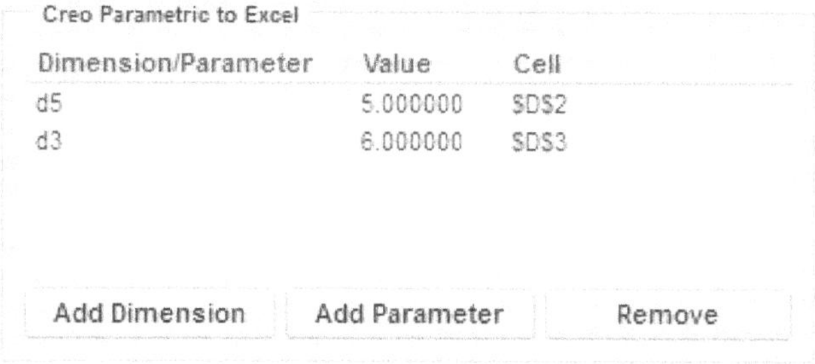

Creo Parametric to Excel		
Dimension/Parameter	Value	Cell
d5	5.000000	D2
d3	6.000000	D3
Add Dimension	Add Parameter	Remove

Figure 6–2

8. Click **Output cells** and select the cell(s) to be recalculated based on the input settings. You can assign more than one cell as output cells. To select multiple cells, press and hold <Ctrl>. Once the cells are selected, click **Done Sel**. Figure 6–3 shows an example of a list of two Output cells.

9. Click **Compute** to run the analysis. The corresponding output values display in the *Results* area, as shown in Figure 6–3.

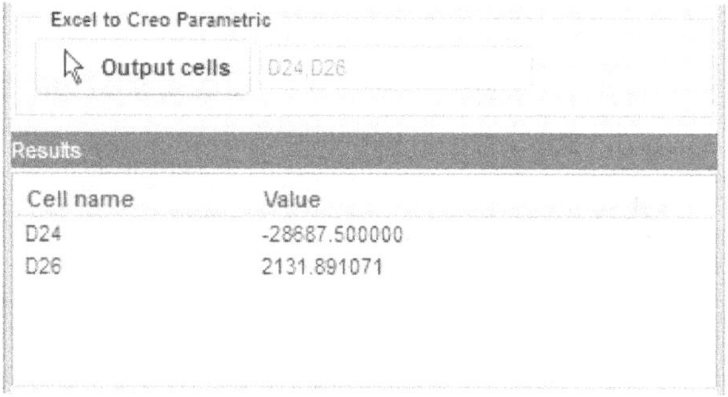

Once an analysis has been calculated, you can save the analysis using the options in the Saved Analysis area.

Excel to Creo Parametric	
⬚ Output cells	D24,D26

Results	
Cell name	Value
D24	-28687.500000
D26	2131.891071

Figure 6–3

10. Click **Close** to complete the calculation. The ANALYSIS dialog box displays, enabling you to create feature parameters based on the results of the calculation.

The default name for a result parameter is XL_<rownumber>_<columnnumber>.

11. To add a result parameter to the model, select **YES** in the *Create* area and enter a *Param Name*. To prevent a result parameter from being added to the model, select **NO**. Figure 6–4 shows an example of result parameters added to the model.

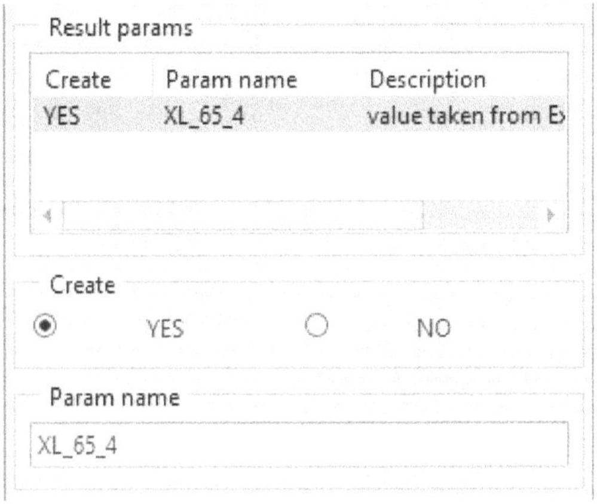

Figure 6–4

12. Click ✓ (OK) to complete the Excel analysis feature.

Once used, the Excel file is not modified with the results of an analysis. The file remains a read-only file while it interacts with Creo Parametric. Each calculation is rerun based on the input settings and the equations in the cells of the file. This enables multiple analysis features and models to reference the same spreadsheet while ensuring accurate results.

Excel Analysis vs. Excel Analysis Feature

An Excel Analysis feature enables you to create parameters in the model. It also adds features to the feature list. If you are only interested in running an Excel analysis without creating a

parameter, click ▦ (Excel Analysis) from the Custom group. This analysis is set up in the same way as an Excel Analysis analysis feature. You can save the results in the *Saved Analyses* area. At any time, you can use this analysis to create an Excel Analysis feature. To do this, retrieve the saved analysis, select **Add Feature** at the bottom of the Excel Analysis dialog box, and enter a name. Rerun the calculation to generate the parameters. In either situation (Excel analysis or Excel analysis feature), a change made to the model is reflected in both.

Excel File Locations

When an Excel analysis is saved or when an Excel analysis feature is created, the system saves the complete path to the .XLS file. When the saved analysis is retrieved, or when the model containing the Excel analysis feature is regenerated, Creo Parametric looks for the Excel file.

Creo Parametric searches the following locations for the Excel file:

- An Excel Analysis/Excel analysis feature's saved path.

- The working directory.

- The directory specified by the *excel_analysis_directory* config.pro option.

If the Excel file cannot be found, the feature remains at the last known values. You must redefine and set up the analysis again. As an alternative, you can close the Creo Parametric file, return the .XLS file to the correct directory and reopen the file. This prevents you from having to set up the analysis again.

Config.pro Options

The *bm_graph_tool* configuration option specifies how graphs generated by the various analyses and studies display. The options for this configuration file option are described as follows:

Option	Description
default	By default, the graphs displays in a regular Creo Parametric window.
excel_embedded	Displays the graphs in an Excel window that is embedded in the Creo Parametric screen.
excel_linked	Launches Excel and displays the graphs in Excel. Excel also shows the input and output values used to create the graphs. This Excel spreadsheet can be saved for documentation purposes or for reference.

Practice 6a Excel Analysis

Practice Objectives

- Create Excel Analysis analysis features.
- Derive tables to find an appropriate design.

In this practice, you will analyze a model to calculate the total heat transfer in its current design. You will then perform a Multi-Objective Design Study to find configurations that meet several constraints.

The spreadsheet file is not modified through its use in Creo Parametric. This is a template containing the calculations that need to be performed to find the heat transfer. The values in this spreadsheet can be changed as required for other materials.

To calculate the total heat transfer, the practice references an Excel spreadsheet. This spreadsheet contains a number of predefined equations that are used to calculate heat transfer. This spreadsheet also contains a number of input values that are assigned from the model to perform calculations. During each analysis, the equations are used to generate the results.

The Datum Graph features in the model represent standard efficiency graphs that are available in many engineering references. Graph1 represents the efficiency values for R2c/R1=1, (Graph2 is R2c/R1=2, Graph3 is R2c/R1=3, Graph5 is R2c/R1=5). R2c is defined in the spreadsheet and R1 represents the inner diameter of a fin.

The Efficiency feature is an analysis feature that uses a relation to determine the correct efficiency value from the graphs.

Task 1 - Open the finned_cylinder.prt part.

1. Set the working directory to *Excel_Analysis*.
2. Open **finned_cylinder.prt**.
3. Set the model display as follows:
   - *(Datum Display Filters)*: All Off
   - *(Spin Center)*: Off
   - *(Display Style)*: (Shading With Edges)
4. The model consists of datum features, protrusions, and a pattern, as shown in Figure 6–5.

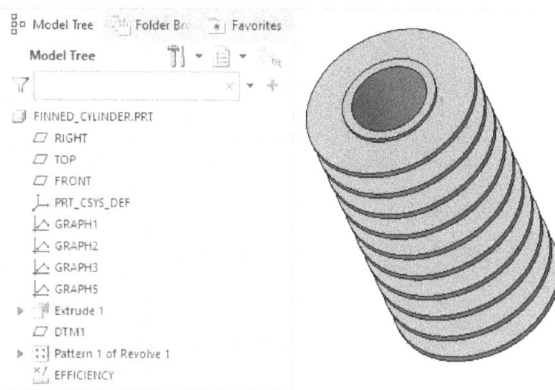

Figure 6–5

5. Examine the Model Tree and review the model.

6. In the Model Tree, right-click on **FINNED_CYLINDER.PRT** and select **Parameters**. Review the model parameters in the Parameters dialog box. The **NUMBER** parameter represents the number of fins on the model.

7. Close the Parameters dialog box.

Task 2 - Create a Relation analysis feature.

---

1. In the Model Tree, drag the **green line** marker so it sits immediately after the pattern.

2. Select the *Analysis* tab.

3. In the Manage group, click ⅗ (Analysis).

4. Edit the name to **FINS_FOR_EXCEL** and press <Enter>.

5. Select **Relation**.

6. Click **Next**.

7. Enter the following relation in the relation editor. N is the dimensional symbol for the number of instances in the pattern.

   FINS=N

8. Click 🗹 (Verify) to verify the relation and click **OK**.

9. Click **OK** in the Relations dialog box.

10. Click ✓ (OK) to complete the analysis feature.

Task 3 - Create an Excel Analysis feature.

1. In the Manage group, click ⚞ (Analysis).

2. Edit the name to **FIND_EFFICIENCY** and press <Enter>.

3. Select **Excel Analysis**.

4. Click **Next**.

5. Click **Load File** and double-click the **heat_transfer1.xls** file. Review the information; it is used to drive the analysis.

6. Select the Creo Parametric window to activate it, but do not close the Excel file.

7. In the *Creo Parametric to Excel* area, click **Add Dimension**.

8. Select both the fin at the bottom of the model and the internal protrusion, as shown in Figure 6–6.

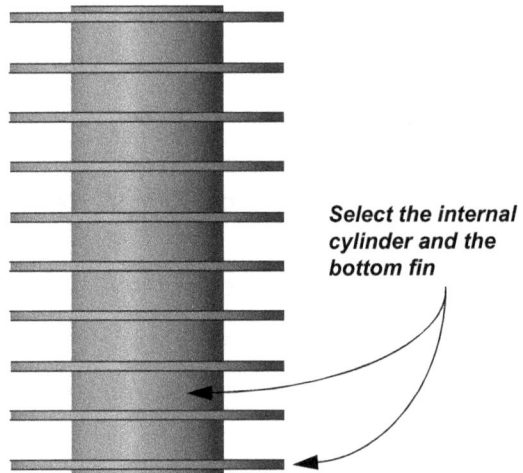

Select the internal cylinder and the bottom fin

Figure 6–6

If the dimensions display in numeric form, select the Tools tab and click ⚞ (Switch Dimensions) to display their symbols.

9. Select the **THICKNESS** dimension. Excel should activate.

10. Select the cell **B4**. Activate the Creo Parametric window and click **Done Sel** from the **EXCEL SELECT** Menu Manager. The **Thickness** parameter updates in the *Input Settings* area with its *Value* and *Cell* location.

Use the window buttons on the bottom of the screen to switch between Excel and Creo Parametric if they do not activate automatically.

11. Select the **R1** dimension. Refer to Figure 6–7 to locate it. Excel should activate.

12. Select cell **B5** and click **Done Sel**.

13. Select the **R2** dimension and select cell **B6**. Click **Done Sel**.

14. Select the **HEIGHT** dimension and select cell **B7**. Click **Done Sel** when finished.

15. Press the middle mouse button to stop selecting dimensions.

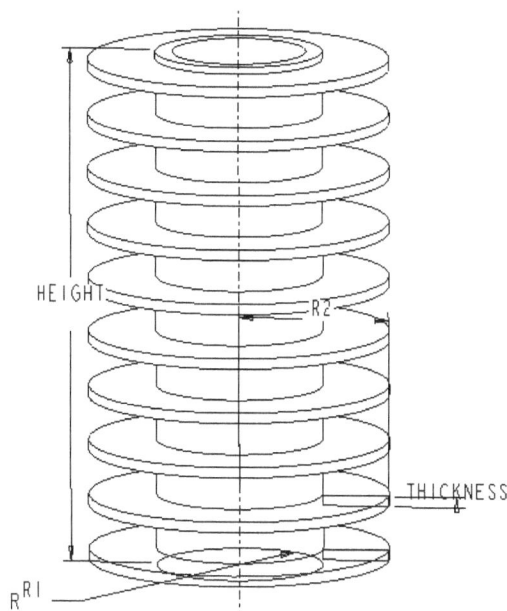

Figure 6–7

16. Click **Add Parameter**. Select **FINS:FINS_FOR_EXCEL** from the Parameters dialog box and click **OK**.

17. Select cell **D8** and click **Done Sel**. The Input Settings are now complete.

18. In the *Output Settings* area, click **Output Cells**.

19. Select cell **B54**, press and hold <Ctrl>, and select cell **B57**. Click **Done Sel**. Review the *Output Cells* area and ensure that cells **B54** and **B57** are the only output cells. If this is not the case, in the *Output Cells* area, reselect the two cells.

20. Click **Compute**. The results display in the *Results* area.

21. Click **Close** in the Excel Analysis dialog box.

22. Create both parameters. Set the Param name for the **XL_54_2** parameter to **XAXIS** and the cell name for the **XL_B57_2** parameter to **LINE**.

23. Click ✔ (OK) to complete the analysis feature.

Task 4 - Redefine the EFFICIENCY analysis feature.

1. In the Model Tree, right-click on the green marker and select **Exit Insert Mode**.

2. Click **Yes** to resume the EFFICIENCY analysis feature. This feature was provided to you to save you from entering extensive relations. However, the relations have errors because the reference feature is missing.

3. In the Model Tree, select **EFFICIENCY** and click ✎ (Edit Definition) in the mini toolbar.

4. Click **Next** to advance to the relations.

5. In the Relations dialog box, click **Edit>Find and Replace** to replace all instances of *1666* with **FIND_EFFICIENCY**.

6. Verify the relations and complete the redefinition of the feature.

Task 5 - Create an Excel Analysis feature to find the total heat transfer.

1. In the Manage group, click ×ƒ (Analysis).

2. Edit the name to **TOTAL_HEAT_TX** and press <Enter>.

3. Select **Excel Analysis**.

4. Click **Next**.

5. Click **Load File** and select the **heat_transfer1.xls** file. Review the information; it is used to drive the analysis.

6. Select the Creo Parametric window to activate it.

7. In the *Input Settings* area, click **Add Dimension**.

8. Select the fin at the bottom of the model and the internal protrusion, as shown in Figure 6–8.

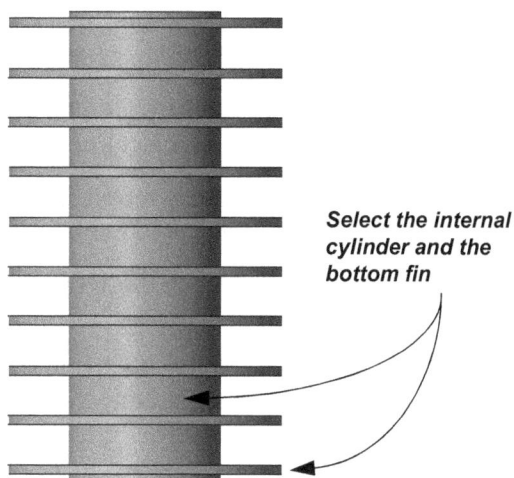

Select the internal cylinder and the bottom fin

Figure 6–8

9. Select the **THICKNESS** dimension and select cell **B4**. Click **Done Sel**.

10. Select the **R1** dimension and select cell **B5**. Click **Done Sel**.

11. Select the **R2** dimension and select cell **B6**. Click **Done Sel**.

12. Select the **HEIGHT** dimension and select cell **B7**. Click **Done Sel**.

13. Press the middle mouse button to stop selecting dimensions.

14. Add the **FINS:FINS_FOR_EXCEL** parameter and select cell **D8**. Click **Done Sel**.

15. Add the **NF:EFFICIENCY** parameter and select cell **D62**. Click **Done Sel**.

16. Set cell **D65** as the only output cell.

17. Click **Compute**. The heat transfer value is **1108W**.

18. Click **Close** in the Excel Analysis dialog box.

19. Edit the name of the Result Parameter to **HEAT_W** and press <Enter>.

20. Click ✓ (OK) to complete the analysis feature.

21. Show the **HEAT_W** parameter in the Model Tree.

Task 6 - View design changes.

1. Modify the **THICKNESS** dimension to **6** and regenerate the model. Note that the heat transfer value increased from *1108W* to **1160W**.

*The **NUMBER** parameter is the number of fins in the model.*

2. Right-click on **FINNED_CYLINDER.PRT** in the Model Tree and select **Parameters**.

3. Modify the **NUMBER** parameter to **5**. Regenerate the model. Note that the heat transfer is reduced from *1160W* to **698W**.

4. Modify the **THICKNESS** dimension to **2**. Regenerate if required.

5. Modify the **NUMBER** parameter to **25**. Regenerate the model. Note that the heat transfer jumps from *698W* to **2356W**.

Task 7 - Create Analysis features to validate the design.

Design Consideration

In this task, you create Analysis features to check the following constraints:

• A maximum of 25 fins with minimum fin thickness of 2mm is permitted.

• The first and last fin must be at least 2mm from the ends.

• The minimum distance between the fins must be 4mm.

A Multi-Objective Design Study will be used. The **LEAD** dimension on the first fin is varied in the design study.

1. Create an analysis feature named **DC_1** to measure the One-Sided Volume using **DTM1** as the reference. Orient the arrow as shown in Figure 6–9. Create the resulting parameter and set the name to **VOL**. Press <Enter> after typing the name.

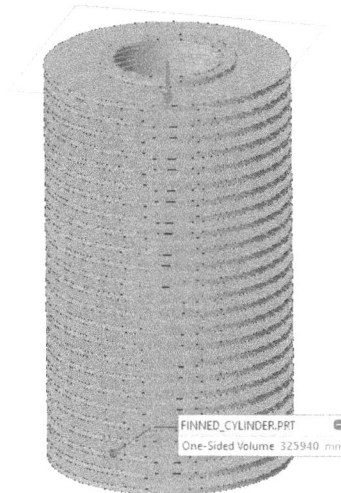

Figure 6–9

2. Create an analysis feature named **DC_2** to measure the distance between the first and second fins. The current distance value should be 4mm. Create the resulting parameter and set the name to **SPACING**.

Task 8 - Create a Model Analysis feature.

1. Create an analysis feature named **MODEL** to calculate the Mass Properties. Create a parameter only for the Mass calculation and set the name to **MASS**.

Task 9 - Create a Multi-Objective Design Study.

1. In the Design Study group, expand ✎ (Feasibility/ Optimization) and select ✕ (Multi-Objective Design Study).

2. Click ☐ (New Design Study) to create a new design study. Set the name to **STUDY5**.

3. Click ☐ (Setup Master Table) to create the Master Table.

4. Click **Select Goals**. The Parameter Selection dialog box displays. Select the following parameters:

- **HEAT_W:TOTAL_HEAT_TX**
- **VOL:DC1**
- **SPACING:DC2**
- **MASS:MODEL**

5. Click ⟦✎⟧ (Add Dimension). Add the **THICKNESS** dimension. Enter **2** and **8** as the *Min* and *Max* values, respectively.

6. Click ⟦✎⟧ (Add Parameter). Add the **NUMBER:FINNED_CYLINDER** parameter. Enter **1** and **25** as the *Min* and *Max* values, respectively.

7. Click **OK** in the Master Table dialog box.

   To capture an adequate range of design options, the study should be run to generate 200 experiments. **This can be time-consuming and can range anywhere between 5-30 minutes, depending on the hardware configuration.** This practice provides a complete design study (if you would like to run your study, please feel free to do so in your free time.)

8. Close the model and erase it from memory.

9. Open **finned_cylinder_final.prt**.

10. Select the *Analysis* tab.

11. In the Design Study group, expand ⟦🔍⟧ (Feasibility/ Optimization) and select ⟦🎲⟧ (Multi-Objective Design Study).

12. Click ⟦📂⟧ (Open Design Study) and select **STUDY5**.

13. Click **OK**. The Multi-Objective Design Study dialog box displays as shown in Figure 6–10.

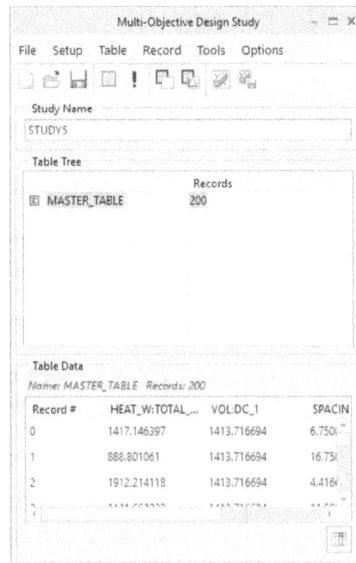

Figure 6–10

Task 10 - Derive a table to find all acceptable designs.

1. Click 🖿 (Derive New Table) to derive a new table.

2. Select **Constraints** to derive the table and select **SPACING:DC_2**.

3. Enter **4.00** as the *minimum* value.

4. Set the table name to **VALID_DESIGNS**.

5. Click **OK**. There are now 133 valid design options.

*If the **LEAD** dimension was also varied, all designs in that **VOL:DC_1** were greater than **1414** are also filtered. Otherwise, **VOL:DC_1** does not need to be added.*

Task 11 - View the Graph of this study.

1. Select **VALID_DESIGNS** in the *Table Tree* area of the dialog box.

2. Click 🖺 (Graph Study).

3. Select **MASS:MODEL** from the *Goals* area to define the X-axis for the graph.

4. Select the *Y-Axis* tab and select the **HEAT_W:TOTAL_HEAT_TX** Goal to define the Y-axis for the graph.

5. Click **Graph**. All design records appear on the graph, as shown in Figure 6–11.

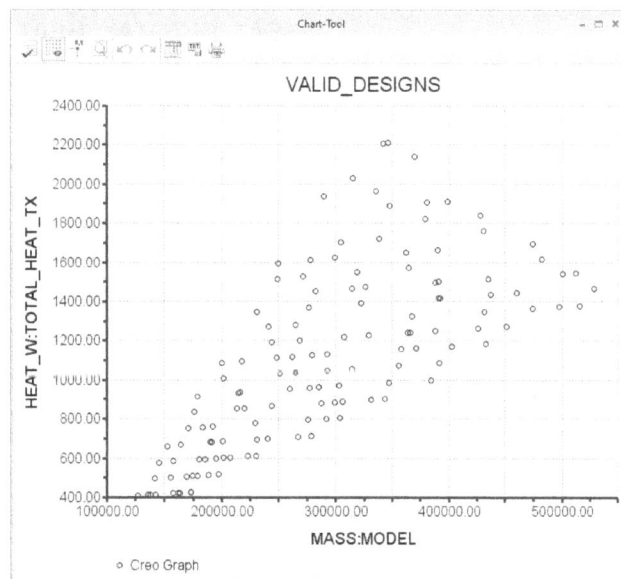

Figure 6–11

6. Close the Chart-Tool dialog box.

7. Close the Graph dialog box.

Task 12 - Derive the table to find the best design.

1. With **VALID_DESIGNS** is still selected in the Multi-Objective Design Study dialog box, click ⬚ (Derive New Table) to derive a new table.

2. Select **Pareto** to derive the table.

3. Select the **HEAT_W:TOTAL_HEAT_TX** parameter and set the option to **Maximize**.

4. Select the **MASS:MODEL** parameter and set the option to **Minimize**.

5. Set the table name to **MIN_MASS_MAX_HEAT**.

6. Click **OK**. Twenty designs now meet the criteria.

7. Select **MIN_MASS_MAX_HEAT** in the *Table Tree* area of the dialog box.

8. Click ⬚ (Graph Study).

9. Select **MASS:MODEL** from the *Goals* area to define the X-axis for the graph.

10. Select the *Y-Axis* tab and select the **HEAT_W:TOTAL_HEAT_TX** Goal to define the Y-axis for the graph.

11. Click **Graph**. The resulting graph displays as shown in Figure 6–12.

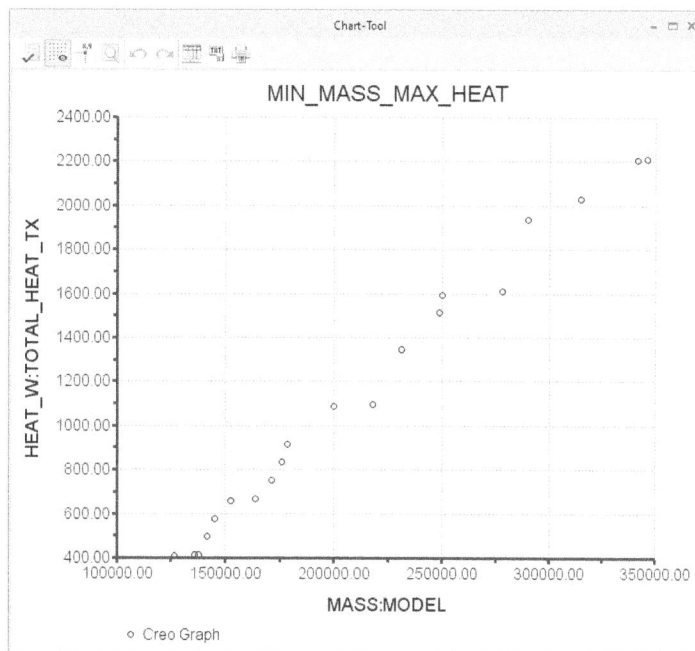

Figure 6–12

12. In the Model Tree, click 🔽 ▾ (Settings)>**Reset Tree Settings>Reset Tree Settings**.

13. Save the study and close the model.

Task 13 - (Optional) Derive additional tables.

Any of the 20 remaining models can be used as an appropriate design. Each design maximizes the heat transfer while minimizing the mass. In reaching these 20 models, one goal may be sacrificed at the expense of another. It is up to the designer to decide on a final design. If required, this table can be derived again to further refine the model.

Practice 6b

Cantilevered Plate

Practice Objectives

- Create an Excel Analysis analysis features.
- Derive tables to find an appropriate design.

In this practice, you will analyze and calculate the maximum bending stress and maximum deflection of a cantilevered plate. The plate is loaded at the free end with a single concentrated force (F=5 KN), as shown in Figure 6–13.

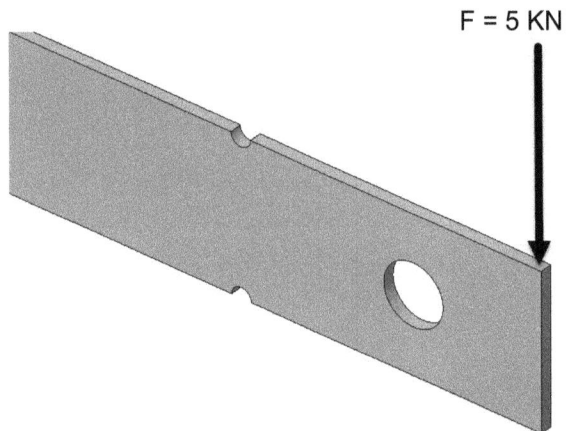

F = 5 KN

Figure 6–13

To calculate the maximum bending stress and maximum deflection, the practice references an Excel spreadsheet. This spreadsheet contains a number of predefined equations that calculate the maximum bending stress and the maximum deflection. It also contains a number of input values that are assigned to perform calculations during each analysis. You will also perform Multi-Objective Design Studies to find configurations that meet several of these constraints.

Task 1 - Open the notched_plate.prt part.

1. Set the working directory to *Cantilevered_Plate*.

2. Open **cantilivered_plate.prt**.

3. Set the model display as follows:

- 	 *(Datum Display Filters)*: 	 (Point Display) Only

- 	 *(Spin Center)*: Off

- 	 *(Display Style)*: 	 (Shading With Edges)

Task 2 - Create a model analysis feature.

1. Select the *Analysis* tab.

2. Create an Mass Properties analysis feature to calculate the plate's mass and to locate the plate's center of mass. Set the analysis name to **MODEL_MASS**.

3. Click **Preview**.

4. Select the *Feature* tab.

5. Create only the mass analysis parameter and leave **MASS** as its name.

6. In the *Datums* area, enable the checkmark next to **PNT_COG**.

7. Click **OK**. The model displays as shown in Figure 6–14.

The model weight = 134.368 kg in SI units.
1 tonne = 1000kg
1lb = 0.4536kg

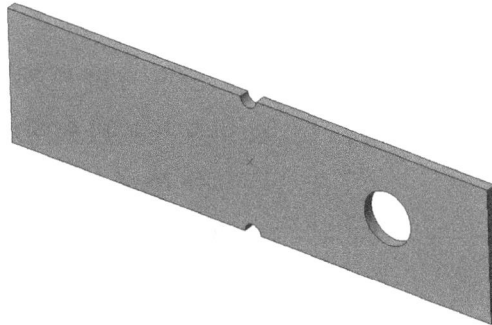

Figure 6–14

8. Display the mass parameter in the Model Tree.

Task 3 - Perform Sensitivity analyses.

Perform three sensitivity analyses that vary the **d25**, **d30** and **d37** dimensions within their permitted range. Which of these variables has the greatest effect on the plate's mass?

1. Select the *Tools* tab and click (Switch Dimensions) to display dimensions using their symbols.

2. Select the *Analysis* tab.

3. Perform a sensitivity analysis for **d25** (width of the plate). Enter its variable range (*5mm to 6mm)* and plot it against the **MASS:MODEL_MASS** parameter. Note the change in plate mass.

4. Perform a sensitivity study for **d30** (radius of the notch). Enter the variable range *(5mm to 10mm)* and plot it against the **MASS:MODEL_MASS** parameter. Note the change in plate mass.

5. Perform a sensitivity study for **d37** (diameter of hole). Enter its variable range *(30mm to 35mm)* and plot it against the **MASS:MODEL_MASS** parameter. Note the change in plate mass.

Task 4 - Create an Excel Analysis Feature.

Design Consideration

The Excel analysis feature that is created in this task calculates the maximum bending stress and maximum deflection, then assigns these values as parameters that can be used in future studies.

1. Select the *Analysis* tab and in the Manage group, click ⌗ (Analysis).

2. Set the name to **MOM_DEF** and press <Enter>.

3. Select **Excel Analysis** as the analysis feature Type.

4. Click **Next**.

5. Click **Load File** and select the **cantilevered_plate.xls** file.

6. Activate the Creo Parametric window and in the *Input Settings* area, click **Add Dimension**.

7. Select both the plate (**Extrude 1**) and the notch (**Extrude 2**) from the Model Tree to display the dimensions, as shown in Figure 6–15.

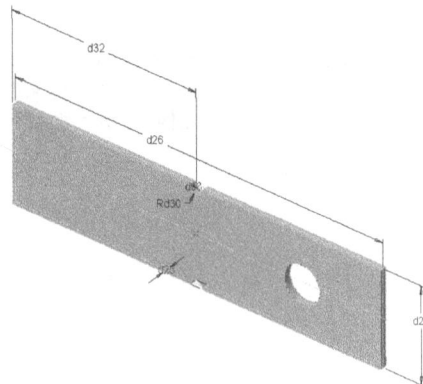

Figure 6–15

8. Select the **d30** dimension and select cell **D2**. Click **Done Sel**.

9. Select the **d25** dimension and select cell **D4**. Click **Done Sel**.

10. Click **Output Cells**, select cell **D22**, press and hold <Ctrl> and select **D26**.

11. Click **Done Sel**.

12. Click **Compute**.

13. Close the Excel Analysis dialog box.

14. Create the two parameters for this analysis feature. Set the cell name for the **XL_22_4** parameter to **MOMENT** and the cell name for the **XL_26_4** parameter to **DEFLECTION**.

15. Click ✔ (OK) to complete the analysis feature.

16. Show the Excel parameters in the Model Tree. The Model Tree displays as shown in Figure 6–16.

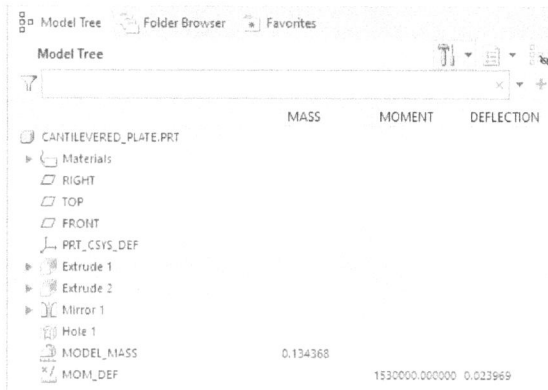

Figure 6–16

Task 5 - Create a Feasibility study.

This study analyzes the Feasibility of varying the **d25**, **d30**, and **d37** dimensions to maintain a mass of 110Kg.

d3 (5mm to 6mm)
d5 (5mm to 10mm)
d18 (30mm to 35mm)

1. Run a feasibility study with the **MASS:MODEL_MASS** design constraint set to **0.110** (110kg). Set the **d25**, **d30** and **d37** design variables using their predefined range (see the margin note located on the left). Graph the design constraints.

2. Study the effect of the weight reduction on parameters **MOMENT** and **DEFLECTION**. The values should update in the Model Tree.

3. Click **Undo** in the Optimization/Feasibility dialog box to undo the dimensional changes.

4. Click **Close** to close the dialog box.

The values may not immediately update in the Model Tree to reflect the Undo operation. To update the values, you can force a model regeneration using the Model Player.

Task 6 - Create a measure analysis feature and feasibility study that set the distance between the center of the model and center of mass at 1.5mm.

1. Create an ⌖ (Offset Coordinate System) datum point (**PNT0**) at the center of the model. Create the point offset from the default coordinate system 152.5; 0; 0.

2. Create a Measure analysis feature to measure the distance between **PNT_COG** and **PNT0**. Set the analysis name to **MEAS_1**. Set the distance parameter name to **DIST**. Do not create any datum features. The distance = 2.76183mm.

d39 (50mm to 150mm)
d32 (20mm to 180mm)

3. Run a feasibility study to determine values of the variable **d39** and **d32** when the design constraint **DIST:MEAS_1** is set to 1.5mm (see the margin note).

4. Click **Undo** in the Optimization/Feasibility dialog box to undo the dimensional changes.

5. Select **Close** to close the dialog box.

Task 7 - Create a Multi-Objective Design Study.

1. In the *Analysis* tab, expand ⬃ (Feasibility/Optimization) and select ⬂ (Multi-Objective Design Study).

2. Click ▢ (New Design Study) to create a new design study. Set the name to **NOTCH**.

3. Click ▤ (Setup Master Table) to create the Master Table.

4. Click 🖉 (Add Dimension). Add the following design variables. Enter variable range as the *Min* and *Max* values.

- hole diameter (d37) = 30mm to 35mm
- plate thickness (d25) = 5mm to 6mm
- notch radius (d30) = 5mm to 10mm
- center of the hole to the free end of the plate (d39) = 50mm to 100mm
- center of the notch to constrained end of the plate (d32) = 100mm to 170mm

5. Click **Select Goals**. The Parameter Selection dialog box displays. Select the following parameters:

- **MASS:MODEL_MASS**
- **MOMENT:MOM_DEF**
- **DEFLECTION:MOM_DEF**
- **DIST:MEAS_1**

6. Click **OK** to close the Master Table dialog box.

7. Click ❗ (Compute Master Table) to run the study.

8. Enter **200** as the number of experiments to run.

Task 8 - Derive tables from the results.

---

1. Derive a table to minimize the plate deflection. Set the table name to **MIN_DEFLECTION**.

2. Select the record for the **MIN_DEFLECTION** table and click **Record>Show Model**. Note the design variable values required to achieve the minimum deflection.

3. Derive another table to minimize the plate deflection and the **DIST** parameter. Set the table name to **MIN_DEFLECTION_DIST**.

4. Graph this study to view the effects of each design variable on the minimum deflection.

5. Derive a table in the **MIN_DEFLECTION_DIST** table and minimize only the deflection. Set the table name to **MIN_DEFLECTION_D1**.

6. Select the record for the **MIN_DEFLECTION_D1** table and click **Record>Show Model**. Note the design variable values required to achieve the minimum deflection.

7. Save the study.

8. In the Model Tree, click ⏚ ▾ (Settings)>**Reset Tree Settings>Reset Tree Settings**.

9. Close and erase the model.

   This application of BMX used a spreadsheet to make multiple calculations for the maximum bending stress and deflection. These could also have been done using Creo Simulate; however, this application enabled you to easily set up the same criteria without using an FEA solution. When changes are made to the model, the maximum bending stress and deflection are easily recalculated.

Chapter 7

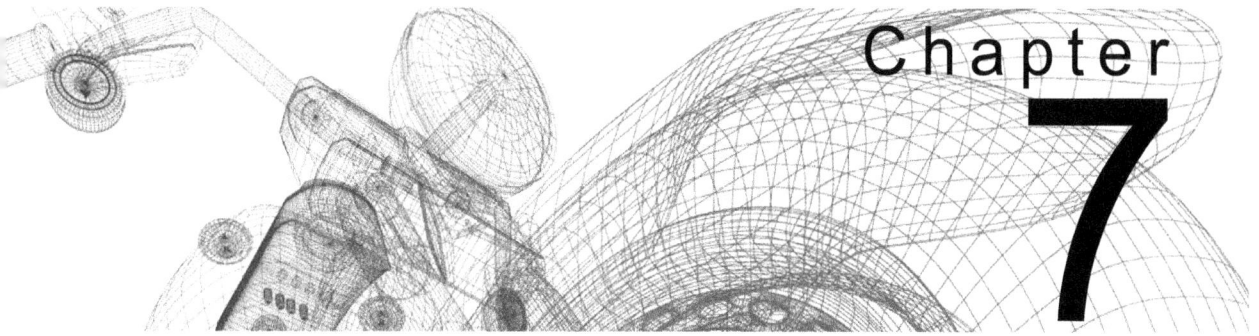

Motion Analysis Features

In previous chapters, analyses were performed on static models. It is often required to evaluate parameters based on the entire range of motion for an assembly. This type of analysis can only be performed in the Assembly mode using a Motion Analysis analysis feature in the top-level assembly. The values of the analysis feature parameters are calculated at each frame throughout the motion definition.

Learning Objective in This Chapter

- Create a Motion analysis feature.

7.1 Motion Analysis Features

To run a Motion Analysis, an assembly must be created using Mechanism connections and drivers to define the required motion. Creating a mechanism in Creo Parametric requires the use of the Mechanism Design Extension (MDX).

For example, you can use MDX to set up connections and drivers, and use BMX to study the effects on the models center of gravity as it moves through its full range of motion. You can also use BMX to study the clearance of the moving assembly relative to other components. Figure 7–1 shows an example of components in a tractor assembly.

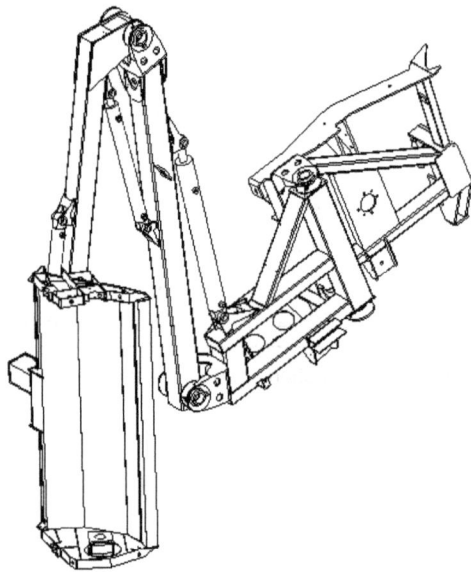

Figure 7–1

If you have a Mechanism Dynamics Option (MDO) license, you can study the effect that applied forces have on the motion of your mechanism. For example, you can set up connections and drivers and modeling entities that are not available in the kinematics-based version of Mechanism Design. These include springs, dampers, force/torque loads, and gravity. Using MDO and BMX, you can study the effects on the kinematic connections reaction force as it moves through its full range of motion.

Creating a Motion Analysis Feature

How To: Create a Motion Analysis Feature

1. In the *Analysis* tab, in the Manage group, click ⌗ (Analysis). The ANALYSIS dialog box displays.
2. Type a new name for the analysis feature and press <Enter>.
3. Select **Motion Analysis** in the *Type* area.
4. Select a *RegenRequest* option to define the regeneration option for the analysis feature.
5. Click **Next**. The Motion Analysis dialog box displays as shown in Figure 7–2.

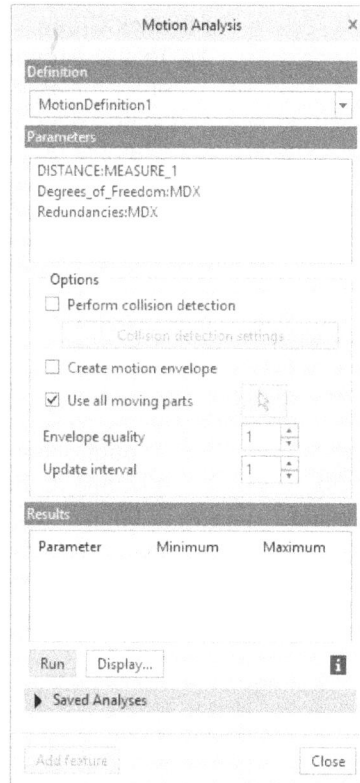

Figure 7–2

6. Select the parameters to evaluate. The parameters must exist in the top-level assembly.
7. To check for collision between components, enable the **Perform collision detection** option.
8. To create a motion envelope, select **Create motion envelope** in the *Options* area of the dialog box. A motion envelope generates a surface quilt that defines the entire range of motion. If the motion envelope is created, you can use all moving parts (select **Use all moving parts**) or select the parts that you want to include in the envelope.

Frames are the number of computation points used in the motion definition.

9. If required, specify the *Envelope quality*. The higher the number, the longer it takes to create.
10. Specify the update interval. The update interval refers to how often the display is recalculated.
11. Click **Run**. The predefined motion begins. A graph displays showing the feature parameter value through each frame.
12. When finished, the *Results* area lists the maximum and minimum value for each of the selected feature parameters along with the time at which they occurred. If a motion envelope was created, it temporarily displays on the screen as a surface.
13. Click **Close**.
14. To add a result parameter, select **YES** in the *Create* area and enter a *Param Name*. To prevent a result parameter from being added to the model, select **NO**. Figure 7–3 shows an example of result params being included and excluded.

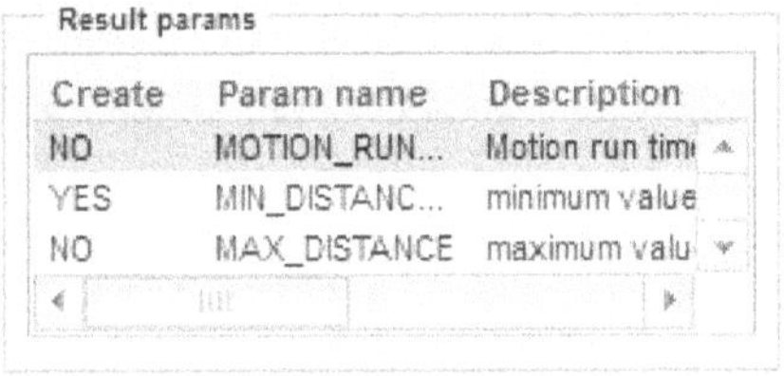

Create	Param name	Description
NO	MOTION_RUN...	Motion run tim⸱
YES	MIN_DISTANC...	minimum value
NO	MAX_DISTANCE	maximum valu⸱

Figure 7–3

Next became active when Create motion envelope was selected in an earlier step.

15. To control the motion envelope's display, click **Next** to advance to the result datum element. To add a result datum (motion envelope), select **YES** in the *Create* area and enter a *Datum Name*. To prevent a result datum from being added to the model, select **NO**. Figure 7–4 shows an example of result datum being added to the model. This is only available if the motion envelope was generated.

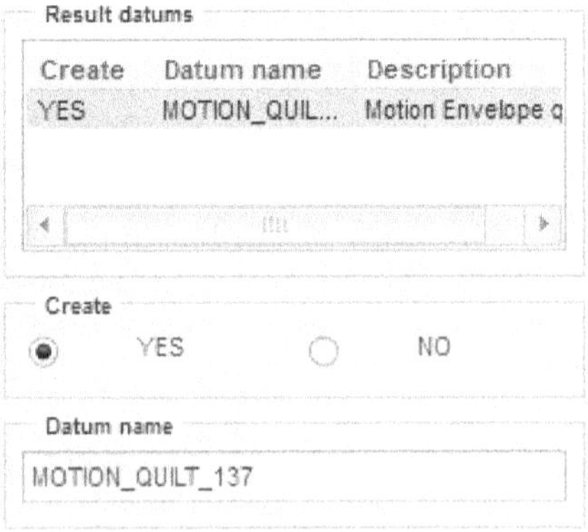

Create	Datum name	Description
YES	MOTION_QUIL...	Motion Envelope q

Create

⦿ YES   ○ NO

Datum name

MOTION_QUILT_137

Figure 7–4

16. Click **Close** to complete the feature.

Practice 7a | Motion Analysis

Practice Objective

- Create and run a motion analysis.

In this practice, you will apply behavioral modeling techniques to analyze a doorknob assembly. The following constraints have been set for the assembly:

- The handle of the doorknob is returned to its original position using a spring. The minimum distance required for the compressed spring is 0.2 inch.

- In order for the door to open, the slider must clear the plate.

Task 1 - Open the doorknob assembly.

1. Set the working directory to *Motion_Analysis*.

2. Open **doorknob.asm**.

3. Set the model display as follows:

   - ⁺ᴵ⁄ (Datum Display Filters): All Off

   - ⤙ (Spin Center): Off

   - ⬚ (Display Style): ▢ (Shading With Edges)

   The model displays as shown in Figure 7–5.

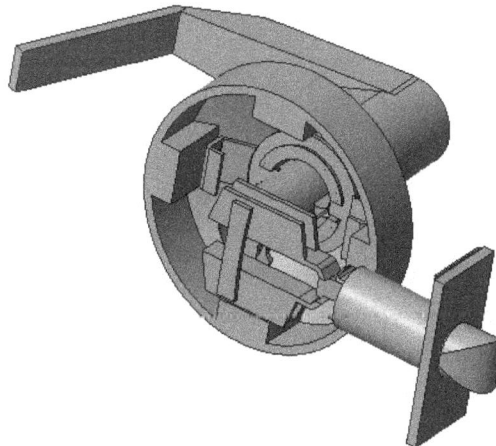

Figure 7–5

4. Assembly features should be displayed in the Model Tree by default. If features are not displayed in the Model Tree, expand (Settings) and click **Tree Filters>Features**. This enables the display of all of the analysis features that are added to the assembly.

Task 2 - Load the MotionDefinition1.pbk file to show an animation of a predefined doorknob movement.

Design Consideration

The Mechanism Design Extension (MDX) of Creo Parametric enables you to simulate kinematic motion in your assemblies. You can drag the mechanisms through their range of motion, or create drivers to define predetermined animations. These motions permit you to examine the behavior of the mechanism. You can use the mechanism in the Behavioral Modeling Extension (BMX) to evaluate important parameters throughout its range of motion.

1. Select the *Applications* tab and click (Mechanism). The connections are **Fixed**, **Pin**, **Slider** and **Cam**. The model driver profile type is **Cosine**.

2. In the Mechanism Tree, select **PLAYBACKS** and click (Play) in the mini toolbar. The Playbacks dialog box opens.

3. In the Playbacks dialog box, click (Restore Result Set) and open **MotionDefinition1.pbk**. The Playbacks dialog box updates as shown in Figure 7–6.

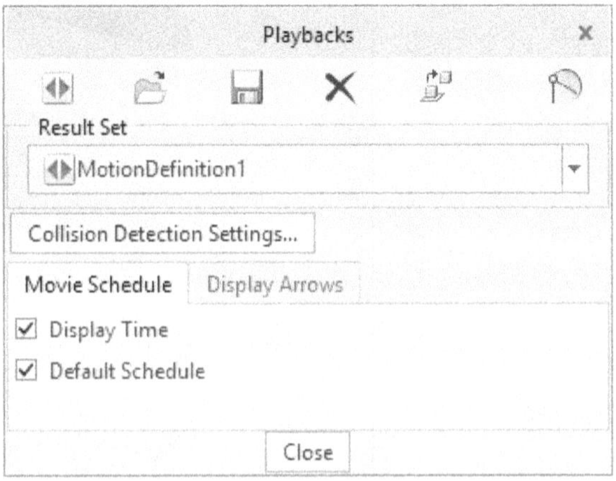

Figure 7–6

4. Click ⊕ (Play Result Set). The Animate dialog box displays as shown in Figure 7–7.

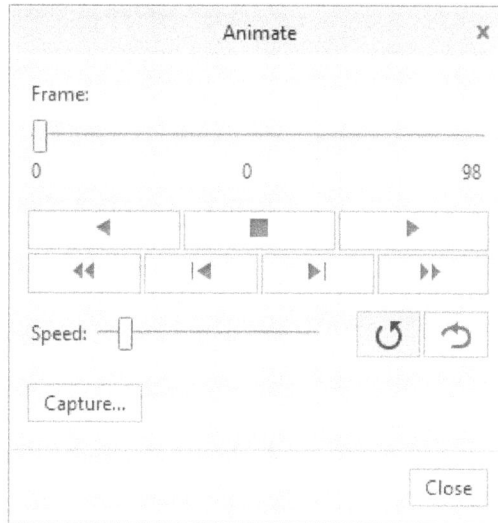

Figure 7–7

5. Click ▶ (Play) to run the animated motion of the doorknob assembly. Note that the slider does not move past the plate during the animation, as shown in Figure 7–8. The slider must clear the plate for the door to open. This is used as a design requirement later in this practice.

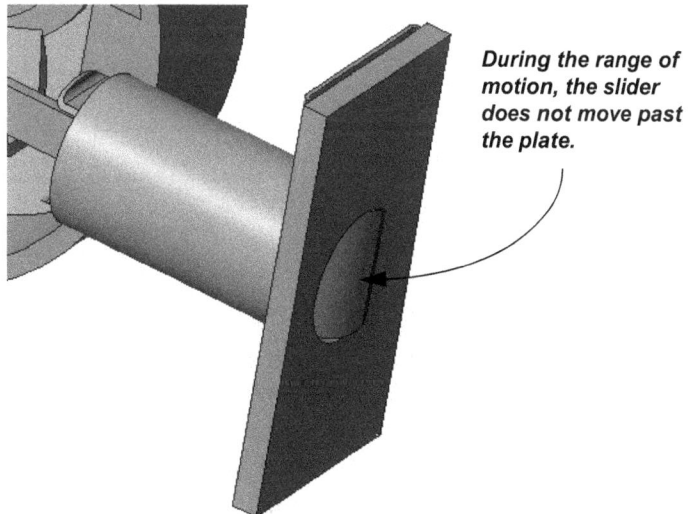

During the range of motion, the slider does not move past the plate.

Figure 7–8

6. Click ◂◂ (Reset to Beginning) to rewind the animation to the beginning once you have reviewed it.

7. Click **Close** to close the dialog box.

8. Click **Close** to close the Playbacks dialog box.

9. In the *Mechanism* tab, click ⊠ (Close).

Task 3 - Create a Measure analysis feature.

1. Select the *View* tab.

2. In the Model Display group, click ▦ (Exploded View).

3. Select the *Analysis* tab.

4. In the Measure group, expand ✎ (Measure) and select ⊓ (Distance).

5. Press and hold <Ctrl> and select the front surface of the **stop.prt** and cut surface of the **slide1.prt**,as shown in Figure 7–9.

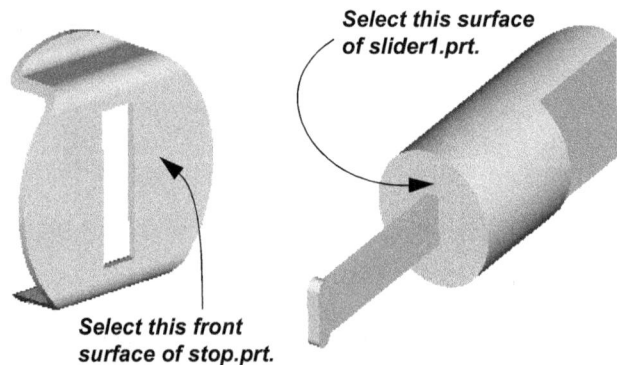

Select this surface of slider1.prt.

Select this front surface of stop.prt.

Figure 7–9

6. The distance between these surfaces displays in the Results window. The *Distance* is approximately **0.5**.

7. Click ▦ (Save) and ensure that **Make Feature** is selected.

8. Edit the name to **MEASURE_1** and click **OK**.

9. Click **Confirm** when prompted to unexplode the view.

10. Select the *Feature* tab.

11. Accept **DISTANCE** as the name of the Distance parameter.

12. Click **Close**.

Task 4 - Create a Motion analysis feature to measure the minimum distance.

---

1. In the Manage group, click ×⟋ (Analysis).

2. Edit the name to **MOTION_1** and press <Enter>.

3. Select **Motion Analysis**.

4. Click **Next**. The Motion Analysis dialog box displays as shown in Figure 7–10.

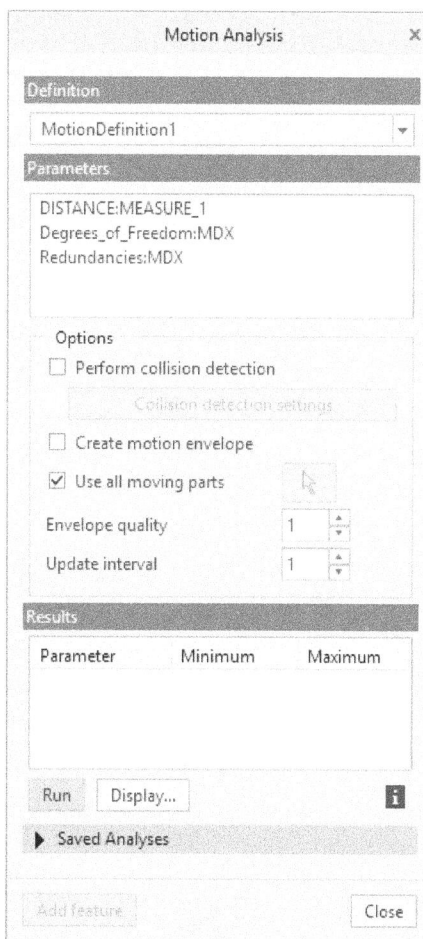

Figure 7–10

5. In the *Parameters* area, select **DISTANCE: MEASURE_1**.

6. Click **Run**. The distance against time graph displays as shown in Figure 7–11.

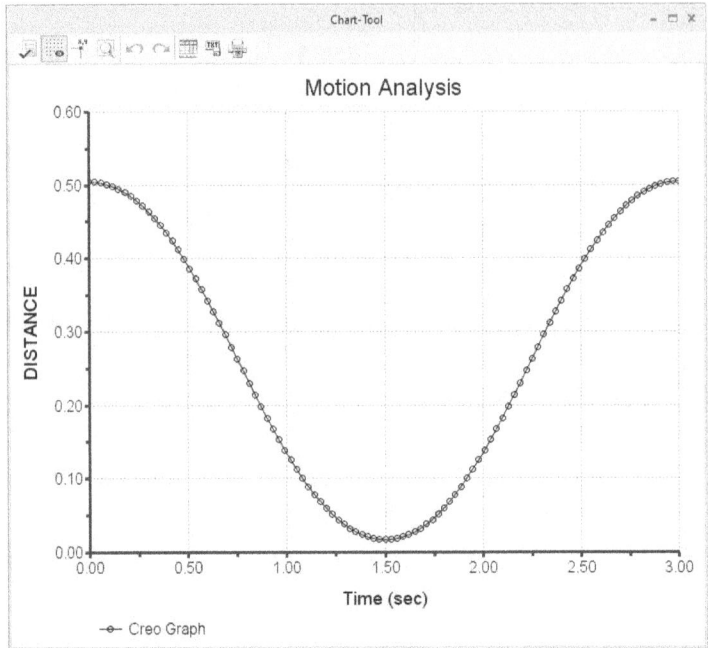

Figure 7–11

The graph in Figure 7–11 shows that the doorknob handle moves to open the door (its extreme position). The minimum distance between front surface of the **stop.prt** and cut surface of the **slide1.prt** is **0.016632 at T = 1.5sec**. You can see the same result in the Results window of the Motion Analysis dialog box, as shown in Figure 7–12.

Results		
Parameter	Minimum	Maximum
DISTANCE:137	0.016632 (t_m...	0.504626 (t_max = 3.000000)

Figure 7–12

7. Close the Motion Analysis dialog box.

8. Set the **Create** cell for the **MIN_DISTANCE** parameter to **YES**.

9. Set the **Create** cell for all other parameters to **NO**.

10. Click ✔ (OK) to complete the analysis feature.

Task 5 - Create a sensitivity study.

Design Consideration

The handle of the doorknob is returned to its original position using a spring. The spring is placed inside of the slider chamber (**CYL1_LATCH.PRT**). The spring is compressed when the handle is moved to open the door. The minimum distance required for the compressed spring is 0.2 inch. In this task, you will vary the design variable **d13** of cut **id 149** in **SLIDER1.PRT** to provide insight into an ideal start for the **d13** when running a feasibility study.

The minimum distance is currently 0.016632 inch, as obtained in the motion analysis.

1. In the Design Study group, click ▣ (Sensitivity Analysis). The Sensitivity dialog box displays as shown in Figure 7–13.

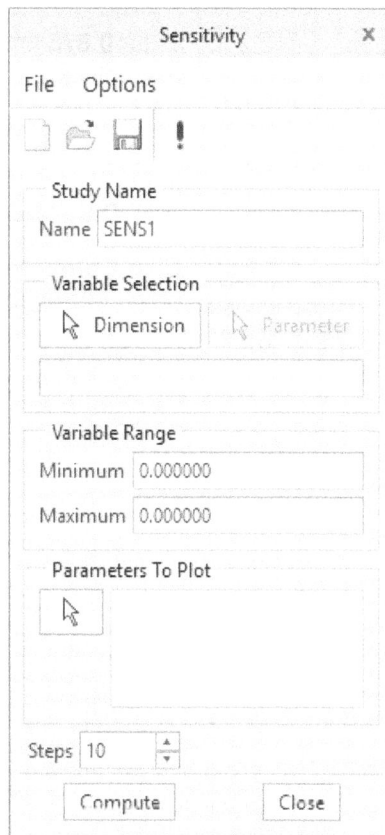

Sensitivity ✕

File   Options

Study Name

Name SENS1

Variable Selection

▷ Dimension   ▷ Parameter

Variable Range

Minimum 0.000000

Maximum 0.000000

Parameters To Plot

Steps 10

Compute   Close

Figure 7–13

2. Maintain the default name for the analysis.

3. Explode the assembly.

4. Click **Dimension** and select dimension **.875** from cut **id 149** in **SLIDER1.PRT**, as shown in Figure 7–14.

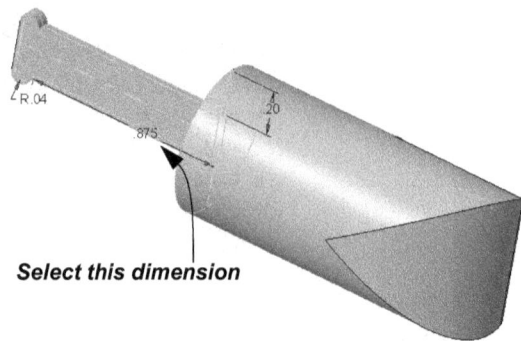

Select this dimension

Figure 7–14

5. Enter **0.875** and **1.1** as the min and max *Variable Ranges*, respectively.

6. Press the middle mouse button to stop selecting dimensions.

7. In the *Parameters To Plot* area, click ▷ (Select) and select **MIN_DISTANCE:MOTION_1**.

8. Click **Compute** to run the analysis. During the analysis, the graph shown in Figure 7–15 displays.

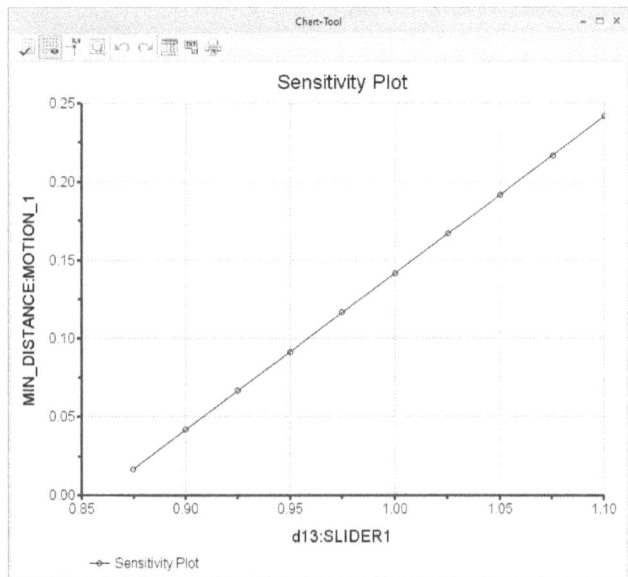

Figure 7–15

Note that the required compression distance of 0.2 (Y-axis of the graph) is within the specified range.

By saving this design study, you can recall and rerun without having to set it up again.

9. Save the design study.

10. Close the Sensitivity dialog box.

Task 6 - Create a Feasibility study.

In this task, you adjust the design variable (0.875) to meet the required compressed distance (design constraint).

1. In the Design Study group, click ▧ (Feasibility/Optimization). The Feasibility/Optimization dialog box displays.

2. Select **Feasibility**.

3. In the *Design Constraints* area, click **Add**.

4. Select the **MIN_DISTANCE:MOTION_1** parameter and set its value equal to **0.2**. Click **OK**.

5. Click **Add Dimension** and select the **.875** dimension from cut **id 149** in **SLIDER1.PRT**.

6. Set the *min* and *max* values to **0.875** and **1.1**, respectively.

7. Press the middle mouse button to stop selecting dimensions.

8. Click **Options>Preferences**.

9. In the *Graphs* tab, select **Variables**.

10. Select the *Run* tab. Enter **10** in the *Convergence %* field.

11. Click **OK**.

12. Click **Compute** to run the analysis. During the analysis, the graph shown in Figure 7–16 displays.

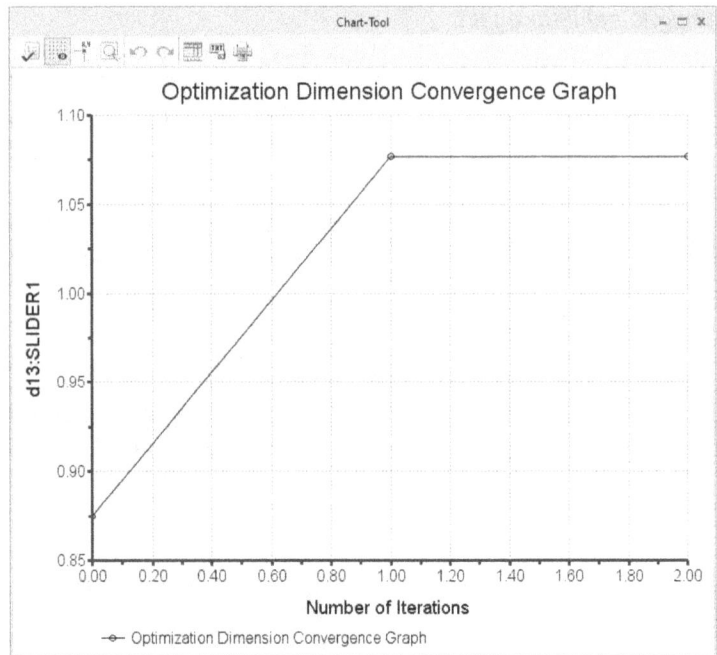

Figure 7–16

The graph shows that, after two iterations, the **dimension** needs to be modified to **1.0767** to satisfy the design constraint.

13. Close the Feasibility/Optimization dialog box.

14. Click **Confirm** when prompted regarding modification to the model.

15. Verify that the **d13** dimension is now **1.077**.

Task 7 - Create a Measure analysis feature to ensure that the slider clears the plate to permit the door to open.

---

1. In the In-graphics toolbar, click ×͞ₒ (Point Display) to enable the display of points.

2. In the Measure group, expand ✎ (Measure) and select ꓻ. (Distance).

3. Press and hold <Ctrl> and select the front surface of the **plate.prt** and the point shown in Figure 7–17.

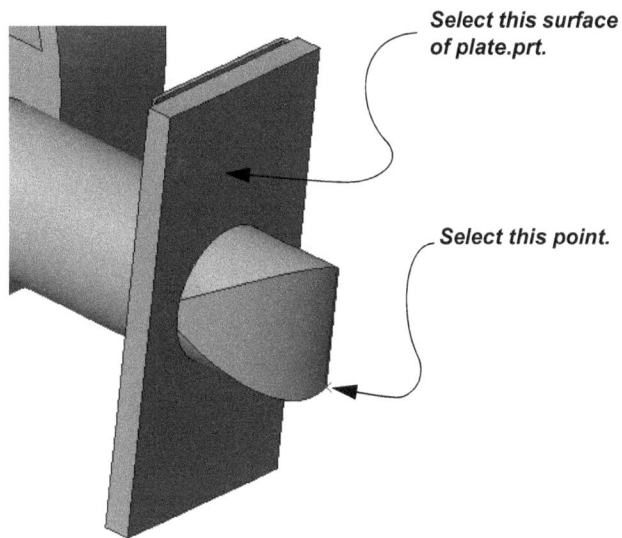

Select this surface of plate.prt.

Select this point.

Figure 7–17

The distance between these references displays in the Results window. The *Distance* is approximately **0.5**.

4. Click ⊟▾ (Save), ensure that **Make Feature** is selected, edit the name to **MEASURE_2**, and press <Enter>.

5. Select the *Feature* tab.

6. Leave the parameter name as **DISTANCE**.

7. Click **Close** to complete the feature.

Task 8 - Create a Motion Analysis feature to measure the minimum distance.

---

1. In the Manage group, click ×⁄ (Analysis).

2. Edit the name to **MOTION_2** and press <Enter>.

3. Select **Motion Analysis**

4. Click **Next**.

5. Highlight **DISTANCE: MEASURE_2** in the Parameter window.

6. Click **Run**. The distance against time graph displays as shown in Figure 7–18.

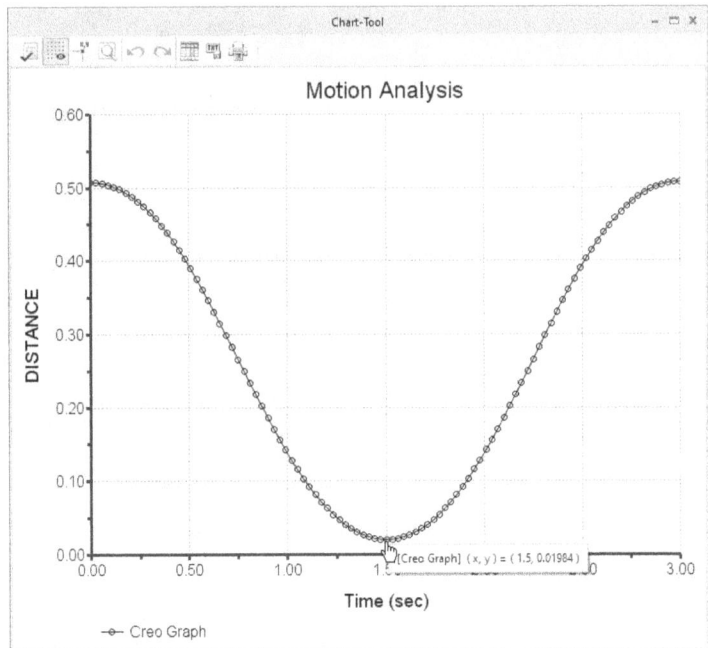

Figure 7–18

The graph in Figure 7–18 shows when the doorknob handle is moved to open the door (its extreme position). The minimum distance between front surface of the **plate.prt** and **PNT0** is **0.01984** inch at T = 1.5sec. You can see the same result in the Results window in the Motion Analysis dialog box.

7. Close the Motion Analysis dialog box.

8. Create only the **MIN_DISTANCE** parameter to **YES**.

9. Leave the parameter name as **MIN_DISTANCE**.

10. Click ✔ (OK) to complete the analysis feature.

Task 9 - Create a Feasibility study.

Design Consideration

In this task, you modify a design variable to set the minimum distance between the front surface of the plate.prt and the point to zero.

1. In the Design Study group, click ✐ (Feasibility/Optimization). The Feasibility/Optimization dialog box displays.

2. Click ☐ (New Design Study) to create a new Feasibility study.

3. Select **Feasibility**.

4. Click **Add** in the *Design Constraints* area.

5. Select the **MIN_DISTANCE:MOTION_2** parameter and set its value equal to **0**. Click **OK**.

6. Click **Add Dimension**, select **SLIDER1.PRT**, and select the **d1** dimension (**Protrusion id 39**), as shown in Figure 7–19.

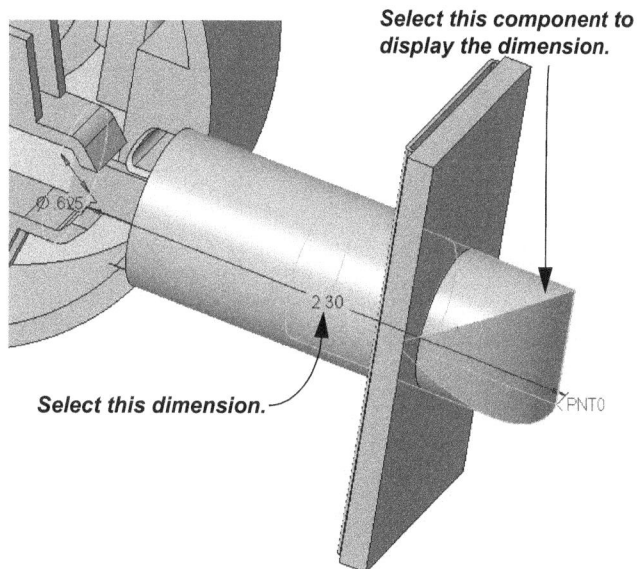

Select this component to display the dimension.

Select this dimension.

Figure 7–19

7. Set the *min* and *max* values to **2.25** and **2.3**, respectively.

8. Press the middle mouse button to stop selecting dimensions.

9. Click **Options>Preferences**.

10. In the *Graphs* tab, select **Variables**.

11. Select the *Run* tab. Enter **0.1** in the *Convergence %* field.

12. Click **OK**.

13. Click **Compute** to run the analysis. During the analysis, the graph shown in Figure 7–20 displays.

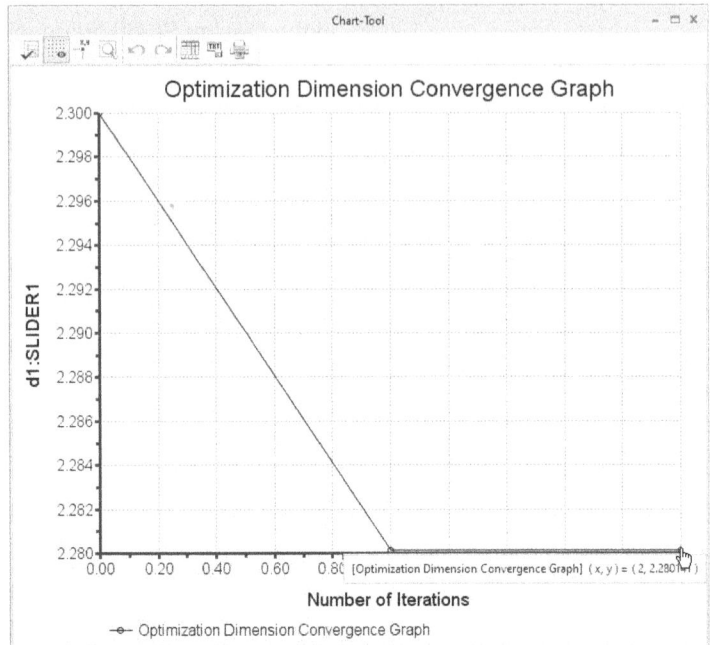

Figure 7–20

The graph shows that, after two iterations, the variable **d1** needs to be modified to **2.28014** to satisfy the design constraint.

14. Close the Feasibility/Optimization dialog box.

15. Confirm the modification to the model. Verify that the **d1** dimension is now **2.28**.

16. Close the model and erase it from memory.

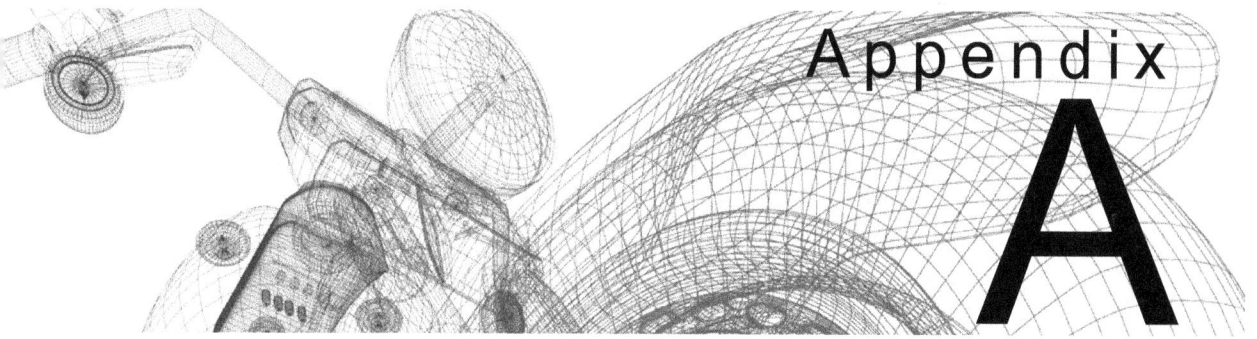

Additional Practices

In this appendix, you will find additional practices.

Practice 1a

Project 1

Practice Objective

- Apply the behavioral modeling techniques to control the diameter size of cylindrical packaging surface.

In this practice, you apply the behavioral modeling techniques to control the diameter size of cylindrical packaging surface for a vase.

Task 1 - Open the part vase.prt.

1. Set the working directory to *Project_1*.

2. Open **vase.prt**. The model displays as shown in Figure A–1.

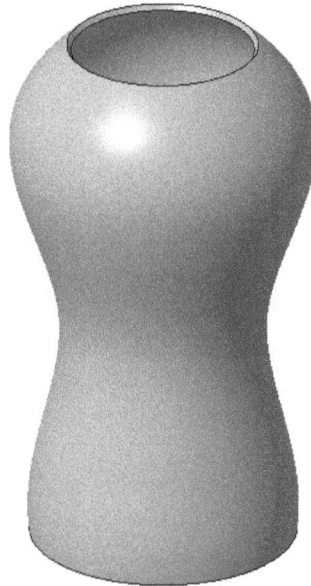

Figure A–1

Task 2 - Create features to measure the maximum vase diameter.

1. Create a field point on the outside surface of the vase.

2. Create an analysis feature to measure the distance between **FPNT0** and **A_1**. Name the analysis **MEASURE_1**. Create a distance analysis parameter and enter **DIST** as its name. Do not create any datum points.

3. Create a construction group that includes both the **FPNT0** and the **MEASURE_1** analysis feature.

4. Create a UDA analysis feature to measure the maximum value of **MEASURE_1** (maximum value of the vase diameter). Name the analysis **UDA**. Create a **UDM_max_val** parameter and enter **UDM_MAX** as its name. Do not create any datums.

Task 3 - Create a revolved surface to represent the packaging for the vase.

---

1. Create a 360° revolved surface that is one sided and has open ends. Sketch the section as shown in Figure A–2.

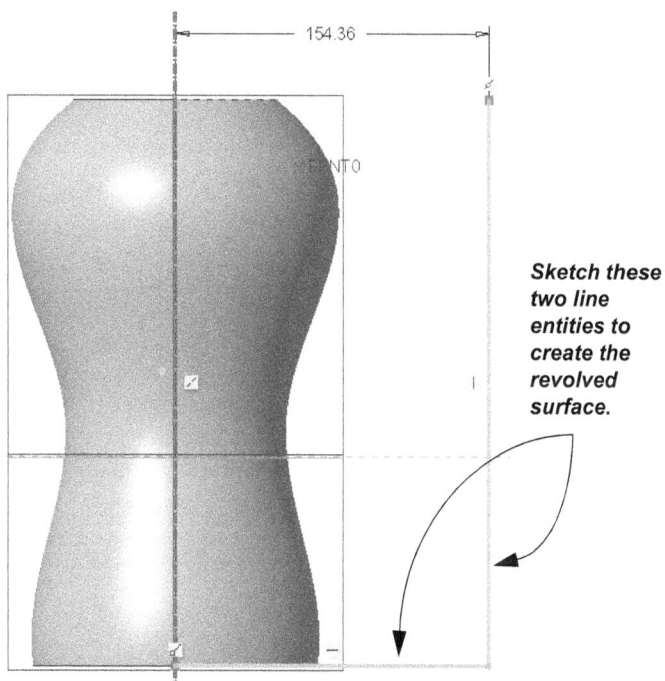

Sketch these two line entities to create the revolved surface.

Figure A–2

Relation_1 = maximum value of the vase radius +10

2. Create a relation analysis feature and name the analysis **RELATION_1**. Enter the relation d# =(UDM_MAX:FID_UDA +10) in the editor, where d# represents the radius dimension for the revolved surface, as shown in Figure A–3. The dimension symbol may vary in your sketch.

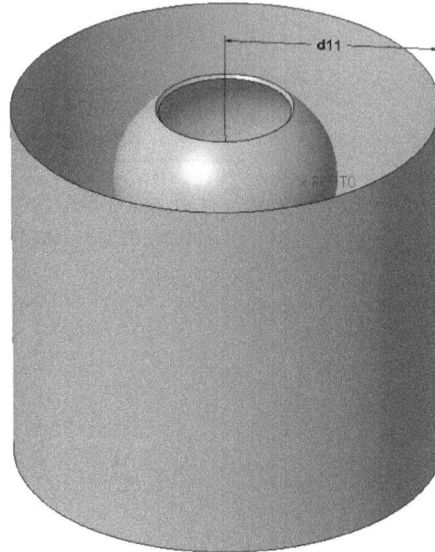

Figure A–3

3. Verify the relation and complete the analysis feature.

4. Regenerate the part. The diameter of the revolved surface updates according to the relation that you have created. The model displays as shown in Figure A–4.

Figure A–4

5. Modify the vase surface id 39 and note the effect on the revolved surface. The surface does not update automatically; therefore, select the revolved surface and click 🖌 (Edit Definition) in the mini toolbar. When the dashboard displays, complete the feature. The surfaces updates to reflect the change to the vase.

6. Design a lid for the vase. Ensure that the diameter of the lid updates as changes are made to the vase.

7. Create solid geometry from the surfaces to create a solid storage container for the vase.

8. Save the model and erase it from memory.

Practice 1b

Project 2

Practice Objective

- Apply behavioral modeling techniques to align the center of mass for a pulley model with a datum plane.

In this practice, you apply behavioral modeling techniques to align the center of mass for a pulley model with the default datum plane FRONT. The design variables have the following constraints:

- Tolerance on pulley flange thickness (d13, d37) is -0, +0.2

- Tolerance on pulley rounds (Rd110) is -0, +0.5

You will use the above design variable constraints to study the design and find a feasible result to meet your design intent.

Task 1 - Open the pulley part.

---

1. Set the working directory to *Project_2*.

2. Open **pulley.prt**. The model displays as shown in Figure A–5.

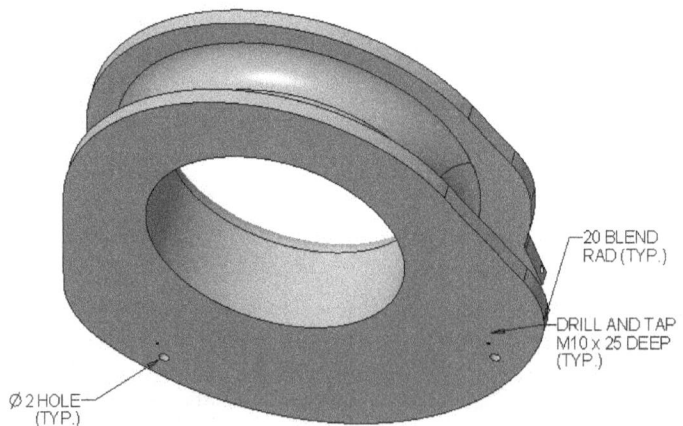

Figure A–5

3. Create a datum point through the default coordinate system for the model.

Task 2 - Create a model analysis feature to locate the center of mass for the pulley.

1. Create a model analysis feature to locate the pulley center of mass. Name the analysis **MODEL_COG**. Create a mass analysis parameter and set the name to **MASS**. Create a datum point on the center mass and set the name to **PNT_COG**. The model displays as shown in Figure A–6.

The image is shown with datum point tag display enabled.

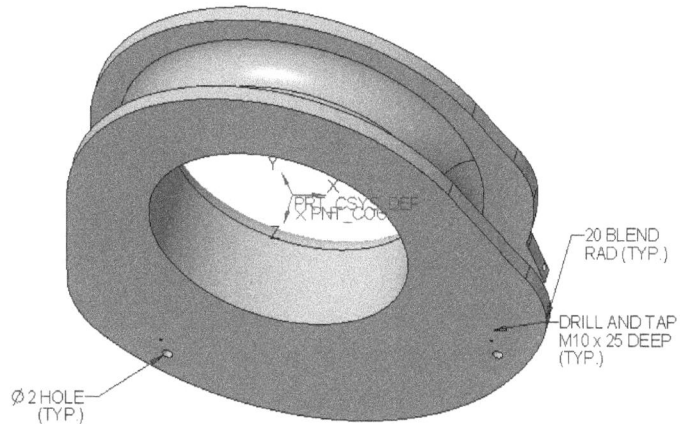

Figure A–6

Task 3 - Create a measure analysis feature.

1. Create a measure analysis feature to measure the distance between **PNT_COG** and default datum plane **FRONT**. Set the analysis name to **HORIZONTAL**. Create a distance parameter and set the name to **H_DIST**. Do not create a datum point. The computed distance equals 0.277.

Task 4 - Create a sensitivity study.

1. Create a sensitivity study on the flange thickness values (**d37**). Enter **3.2** as the maximum flange thickness and **3.0** as the minimum flange thickness. Plot this thickness against the **H_DIST** parameter. The distance between **PNT_COG** and default datum plane **FRONT** reduces to 0.057.

Task 5 - Create a sensitivity study.

1. Create a sensitivity study with **Rd110** as the variable, as shown in Figure A–7. Enter **6.5** and **6.0** as the maximum and minimum values, respectively. Plot this value against the **H_DIST** parameter. The distance between **PNT_COG** and default datum plane **FRONT** reduces to 0.235.

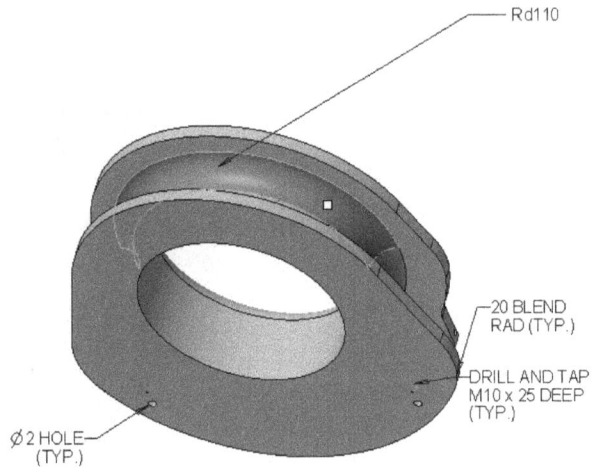

Figure A–7

Task 6 - Create a feasibility study.

Rd110 (6in to 6.5in)
d37 (3in to 3.2in)

1. Create a feasibility study with the **H_DIST** parameter set to 0, and variables **Rd110** and **d37** set to their maximum and minimum values. No feasible solution is found; however, the distance between **PNT_COG** and default datum plane **FRONT** reduces to 0.017.

Rd39 (3.6in to 4.4in)

2. Include the variable **Rd39** in your study to achieve feasibility.

3. Save the model and erase it from memory.

Practice 1c

Project 3

Practice Objective

- Ensure that the center of gravity is below the waterline to increase stability.

In this practice, you work with a toy boat assembly to determine the waterline, then ensure that the center of gravity is below the waterline to increase stability. You will first create analysis features and a feasibility study to find the waterline of the boat. Once the waterline has been found, you will create a second feasibility study to position the model's center of gravity.

Task 1 - Open the boat.asm model.

1. Set the working directory to *Project_3*.

2. Open **boat.asm**. Note the toy boat assembly consists of three parts: a hull, cabin, and weight. The assembly displays as shown in Figure A–8.

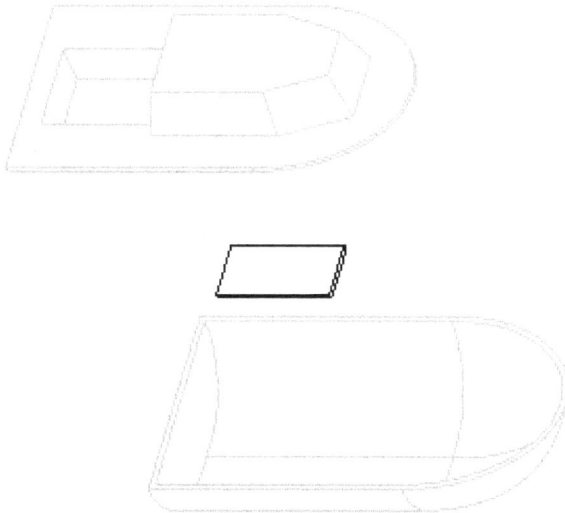

Figure A–8

Task 2 - Investigate the hull model in the assembly.

1. Display datum planes and tags.

2. Select the hull model in the Model Tree and click 🖾 (Open) in the mini toolbar. The hull part opens in a new window, as shown in Figure A–9.

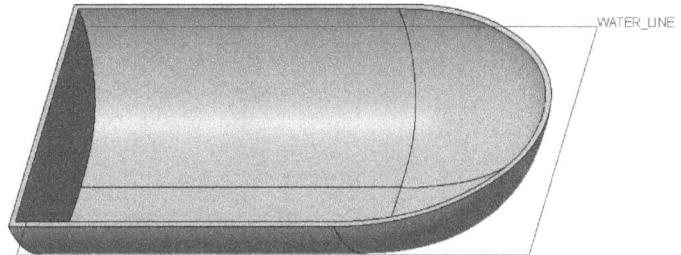

WATER_LINE

Figure A–9

Task 3 - Create an analysis feature to measure the displacement of the hull.

1. In the Model Tree, activate Insert Mode before the shell feature.

2. Create a Measure analysis feature to measure the One Sided Volume below the **WATER_LINE** datum plane. Create the **ONE_SIDED_VOLUME** parameter. Set the analysis name to **DISPLACEMENT**.

3. Cancel the Insert Mode.

4. Save **hull.prt** and close the window.

Task 4 - Measure the total mass of the assembly.

1. In the **BOAT** window, switch to the **FRONT** saved orientation.

2. Display Coordinate Systems.

3. Create a Mass Properties analysis feature to measure the assembly mass properties. Set the analysis name to **TOTAL_MASS**. Create the **MASS** parameter and a datum coordinate system at the center of gravity. The model displays as shown in Figure A–10.

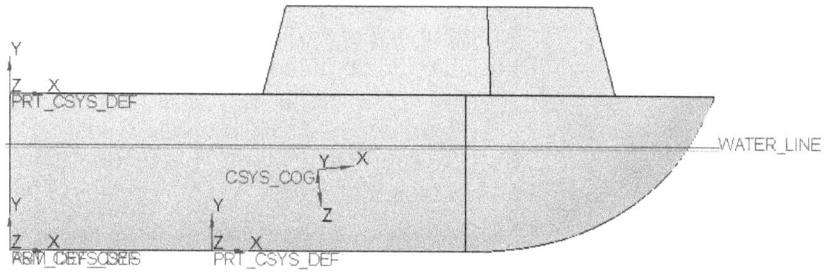

Figure A–10

Task 5 - Calculate the difference in mass using a relation analysis feature.

---

1. Create a relation analysis feature and name it **MASS_DIFF**.

0.04 (lbm/in^3), is the approximate density for water.

2. Enter the following relation:
   MASS_DIFF=(ONE_SIDE_VOL:FID_DISPLACEMENT:0
   *0.04)-MASS:FID_TOTAL_MASS

3. In the Relations dialog box, Select Utilities and remove the check mark next to **Unit Sensitive**.

4. Click ✓ (Verify) and click **OK**.

Task 6 - Find the waterline using a feasibility study.

---

1. Create a feasibility study.

2. Set the **Design Constraint** as *MASS_DIFF:MASS_DIFF* equal to **0**.

3. The only design variable is the **d57** dimension, which locates the **WATER_LINE** datum. Its range is from *0* to *5*.

4. Run the study. The model displays as shown in Figure A–11.

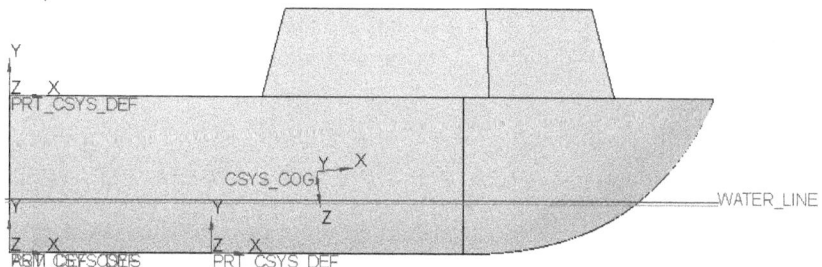

Figure A–11

The computer has found the position of the waterline by making the mass of the submerged and non-submerged portions equal. It should be noted that in this example, the waterline datum is only approximate, as you are not taking into account the slight rotation of the COG coordinate system with respect to the **WATER_LINE** datum. This rotation is insignificant and can be ignored.

Note that the COG for the boat assembly is above the waterline. For added stability, you can optimize the weight part to bring the center of gravity to be .15 below the waterline.

5. Click **Confirm** after closing the analysis dialog box.

Task 7 - Create a datum plane for the required COG position.

---

1. Create an Offset datum plane from **WATER_LINE**.

2. Enter a value of **-0.15** to offset below the **WATER_LINE** datum. The assembly displays as shown in Figure A–12.

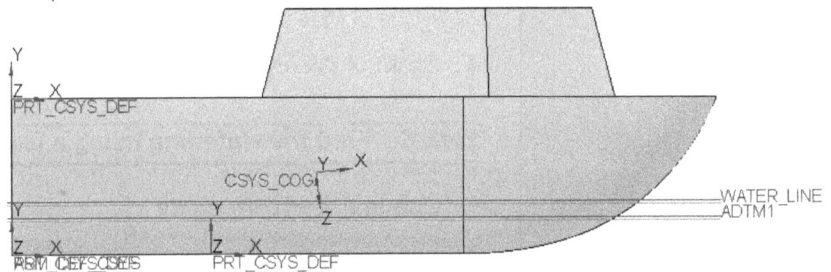

Figure A–12

Task 8 - Create another analysis feature.

---

1. Create a Measure analysis feature named **COG_DISTANCE** that measures the distance from the CSYS_COG coordinate system to the **ADTM1** datum plane. Create the distance parameter using the default name.

Task 9 - Position the COG on ADTM1 using a feasibility study.

1. Create a feasibility study. The constraints and variables from the previous study should still be present.

2. Add *DISTANCE:COG_DISTANCE* as a **Design Constraint** equal to 0.

3. Select the Hull component in the Model Tree and select ✎ (Hide) in the mini toolbar.

*The **d3** and **d2** dimensions represent the width and height of the weight component.*

4. Add the **d3** dimension from the **WEIGHT** part as a Design Variable. Vary the dimension from **0.09** to **0.25**.

5. Add the **d2** dimension from the **WEIGHT** part for an additional Design Variable. Vary the dimension from **0.90** to **2.50**.

6. Middle-click to stop adding dimensions.

7. Select the Hull component in the Model Tree and select ◉ (Show) in the mini toolbar.

8. Run the study. When completed, the assembly displays as shown in Figure A–13.

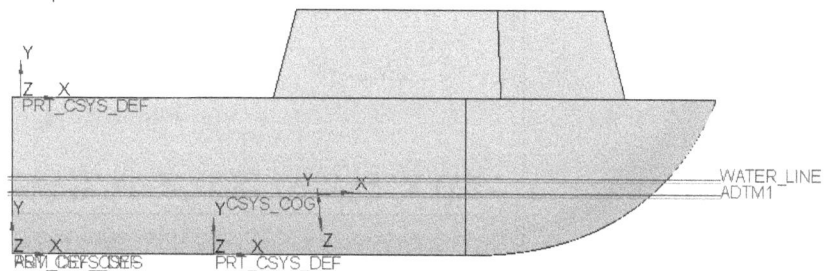

Figure A–13

9. Save the model and erase from memory.

Practice 1d

Project 4

Practice Objective

- Analyze the model and make the required design changes to meet several design criteria.

In this practice, you will analyze the model and make the required design changes for **FORKB.PRT**, shown in Figure A–14, to meet the following design criteria:

- The center of gravity must lie on the **A_1** axis.

- The distance from the end of the counterweight to the **A_3** axis must be less than 350.

- Mass must be minimized.

- Try using both methods of optimization: GDP and MDS.

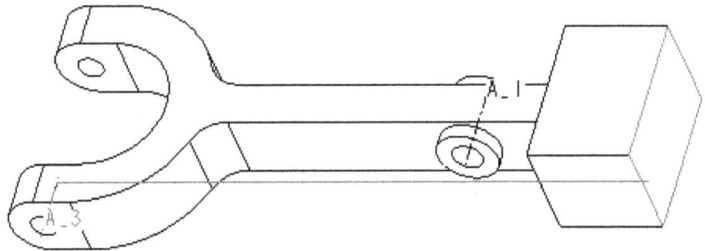

Figure A–14

Task 1 - Open the engine3.asm assembly.

1. Set the working directory to *Project_4*.

2. Open **forkb.prt**.

Task 2 - Using the above design criteria, make the required design changes without step by step instructions.

Practice 1e

Project 5

Practice Objective

- Analyze a model and make the required design changes for it to meet several design criteria.

In this practice, you will analyze **SURFACEB.PRT**, shown in Figure A–15, and make the required design changes for it to meet the following design criteria:

- The revolved protrusion must follow the contours of the existing surface, while still maintaining its inherent shape.

- The protrusion should deviate from the surface by as much as **3** and as little as **0**.

The error in calculations can vary by 5%.

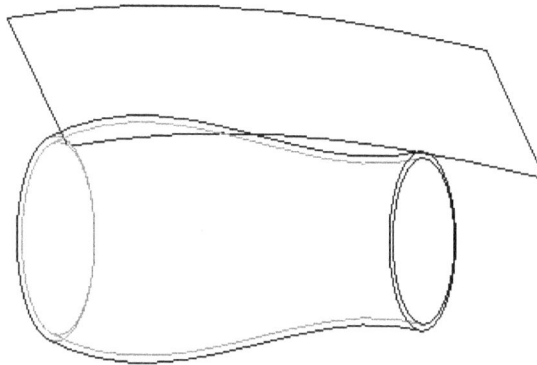

Figure A–15

Task 1 - Open the engine3.asm assembly.

1. Set the working directory to *Project_5*.

2. Open **surfaceb.prt**.

Task 2 - Using the above design criteria, make the required design changes without step by step instructions.

Practice 1f | Project 6

Practice Objective

- Apply behavioral modeling techniques to a slider-crank assembly to study how crank length affects several design elements.

In this practice, you will apply behavioral modeling techniques to a slider-crank assembly to study how crank length affects the following:

- Clearance between the piston and the connecting rod.

- Distance between the crank's center line and the pin's center line.

- Velocity of the reciprocating component (piston).

The following constraint has been set for the assembly:

- Clearance between the piston and the connecting rod cannot be less than 0.0802in (2mm).

Task 1 - Open the engine3.asm assembly.

1. Set the working directory to *Project_6*.

2. Open **engine3.asm**. The model displays as shown in Figure A–16.

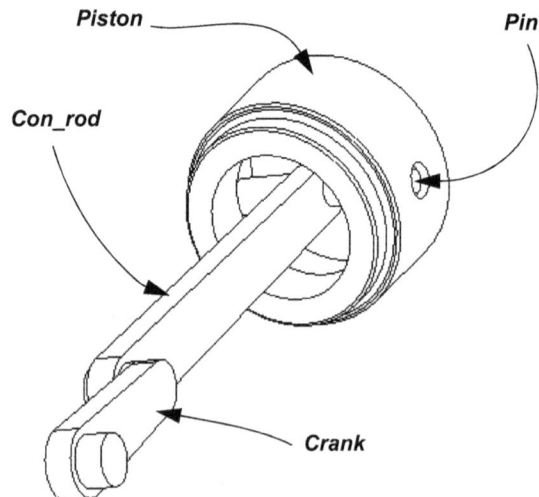

Piston

Pin

Con_rod

Crank

Figure A–16

3. Display features in the Model Tree (by default, they are not displayed). This enables the display of all of the analysis features that are added to the assembly.

Task 2 - Load the MotionDefinition1.pbk file to show an animation of a predefined doorknob movement.

The connections are Fixed, Pin and Slider The model driver profile type is Cosine.

The Mechanism Design Extension (MDX) of Creo Parametric enables you to simulate kinematic motion in an assembly. You can drag the mechanism through its range of motion or create drivers to define predetermined animations. These motions enable you to examine the behavior of the mechanism. The mechanism that is in the Behavioral Modeling Extension (BMX) is used evaluate important parameters throughout its range of motion.

1. In the *Application* tab, select ☼ (Mechanism). Select
PLAYBACKS from Model Tree and click ▶ (Play) in the mini toolbar. The Playbacks dialog box opens as shown in Figure A–17.

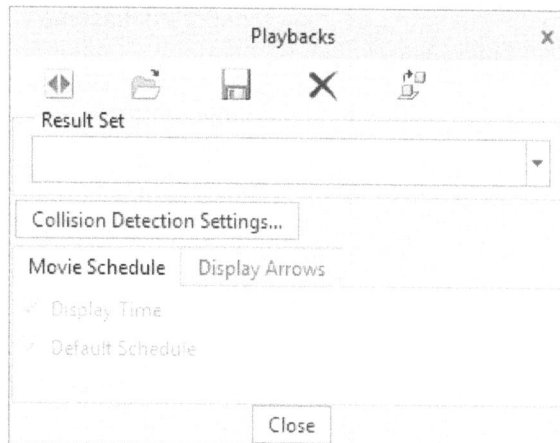

Playbacks	✕
◀▶ ☐ ☐ ✕ ☐	
Result Set	
▼	
Collision Detection Settings...	
Movie Schedule Display Arrows	
✓ Display Time	
✓ Default Schedule	
Close	

Figure A–17

2. In the Playbacks dialog box, click ☐ (Restore Result Set) and open **MotionDefinition2.pbk**.

3. Click ⊕ (Play Result Set). The Animate dialog box displays as shown in Figure A–18.

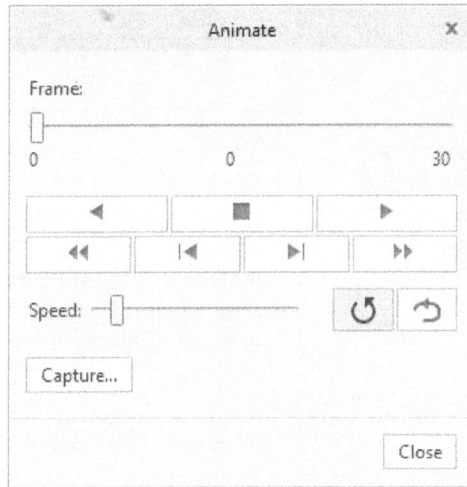

Figure A–18

4. Select the ▶ (Play) icon to run the animated motion of the slider-crank assembly.

5. Select the ◀◀ (Reset to Beginning) icon to rewind the animation to the beginning once you have reviewed it.

6. Select **Close** to close the dialog box.

7. Select **Close** to close the Results Play dialog box.

8. Return to the top-level assembly and regenerate the assembly.

Task 3 - Create a Measure analysis feature.

---

1. Create an analysis feature named **C_MEASURE** to measure the distance between the crank center line and pin center line. Create a distance analysis parameter named **C_to_C**. Do not create any datum points.

2. Show the **C_to_C** parameter in the Model Tree.

Task 4 - Create a Measure analysis feature.

1. Create a datum point on edge vertex, as shown in Figure A–19.

2. Create an analysis feature named **P_R_MEASURE** to measure the clearance between the connecting rod and piston. Select the surface for the connecting rod and the vertex point on the piston, as shown in Figure A–19. Create a distance analysis parameter named **P_R**. Do not create any datum points. Set the clearance to **0.82166in**.

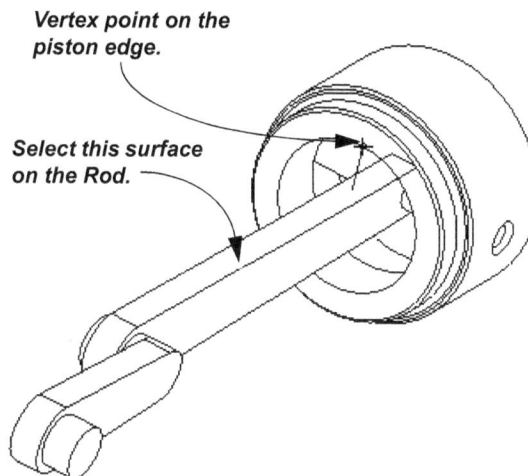

Vertex point on the piston edge.

Select this surface on the Rod.

Figure A–19

Task 5 - Create a Motion analysis feature.

Refer to Task 4 in practice 7a for reference.

The minimum clearance = 0.1573in.

1. Create and run a motion analysis feature named **MOTION** to measure the minimum clearance between the connecting rod and piston.

2. Create only the **MIN_P_R** parameter. Set the name to **P_R_DIST**.

Task 6 - Create a sensitivity study.

Refer to Task 5 in practice 7a for reference.

1. Create and run a sensitivity study to provide insight into an ideal start for the crank length **crank_length:0** when running a feasibility study. Enter **3.00** and **4.00** as the minimum and maximum variable ranges, respectively. Select the **P_R_DIST:MOTION** parameter to plot. Note that the required minimum clearance of 0.802in (Y-axis of the graph) is within the specified range.

Task 7 - Create a feasibility study.

Refer to Task 6 in practice 7a for reference.

1. Create and run a feasibility study to adjust the design variable **crank_length:0** to meet the required minimum clearance. Select the parameter **P_R_DIST:MOTION** and set its value equal to **0.0802**. Set the minimum and maximum values for **crank_length:0** to **3.00** and **3.50**, respectively.

(crank_length:0) dimension was 3in originally.

2. Verify that the **crank_length:0** dimension is now 3.30inch.

Task 8 - Create an Excel Analysis feature.

Refer to Task 5 in practice 6a for reference.

1. Create and run an Excel analysis named **VELOCITY** to find the velocity of the piston after adjustment to the crank length in Task 7. Load and open **velocity.xls**. Select the **crank_length** and cell **B4**. Select **rod_length** and cell **B5**. Select cell **B30** as the output cell and set its name to **VEL**.

Piston velocity = 0.97316in/sec

2. Show the **VEL** parameter in the Model Tree.

Task 9 - (Optional) Add piston acceleration to Excel analysis.

1. Add piston acceleration to the excel spread sheet:

   Piston acceleration = w^2*acosB + 1/q*cos2B

   Where q = b/a

2. Create and run an Excel analysis to find the acceleration of the piston after adjustment to the crank length in Task 7.

Task 10 - (Optional) Add piston total force to Excel analysis.

1. Add the total force for the reciprocating part (piston) to the spreadsheet.

   Total force (F) = m*w^2*acosB + 1/q*cos2B

   Where m = mass of the piston

2. Create and run an Excel analysis to find the total force on of the piston after adjustment to the crank length in Task 7.

3. Save the assembly and erase it from memory.

www.ingramcontent.com/pod-product-compliance
Lightning Source LLC
Chambersburg PA
CBHW061414210326
41598CB00035B/6206